AF480948

The
Genesis Program

Lizhong Liao

Veronica Lane Books
www.VeronicaLaneBooks.com
Books That Make a Difference!
11420 US-1, Suite 124, N. Palm Beach, FL 33408 USA
Tel: +1(833) VLBOOKS (+1 833-852-6657

Table of Contents

Introduction

Mom, I guess life is like a game; the game is over when you die.

I was instantly shocked when I heard these words that a boy of 8 or 9 said to his mom in the courtyard of my apartment building that afternoon.

I believe in their childhood many people cherished curiosity and fantasy about Nature. When I was a child, I often sat up late on the ground of the harvest yard in front of my house, watching the ethereal Milky Way flickering in the night sky, wondering what there should be up there in the sky.

Looking up into the starry sky, innumerous sages and poets for centuries have been wondering how vast the universe is and how humble human life is, saddened by the transiency of life against the eternity of time. They have been intrigued by the same eternal question:

Who created the universe? Where do humans come from?

Preface

In the last few hundred years, many more English books have been translated into Chinese than vice versa. The translation of this Chinese book into English is contributing to addressing this imbalance.

The exchange of ideas between different cultures has contributed significantly to the progress of human civilization. A good case study is that European Enlightenment in the 17th century happened following systematic cultural exchange between Europe and China.   During this time Jesuits were starting to translate ancient Chinese classics into European languages for the first time. This opened up a huge opportunity for the Europeans to learn from the Chinese.

The thought that human beings are able to come to meaningful conclusions about the nature of the Universe, on their own, was introduced to Europe through these translations.   This is in contrast to divine revelation derived from the revealed theology of Christianity. These translations had a big impact on the imaginations of European intellectuals. What happened during this period of time was that European intellectuals were turning away from religious explanations of nature and started to look for a scientific explanation of the Universe.

Since the Scientific Revolution, science has established itself as a reliable collective attempt at understanding the physical world. The scientific methodology ensures that data are gathered rigorously by avoiding delusion and illusion as much as possible. Scientific theories are established only when a hypothesis that gives testable predictions has been independently verified.

Science has demonstrated the potential for humanity to understand and manipulate the physical world around us. As a result of scientific development, we have a tremendous amount of knowledge about the world we didn't have before. It has accomplished unprecedented goals of improving the quality of life of humanity.   Because of its huge success, it has brought with it a culture that only science has the authority and reliability to generate knowledge and answer questions.

It is worth noting that in the last few hundred years science has been restricting its focus on physical data that are gathered using our physical senses and by extending and amplifying our physical senses using instruments.

However, having a science which is limited only to the physical world ignores a whole spectrum of human experience, as physical data is only a subset of data we experience as humans.

In addition to experiencing the outer physical world using our physical senses, we also experience the inner non-physical world when our physical senses are not in operation, for instance, during dreaming. Many also experience visions in their meditation, while doing psychic viewing, under the influence of psychedelics, and during dying. These non-physical visual experiences have been categorized as subjective, implying they don't really exist. Some non-physical visual phenomena are even regarded by the mainstream scientific community as 'hallucinations', fantasies or even 'mental illnesses'. By doing so these experiences can be hopefully "explained away" by scientists.

It is obvious that there is no space for nonphysical experiences in the existing paradigm of science. Existing tools are not adequate to handle nonphysical data. If we want to study our inner experience systematically, we will need new theoretical frameworks that provide structures for the investigation of our inner experience.

The history of science tells us that the establishment of theoretical frameworks relies heavily on metaphors. Observation of the world gives us conceptual metaphors that are often used to propose theories and models. Light as a wave, light as particles, gas as billiard balls, electric current as flow and the atom as a planetary system are all examples of metaphor-based hypotheses that have been accepted as mainstream scientific theories.

The development and application of computation and data science has given us a new metaphor to comprehend and describe the world. Since the second half of the 20th century, some computer scientists and physicists have proposed new ideas for the world. Konrad Zuse (1969), one of the earliest pioneers of the modern computer, first suggested the idea that the entire universe is being computed on a computer. John Wheeler (1990) proposed a famous remark 'it-from-bit'. Nowadays, more scientists and philosophers are taking the computational universe hypothesis seriously.

The computational universe hypothesis provides a new perspective to see the world. From the new perspective, we have a new understanding of our experiences. For example, laws of nature expressed in physics can be seen as an expression of underlying programming. Physical properties of matter can be seen as derived from programming.

As discussed in this book, many paradoxes in the existing scientific paradigm can be resolved, including issues in the Big Bang theory, theory of evolution, quantum mechanics, entanglement, relativity, etc. It is also shown that many nonphysical, psychological and parapsychological phenomena can be explained using the computational universe hypothesis.

It is worth noting that computation is developed based on the binary system developed by Leibniz in the 17th century when the Chinese Ying Yang philosophy was introduced to Europe.

The first book that introduced Chinese history from the earliest age to Europe was *Sinicæ historiæ decas prima* published in Munich in 1658 and written by Martino Martini, a 17th-century Italian Jesuit priest. The book introduced the Chinese concept of Yin and Yang, two polar opposites, as the source of creation. It also introduced Yi Jing (also known as I Ching or Book of Changes), an interpretation of a set of all 64 possible combinations of Yin and Yang, symbolized by six broken or unbroken lines.

In 1697, Leibniz designed a medallion titled *imago creationis* (Image of Creation) which contains a table in the center. In the table are the binary numbers up to 10001 and their decimal correspondence up to 17. The invention of the binary system allowed decimal numbers to be represented by binary polar opposites represented by 0 and 1. In this way, Leibniz unified the Chinese philosophy of creation by Yin and Yang with the Pythagorean philosophy of creation by numbers.

Leibniz attempted to show how God created the world out of nothing, the zero, by creating one. The caption on the medallion reads: "For everything to be drawn out of nothing, the one suffices." Leibniz's unification of Yin Yang philosophy and Pythagorean philosophy made God's creative act transparent.

Leibniz's formal work on binary arithmetic appeared in his article *Explication de Arithmétique Binaire,* published in 1703. The full title of Leibniz's article is translated into English as the "Explanation of Binary Arithmetic, which uses only the characters 1 and 0, with some remarks on its usefulness, and on the light, it throws on the ancient Chinese figures of Fu Xi". As a Sinophile, Leibniz was fascinated by how hexagrams in I-Ching correspond to the binary numbers from 0 to 111111 and concluded that this mapping was evidence of major Chinese accomplishments in the sort of philosophical mathematics he admired.

The Binary system was later deployed as the principle of the digital computer.

Essentially, computation is the determination of a choice of binary according to a set of rules, i.e., programming. Modern electronic computers enabled the binary states using the presence (1) and absence (0) of electrical current. It can be said that the computer as technology has its roots deeply connected to Chinese Ying Yang philosophy.

It is worth mentioning that the computational universe hypothesis also has its roots deeply associated with Lao Tze's thoughts, as revealed by the author. According to Lao Tze, Tao exists prior to the universe as a "mixture of things" (combination of 1s and 0s), it is independent of the Universe and is "the mother of the universe" (software that is outside of computer display). It "runs cyclically and never stops" (processing of computation). The author pointed out that the Tao can be understood as the "creation program" in the computational universe theoretical framework.

How did Lao Tze obtain such profound insight so far ahead of his time? It appears that he didn't rely on physical sense perception or empirical experience, instead, his knowledge about the universe came from introspection and contemplation - "Knowing the world without going out; seeing the way of heaven without looking out of windows; if you go far away, you may know less."

The scope for exploration of our inner space is enormous when we readdress our focus of attention from the outer material world to the inner nonphysical world. If the first scientific revolution in the 17th century ushered in an era of understanding and manipulation of the outer physical world, the second scientific revolution will open up the knowledge and understanding of the workings of our inner world.

We will need a new, robust methodology to reliably investigate our inner experiences with the same rigor and thoroughness used when researching the outer world.   We also need new theories to structure our understanding of our inner experience. When we are successful in establishing the new paradigm, it will allow us to have breakthroughs in life science, biology, energy, artificial intelligence, etc.

As discussed in this book, the computational universe hypothesis can be a potential candidate theory for such a new paradigm. It has the potential to break through the barriers between philosophy, religion, and science, and becomes an inclusive theoretical framework that reflects the truth of the world.

The new paradigm will also bring changes in our culture of producing and consuming, and the associated ethics of both. If we understand that the physical universe is a processing output of computation, akin to virtual reality, we probably won't be treating the accumulation of material wealth as the main purpose of our lives, destroying our planet in the process.

As we have seen across history, cross-culture fertilization brings significant progress in human civilization. As Leibniz put it when he commented on cultural exchange with China: "For this is commerce of light, and which could give to us at once their work of thousands of years and render ours to them, and double so to speak our true wealth for one and the other. This is something greater than one imagines."

I do not doubt publication of this book in English will contribute to this process.

Simon Duan PhD
Metacomputics Labs, UK

Chapter 1

The Ultimate Questions:
Where Does the Universe Come From?
What is the Meaning of Human Life?

I don't know why Heaven lets me come across the secret. I believe there must be some reason.

I want to share with you the ultimate secret of the universe.

From antiquity to the present, humans have been contemplating the following questions: how does the universe come into being? Where do humans come from? What is the meaning of human life? These questions are considered the ultimate questions of the human being.

Up to now, the answers to these ultimate questions come from two systems of thinking, religion, and science. The first answers systematically addressing these questions are from religion.

All three religions give their answers to these questions. The Christian answers are God created the universe and man, and man was born with the original sin, as man did not obey God's will after they were created. As a result, the meaning of human life is to believe in God, to cleanse his sins so as to be redeemed and accepted back again by God into Heaven.

Islam believes that Allah is the supreme master of the universe and that there are no other gods. The meaning of life lies in faith in and obedience to Allah, doing more good work while creating a happy life in the world, waiting to be resurrected by Allah after death, and entering heaven after accepting the judgment of Allah.

Buddhism does not directly answer the question of how the world and human beings originate. It only says that all things are born due to the collection of causes and die when the causes disappear and that sentient beings are constantly in reincarnation in the three circles and six paths. The process that dominates this process is *industry*. All beings are suffering, and the meaning of life is to achieve *nirvana* through the ascetic practice of abstinence, so as to go beyond the six reincarnations and get complete relief.

Religion has a very positive meaning for the answer to the ultimate questions. It gives believers the direction of life and makes their lives meaningful and spiritual. Devoted religious people can generally be impetuous, not anxious, not evil, not greedy, living a good life with a peaceful mind, and calmly facing the advent of death.

Because of believing in the supervision of God, everyone's behavior will determine whether they will go to heaven or hell after death; or because of believing that there is karma, the good and evil of this life will affect the fate of the afterlife, so the devoutly religious people have awe. Advocating such values and principles as consciously constraining one's own behavior, obeying religious ethics, and not daring to violate the commandments, religion thus played a positive role in maintaining social order. Until today, many countries in the world are still relying on religion to establish a social moral value system.

For a long time in the history of human civilization, religion dominated people's perception of the world and made us believe that the ultimate problem has a definitive answer. People who live in faith are happy, and whether they are poor or rich, they are always spiritually rich. But unfortunately, religion exposed many problems.

The most fascinating scene of Genesis that Michelangelo painted for the vault of the Sistine Chapel in the Vatican, Rome. The picture shows the moment the sacred spark is about to touch Adam when God descends from the sky and points his finger at Adam.

Exclusiveness is a big problem in religion. Most religions believe that their teachings are absolutely correct. But the teachings of different religions are different. They cannot all be right. Someone must have made a mistake. So, in order to argue who is right and who is wrong, different religions, even among different factions of the same religion, often quarrel and even fight bloody battles to prove the rightness of their religion.

The correctness of religious teachings is also questionable. The founders of religion all claim that their knowledge comes from *the Apocalypse*, but we can easily observe that religion has a strong regional character. As the ancient Greek philosopher Xenophon pointed out in the 6th century BC, the Ethiopian god is a flat-nosed black man, while the Thrace god is red-haired blue eyes. Religions in the same region are like brothers with similar bloodlines, and there are many similarities. Western Christianity, Islam, and Judaism all believe that God created the world and human beings. The difference is simply whether to call it *Jehovah* or *Allah*. Buddhism, Hinduism, and Jainism in India believe that there is *reincarnation* and *industry*, and through spiritual practice, man can be free from the bitter sea, not into reincarnation, and get complete relief. The only difference is whether the path is through "nirvana" or "the union of oneself with Brahma."

We have reason to believe that at least parts of the teachings of these religions were not from *the Apocalypse*, but from the environment in which the founders lived. Otherwise, it is difficult to explain why the religious teachings in the same region are so similar, and the religious teachings in different regions vary widely.

To make matters worse, although all religions claim that their teachings are absolutely correct, their description of the world is not only crude, and ambiguous, but also has many mistakes, and therefore, it is difficult for them to stand the test of time.

The Bible describes the origin of the world in this way: At first, God created the heavens and the earth. In the next six days, it created light, dark, sacred, land and sea, grass and vegetable trees, plants, sun, moon, stars, fish and birds, reptiles, and beasts, and finally created man according to His own image to manage other creatures. The church, therefore, believes that humans have a status above other life, because in God's creation plan human beings are managers, and the earth is the center of the universe.

These claims did not have any problems in the early days of Christianity, but then as science continued to refresh people's perception of the world, it became full of loopholes.

After the Polish astronomer Copernicus proposed the *Solar Center Theory* in the 16th century, the facts gradually proved that the earth is rotating around the sun, and "the earth is the center of the universe" cannot be established. Later, scientists discovered that the universe was born 13.7 billion years ago, and the age of the earth was only 4.6 billion years. The time gap between them appeared too far. The idea that "in the beginning, God created the heavens and the earth" is obviously just pure imagination.

In the 19th century, the British biologist Darwin proposed the Evolution theory. He believed that the species on earth did not appear at the same time in the past, but gradually evolved over a long period of time. In this way, the saying that "God created fish and birds and other creatures, reptiles, and beasts" is not right. Even more troublesome is that Darwin also believes that human beings evolved from ancient times, and if human beings were created by God according to his own image, then this creation should be shaped into being once. Humans couldn't be evolved from other species over a long period of time, so the "God-made man" in the Bible is also denied, and the foundation of Christian doctrine has been completely overthrown.

Religion usually requires the believer to unconditionally believe in it and does not allow any change to the doctrine. This helps to highlight its sacredness and authority, but it also blocks the way for its further development, so that it no longer has room for improvement. Because the teachings cannot be modified according to the new situations, the new discoveries of science make the religion very embarrassing and helpless. "For every step that science takes forward, religion has to retreat the same step." Eventually, science prevails over religion in the realm of reason and dominates human cognition of the world instead.

Many religions regard human beings as the spirit of all things and believe that human beings are above other species and regard the earth as the center of the universe. But now we already know that human beings are only high-level animals. The earth is not the center of the universe. It is just an ordinary planet in the universe.

Scientists believe that it is not the gods that dominate the world; it is *the natural laws*. Scientific research is to observe and experiment in different categories to discover the regularity that exists in the evolution of the universe.

Darwin's theory of evolution has far-reaching influences. Inspired by this theory, scientists began to believe that the emergence of life is only an accident, the result of natural evolution. Later, after studying the evolution of planets, stars, and galaxies, scientists came to realize that the whole universe evolves over time naturally and has nothing to do with the creation of God.

From this, science gives its answer to the ultimate question: the world is naturally formed, and the emergence of human beings is the result of natural evolution and has nothing to do with God. If so, the question of "what is the meaning of life" is not very easy to answer. This is because, since people can only live for a lifetime, and nothing is left after death, then as long as you have a good life in this world, you don't need to think more about your afterlife. We can only say: "The meaning of life is to live your life well. There is no other meaning."

After religion, science once again makes us believe that the ultimate problem has been answered. But unfortunately, now we find that science also has problems.

In fact, some phenomena clearly indicate the latest development trends: although science believes that it has already defeated religion in the realm of reason, it is strange that instead of withering away the world's major religions all have been thriving along with the development of science.

The biggest problem with science is that it cannot satisfy the spiritual needs of people. Science destroys people's beliefs. When a person lacks faith, he is mentally homeless and can only use material things to fill his spiritual emptiness. Those who believe that there is no future life will no longer have awe in their hearts in this life. They will always be madly in pursuit of material desires, even for selfish desires, expecting maximum satisfaction in a short life. This will bring a devastating impact on the maintenance of the proper social-moral system.

The German philosopher Kant in the 18th century had long worried about this. He said: Though neither reason nor experience can prove the existence of God, for the sake of maintaining morality, we should assume that people have immortal souls and God does exist. Perhaps because of this, no matter how advanced science is, the role of religion is still irreplaceable.

In addition, we also find that science itself is limited. Today, science has become so advanced, and the world has been studied so thoroughly, but we have seen that scientific research methods are more applicable to the material world, but little research has been done in the spiritual world. So, for the spiritual world of human beings, we still know very little about it. We even don't know how human consciousness is produced, and what its operating mechanism is.

Because of this, when the body has a problem, we will believe in science and go to the hospital to seek the help of the doctor; but when the spirit is in trouble, we are more willing to turn to religion, to go to churches and temples to find spiritual comfort. Few people will consult a scientist when they are mentally empty and have doubts about the meaning of life. Scientists can't help you in this regard.

Scientists are also aware of this.   So, unlike some people imagine, science and religion are opposites. Many scientists do not reject religion, and they believe that religion is a useful supplement to science.

Another interesting phenomenon in the scientific community is that many famous scientists have finally embarked on the road of coming to terms with religion. Perhaps the most famous example is the British scientist Isaac Newton in the 17th century. The most recent ones are contemporary scientists Li Since, former President of Taiwan University and Zhu Qingshi, former President of the Chinese University of Science and Technology. These scientists eventually moved away from modern mainstream science becoming more and more devoted to religious interpretation.

Is this because these scientists have worn out their sharp minds?

Of course, it is not true. The right and wrong between science and religion are not as simple as they seem. Looking back on history, you will find out that science does not overthrow the answer to the ultimate question given by religion. Science may be able to prove that the description of God's creation in the Bible is wrong, but it cannot prove that God does not exist, nor can it prove that the idea that the universe came into being a world by itself is correct.

Einstein said: "Science without religion is lame, and religion without science is blind." He believed that religion and science are complementary, religion can inject spiritual power into science, and science can help religion to enhance the correctness of its teachings, making it free from blind faith.

Just as no one would believe him anymore when the child twice cried the fake warning call of "the wolf is coming". Because religion has overdrawn its credit in some respects historically, many people now habitually reject it when seeking enlightenment on too many issues and choose to turn to science for answers. But they have not realized that science did not provide sufficient proof for the answers they gave.

To this day, science has many new incredible discoveries. To our astonishment, these discoveries have failed to further destroy religious beliefs. Instead, they have been integrated with religious doctrines to a certain extent, posing serious challenges to science itself. The British physicist Paul Davis once said that the discovery of relativity theory and quantum theory have led physicists to realize that the most basic aspects of reality need to be completely redefined. "They have to learn to solve problems in completely unexpected new methods, and these methods seem to be contrary to common sense; they are closer to mysticism than to materialism."

Some scientists have begun to try to gain wisdom from religious teachings to interpret discoveries in science, but this tendency has been strongly resisted by the scientific community. Just as in the era when religion dominated the ideology of society, Copernicus and Galileo did not dare to express their views freely, now scientists are also afraid to disclose their own arch in this area for fear of being rejected or marginalized by the mainstream scientific community.

From the story of the boy who cried wolf, we can get the lesson that people can easily be judgmental. By experience, they can often form judgments of things as absolutely good or bad, absolutely right or absolutely reality, there are more situations in which the right things are not necessarily correct, and the wrong things are not necessarily all wrong. Though the child shepherd falsely cried wolf twice, how could you know that for the third time he will tell a lie?

Religion advocates unconditional faith and submission, and skepticism was once one of the most well-recognized spirits of science; but when it comes to suspicion, science and religion do not react differently. Many people view science as much as they do religion. A theory that is labeled with science is absolutely correct and unquestionable. Once a concept conflicts with the existing scientific theories, there is no room for negotiation. The stick is wielded to kill it. As a result, science has become a religious belief for some people.

In fact, the original answer to the ultimate question of science has now been negated by the updated scientific findings. We originally thought that science has given a clear answer to the ultimate problem, but now the new discovery of science once again confuses our perception. Fragmented, the situation has once again become confusing. And more importantly, these new scientific discoveries are enough to give us a new understanding of the ultimate problem and a new understanding of the meaning of life.

Paul Davis once said, "I believe that science can point people to a more precise path to God than religion." Perhaps what he said is correct. Science will not become the terminator of religious belief but become a different path other than religion, to find the ultimate truth of the world from different angles.

This book may subvert your worldview, values, and outlook on life. Are you ready?

Human Paranoia is Equally Prominent in Religion and Science.

The vast majority of religions in the world advocate such virtues as love, harmony, and humility, but religious persecution, religious hatred, and religious conflicts are everywhere. Some people are brutally killed only because they propose new thinking and new ideas that are contrary to the doctrines. They even attack each other because of their different understandings of the doctrines. The confrontation between different religions is even more serious. Christianity and Islam have historically carried out a 200-year religious war—the Crusades, which has turned into a tragedy of countless bloodsheds and catastrophes. Even today hatred is still fermenting, leading to constant disputes and conflicts.

Why is this so? In addition to the hiding personal purpose of some religious leaders, a very important reason is people's paranoia. Many religious believers are paranoid and believe that the religious correctness of their beliefs is unquestionable, but it is unreasonable to conclude that the religions of others are absolutely wrong, and they do not want to give people room for justification. This problem still exists today. I wanted to learn about the knowledge of Buddhism a few days ago and so I joined some Buddhist exchange groups. Some councilors just read the scriptures, and the explanations are also standard models, not their own understanding. When I asked some questions, I was told that I should just follow the chanting, and don't ask why. When I tried to propose and explore some of my understandings, I found myself kicked out of the groups very quickly. This blind, fanatical, paranoid problem exists in varying degrees in any religion.

In fact, few religious founders say that they are gods. They at most claim that they have listened to God's teachings in person or speak for God as his spokesperson. Since people are not gods, then how can their words be absolutely correct? What's more, the religious teachings that have been passed down are not their original words, but they are recorded by others according to their memories. You can imagine the accuracy, when you try to recall the lectures, you have heard, try to organize them into text, and then compare them with the original recording to see how accurate it is.

Regrettably, this paranoia is not limited to a religious person. It also exists in many scientific people. It seems that it is a common problem for human beings. Some people unreasonably believe that science and religion are antagonistic and thus bear hostility toward religion. To make matters worse, they also equate pure spirit with religion. When it comes to the role of the spirit, they think that it is the dross of religion. So now there are basically few people in the scientific world who dare to touch the study of pure spirituality. It seems to have become a taboo area of science.

In fact, there is no irreconcilable contradiction between science and religion. Many scientists in history believe in the existence of God, such as Newton, Faraday, Dalton, Mendel, Maxwell, and von Braun. Einstein also believes that religion and science are complementary. He said: "Even if the division of religion and science can be divided, the connection and dependence between the two still exist. Religion can determine the goal, science can be created by man's craving for truth and knowledge, and religious goals can be realized through scientific means.

Religion is good at exploring the spiritual world through intuition and science is good at examining the physical world with reason, so many people will want to combine them. Einstein said: "The road to true religion does not lie in fear of life and death, nor in blind faith, but in the relentless pursuit of rational knowledge." Davis also believes that "science can point out a more precise path to God for humans." However, this combination must have a premise that human beings must be able to overcome their own paranoia and embrace the truth of the world with an inclusive attitude.

Chapter 2

The Supernormal Phenomena:
Why is There Natural Law?
Who Made the Law of Nature?

Zhuang Tzu said: "The well-frog can't be spoken to the sea as its vision is limited by the size of the wellhead; the summer worm can't be spoken to of the ice, as it only lives a short span of one summer." The limitation of time and space has so greatly restricted the ability the understanding of a frog in its well and of insects in the summer so that their level of understanding is limited to a very poor and narrow range.

People often use the saying that "the summer insects cannot be spoken to of the ice" to satirize a person's limit of knowledge. However, if we look at the span of the entire history of the evolution of the universe, it is actually unreasonable for humans to laugh at the well-frog and insects because we are not much better than they are.

From a spatial perspective, human beings are trapped on a small planet with a diameter of only 12,800 kilometers. The vastness of the universe is beyond imagination. If we can fly at a speed of light of 300,000 km/s, it takes only 0.13 seconds to circle the earth, but it will take 12 billion years to reach the farthest celestial body we know from us. The age of the earth is only 4.6 billion years old. By contrast, you will know how big the universe is and how small our scope of activities is.

In terms of time, the existence of human beings can only be said to be short-lived compared to the history of the evolution of the entire universe. If the time span of 13.7 billion years of the evolution of the universe is scaled down to one year, then the history of human civilization only began less than half a minute before the New Year's bell rings.

Only by knowing our position in the universe will we know that the pride that I showed in front of the well-frog and the summer insects is actually like the kind of ignorance that one man having traveled a hundred steps laughed at another man having traveled just fifty steps.

Each illuminating body in the photo may be a galaxy composed of innumerable stars, and the earth is just one planet of one of the stars. A randomly picked star in the universe is much larger than it. The size of the sun is equivalent to 1.3 million times its size. The earth is nothing more than dust in the universe. For a human being trapped on this little planet, it is quite easy to imagine how much vision he can have.

For the well-frog having lived his whole life in the well, he thought that the world is a well of water plus a sky the size of the wellhead; for a summer worm with a short life span of only one summer, all he could see is the flowing water, so he thought this will always be the case, and it is impossible to for him to imagine the white icy scenery of thousands of miles in the winter. The limited and false impressions that they have formed are mainly due to the limit of space and time.

The gaps between the real situation in the world and the visions in the eyes of the frog and the summer worm are so great. Does humanity also have such problems?

The situation is not much different for human beings. Since ancient times, all that the human eyes have seen is flat earth. The sun rises and falls, and the stars are rotating around the earth. Therefore, it is natural for them to think that the earth is a plane and is the center of the universe. For most of the history of human civilization, this concept has dominated people's understanding. How do you know that the truth behind this seemingly normal phenomenon is that the earth rotates around the sun while revolving around it?

When people thought that the earth is a plane, it seemed reasonable for them that the apples on the tree fall down, because there are ups and downs. But now we know that the earth is actually a sphere. Under where you stand, on the other side of the sphere, stand the Americans. And they still stand firm and don't fall down. At this point, will you insist that things should of course fall down?

In the real world, there are some phenomena that we have taken for granted that are not normal. There are secrets behind them. I call these phenomena *supernormal phenomena*.

There are a lot of *supernormal phenomena* in the fields of science and philosophy, but we have long been accustomed to them and have not given them enough attention. Next, I will point out one after another phenomena that you may feel normal and explore the secret behind them. I believe you will be surprised to find that you have never really known the world. When you look into the essence of the world and lift the veil that covers it, the answer to the ultimate question is in sight.

The first phenomenon that many people never bother to give their thought to, I would like to say, is the existence of natural laws.

It has been realized for a long time that there is an invisible hand behind the world that sets in motion the order of the heavens and the earth. From the changing of day and night to the booming and withering of grasses to the grounding of stones and flowing of water to low places, everything seems to have rules to follow. Even more strange is that there are causal relationships between different events in nature, and regularity can be found. Clouds mean rain, and ants can predict the same result. Einstein was surprised by this: "The most incomprehensible thing about this world is that it can be understood."

We usually refer to this orderly performance behind the world as *the natural law*, and in popular science books translated from abroad, it is more expressed as *the natural law* or *the scientific law*. The history of people's understanding of the laws of nature dates back to antiquities. Although the ancient people did not know how the laws of nature were going, they knew very early that they could not violate the laws of nature. The Chinese idiom of "pulling out a bit the seedlings to help their growth" satirized such ignorance of this natural law.

The superb mastery and skillful application of the natural laws by the ancient people sometimes made modern people feel ashamed. Li Bing, who presided over the construction of the river diversion project Dujiangyan Dam in 256 BC, had already understood how to make use of the characteristics of the terrain and the law of water flow, so as to build it into hydraulic works with multiple functions such as automatic diversion, sand discharge, and control of influent flow. Based on a deep understanding of the laws of nature and their ingenious uses, this water conservancy works has gone through flood tests intact for more than 2,200 years and it still works perfectly to its functions.

In modern times, scientific development has given people a deeper understanding of the laws of nature, and its use has also been greatly improved, thereby promoting the rapid advancement of technology. But no matter how successful human beings are in applying the laws of nature, their understanding of them is still at a superficial level.

People often confuse the "rule of nature" with the "law of nature." Although there is a correlation between the rules of nature and the laws of nature, they are completely different concepts. The following is an example.

When you stand at the door of a school, you may observe and find that all the people coming out the gate are girls, with no exception, so you discover a phenomenon that the students from this school are all girls. According to this observation, you can predict that the next one should be a girl. This is called "a rule" which is a summary of people's experience of some common phenomenon in nature and human society.

Why is there such a rule? After learning more and knowing that this is a girls' school, you suddenly understand why this is so. The enrollment rules of the girls' school stipulate that only girls are enrolled. It is this stipulation that causes you to only see the rule of only girls.

It should be noted that the law is the real cause, and the rule is only the phenomenon that the law causes. Because of the existence of laws, the development process of things will show the rules, so the laws determine the rules and the enrollment rules of the girls' school determine that you can only see the rule of only girls. From the rules, you can't draw the laws. If you can only see the girls, it does not necessarily mean it is a girl-only school that must only recruit girls. Or it may be simply because the school gate is just in front of the girls' dormitory.

In the 18th century, the German philosopher Kant realized that "the things per se" are different from the "things in our eyes." He said that what we can know is only what we see in our eyes. We can never know the true colors of things. In the same way, the natural laws we observe are only the appearance of natural laws, and we cannot simply think of them as the laws of nature. Just like in the picture you may see the shadows of a man's head and a woman's head, but is this the truth?

The rule as a phenomenon is likely to change, but the law behind it will not change. The entrance of a few neighboring schoolboys to the girls' school will break the rule of only seeing girls, but this does not mean that its enrollment rules (the law) have changed.

Because the concept of the law is often confused with that of the rule, some people take it for granted that the rule of nature is an iron-firm law. This is not the case. As the angle of observation changes, the natural rules that people summarize will change. What remains unchanged is the natural law that exists behind it. Regrettably, we can discover and summarize the rules of nature, but we can never use them to infer the true laws of nature, as Einstein said: "You can't see the cards in the hands of God."

What needs to be reminded is that scientific laws are just the natural rules that people have summed up, not the laws of nature. Darwin once said: "Science is to sort out the facts, discover the rules, and draw conclusions." This is a good summary. The subject of scientific research is the phenomena existing in the real world. The method adopted is to conduct research in different categories. The result can only be a partial understanding of the rules of nature, rather than an overall understanding of the laws of nature.

History has proven that except for the mathematical field of pure thinking, the violation of scientific laws is commonplace. At the end of the 19th century, the theoretical system of classical physics, which was composed of Newton's classical mechanics, Maxwell's electromagnetic theory, and thermodynamics, achieved such a brilliant success that many people felt that physics was nearing the end, but it was soon overwhelmed by the theory of relativity and the quantum theory.

All the scientific laws that people think have been fully validated are only limited verifications, because people can never exhaust all the phenomena in the universe to prove their correctness. So, in a strict sense, we can never be sure that the laws of science are correct, and at most, we can only say that we have not found its errors yet.

This can even lead to such a frustrating conclusion that science can never give us the truth. It's just because of the enormous practical value of science that we often choose to ignore this fact.

But what is more easily overlooked is this question: Why is there a natural law?

For a long time in human history, people have become accustomed to this kind of order in the world. Finally, someone began to think about this problem. Thomas Aquinas wrote: "People observe a behavioral order that tends to a certain purpose in all objects, and all objects follow the laws of nature, even when they are not aware." Aquinas realized that the world is operating by the laws of nature. He used this as evidence of the existence of God and believed that it was God who made the rules behind the scenes.

Since then, people have slowly begun to consciously discover the laws of nature. By the 17th century, the modern concept of the laws of nature had begun to appear. The German astronomer Kepler and the Italian scientist Galileo were able to understand the meaning of the term in the modern scientific sense. Galileo also found many laws of nature.

The first person who clearly and rigorously expresses the concept of the modern law of nature is Descartes. He believes that all physical phenomena must be explained by the collisions of moving objects. This process is governed by the laws of nature. What he talked about is the forerunners of Newton's laws of motion. Descartes is also very aware of the importance of the initial conditions, knowing that only when the initial conditions are determined, the system will evolve with time under the constraints of the laws of nature, otherwise, the process cannot be inferred by the laws of nature.

In recent centuries, the development of science has made people's understanding of the laws of nature deeper and deeper. The operating mechanism hidden behind the world has gradually become clearer. In the 17th century, for the first time, the British scientist Newton made it clear that the regularity of causality between natural events can be quantified by formula. Later, more and more scientific laws were discovered in various subject areas, and the world that seemed to be somewhat vague in the eyes of the people was gradually more and more clearly described by various formulas.

Where do these laws come from? Early scientists, such as Kepler, Galileo, Descartes, and Newton, share roughly the same idea as Aquinas and generally believed that the natural laws that determine the course of the world are God's masterpieces.

But now, it is difficult for us to hear such a claim that the laws of nature are from the hands of God. Why is there such a change? The reason is also the theory of evolution. Darwin's theory of evolution denies the idea of God's creation, and thus makes people no longer believe that the world is created by God, and at the same time, it denies God's idea of enacting the laws of nature.

According to the theory of evolution, the complex order and biological diversity of the Earth's biological world are automatically formed under the influence of natural selection, not the creation of God's consciousness. Starting from this logic, people began to think, that since the complex natural ecological order can be produced by ordinary natural functions, without a prime mover, is it possible that the complex natural law itself can be automatically generated under natural action?

"Why could your Ace crush my King?"
"This is the rule of playing cards!"
"Where has the rule come from? Why is this determined?"
"The rule has been around for a long time. Don't bother to know where it comes from. Anyway, we have been playing in this way all the time!"

With the theory of evolution becoming more and more popular, its logic has also been widely used in various subject areas. More and more scientists believe that natural laws can be automatically generated, which gradually became the mainstream of thinking. In this way, people have become accustomed to the phenomenon of the existence of natural laws in nature.

But people seem to have intentionally or unintentionally ignored this point: the scientific community's view that natural law is automatically generated has never been proved. Such a rigorous and complicated natural law, like God, can generate itself.

As for the existence of the supernormal phenomenon of natural laws, we have to ask: Why do natural laws exist? Who made them?

Let us Consider Philosophical Thinking, Mathematical Calculations, and Scientific Verifications.

In the beginning, human understanding of the world was irrational. The priest was important in many primitive tribes. It was not until the emergence of philosophers that rationality was brought into people's way of thinking. There emerged a large number of philosophers in ancient Greece in the 6th century BC, beginning with Thales. Almost in the same period, there also appeared a large number of philosophers in China, with Lao Tzu and Confucius as the most famous ones. An unprecedented age of boom of schools of thought came to age.

This kind of understanding of the world obtained through philosophical thinking is generally based on experience. They are pure thoughts. People are used to testing them through debate, rather than proving them through practice. That's what it means by saying debate leads to truth. Philosophers can often also be called thinkers. They focus on ideas but not on practice; they focus on determining the nature of a phenomenon without paying attention to its quantity. Plato believes that the role of perception is limited to the understanding of phenomena, and it cannot be a tool for acquiring rational knowledge. Truth is the product of pure thinking and can only be obtained through reflection and contemplation.

This characteristic of philosophical thinking enables it to stand in a relatively high position and to observe the world as a whole, but its understanding is rough and vague, neither precise nor accurate.

Later, people began to question this way of knowing the world. Galileo believes that the language of nature is mathematics. The best way to observe and study nature is through scientific experiments. Mathematical formulas and experimental data should be used to express the laws of natural motion. There is a story that people long to relish. Galileo loosened his hands on the Leaning Tower of Pisa, letting two iron balls one big and one small fall down at the same time. As a result, two iron balls landed on the ground at the same time, so an extremely simple experiment smashed the idea that people had held fast for two thousand years -- Aristotle's idea that "heavy objects fall fast".

Since then, scientific experiments and mathematical language have gradually replaced philosophical speculation and become the main tool for human beings to understand nature. People have shifted from focusing on *qualitative* to focusing on *quantitative*, and the understanding of the world has begun to become clear and concrete.

The first person to establish a complete scientific theoretical system of the universe in mathematical language is Newton. In 1687, Newton published the book *The Mathematical Principles of Natural Philosophy*. Following the framework of Euclidean *Geometry Original*, the book, starting from the most basic definitions and axioms, almost depicts a complete universe in his heart in mathematical language with propositions, formulas, and proofs.

This is undoubtedly a breakthrough in human understanding of the world.

From then on, people are no longer limited to the philosophical language's general expression of the world. Instead, they use accurate mathematical methods to calculate the world's operation, and scientific experiments to verify their understanding of the world. This method has greatly promoted the development of science and revolutionized the way people think about the world.

However, there is not an absolute thing in the world. This kind of transformation also brings some problems.

One problem that people often overlook is that not all phenomena in the world can be verified. The scientific laws that people have summed up can be verified by the re-enactment of experiments, but for many things, such as history, you have no way to verify them. You can't use experiments to prove whether your own opinion on the causes of the Ming Dynasty's demise is right or wrong.

There are also other things like social political and economic phenomena, literature, and art that cannot be expressed by formulas and accurately mathematically calculated. What is purely spiritual is more complicated; it cannot be calculated, and it is difficult to verify with experiments. Because of its inability of it to perform calculations and verification, in many people's minds, these areas are naturally excluded from the scope of scientific research. So now science in the general sense refers to the natural sciences, and in fact, it just reflects only part of the world.

Over time, people's obsession with mathematical calculations and scientific evidence has gradually evolved to the point where they can't be added. Many prestigious scientists have thought about using a simple set of equations to describe the whole world. While scientific experiments and mathematical calculations are popular, philosophical thinking is increasingly forgotten. The most direct consequence of this is that it has created a gap between science and humanities, science and the public, and natural sciences and social sciences. Science has become something that only experts can understand.

In the time when Confucius lived, a woodcutter in the mountains and a farmer in the field could be philosophers who had a deep understanding of life and the universe, but this situation has long ceased to exist. The right of interpretation of the world has become the private property of the experts, and a high wall was built up in all fields to block the line of sight from outside.

Some people complain that people don't care about science, but few people reflect: Is this due to that the public does not love science, or is this because science is out of the reach of the public?

Logical thinking is the way of thinking that most people are used to. The mathematical formula and scientific verification are far away from daily life. *Sherlock Holmes* is easier to understand than *the Philosophy Principles of Natural Science* because the logical reasoning in the former is more in line with people's thinking habits. But now many people believe that only science that can be calculated and verified is called science, and the role of thought is completely ignored. They are accustomed to using mathematical formulas to express them. They don't use logical language to discuss them. It's no wonder that ordinary people can't understand science. Just like in China, people are used to speaking Chinese, but you insist on speaking English. How can you blame others when they can't understand what you are saying?

At present, in the scientific world, philosophical thinking lags far behind the paces of experimentation. Many scientific discoveries cannot be reasonably explained. This phenomenon is not unrelated to the extreme attitude towards philosophical thinking and the deliberate avoidance of research in some special fields.

How to solve these problems? We can expand the scope of scientific research by including all phenomena of the world in our scope of the study, not just those that can be described by scientific laws. We must admit that scientific verification and mathematical calculations are not the only way to study science. Science is not only something that can be verified and calculated, but philosophical thinking and even intuition are equally important.

Of course, we can also insist that the scope of scientific research can only be those areas where c calculations and verifications can be made. But, in this way, we must understand that science is not the only way to explain the world. There are philosophy, religion, and even some more mysterious things outside science that are equally important for understanding the world. We should not equate "science" with "correctness" and believe that only the conclusions obtained by scientific methods are credible, but we should encourage people to explore the blind spots and unknown areas of science regardless of the ways of these inquiries.

Chapter 3

The Creation of the Universe:
Is the Universe Born Out of Nothing?
What is There Outside the Universe?

The abnormal "supernormal phenomenon that is hardest for us to feel abnormal is not the existence of the natural laws, but the world in which we live—the universe. Why does it exist?

For most people, the existence of the universe may be a normal thing, and they will not doubt that they are secrets behind it.

But we have to start to doubt now because science has a discovery—the Big Bang Theory.

Let us look at the formation of this theory first.

In 1666, Newton discovered that white light is a kind of composite light. When passing through a triangular prism, it can be decomposed into a plurality of colors like a rainbow. This phenomenon is called "dispersion", and the separated monochromatic lights are sequentially arranged. It is called "spectrum".

After passing through the triangular prism, the white light will be decomposed into seven colors: red, orange, yellow, green, blue, enamel and purple.

Later, people turned the focus of the telescope to a single star or galaxy and observed the spectrum of the light coming from it. According to the Doppler Effect, by analyzing these spectra, it can be determined whether these stars are stationary or moving relative to us, or whether they are coming toward us or away from us. If they are leaving us, then the light we receive will have a longer wavelength and will move to the red end of the spectrum. This is called "the redshift; otherwise, it will move to the blue end, which is called "the blue shift".

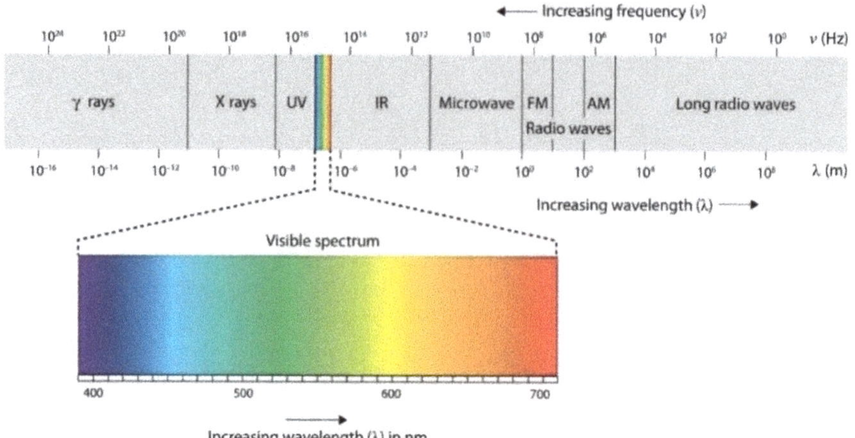

The figure above shows the electromagnetic spectrum. Electromagnetic waves are also called electromagnetic radiation. Radio waves, microwaves, infrared rays, visible light, ultraviolet rays, X-rays, and gamma rays are all electromagnetic waves. The difference between them is that the frequency and wavelength are different. Radio waves have the longest wavelength and the lowest frequency; gamma rays have the shortest wavelength and the highest frequency. The electromagnetic wave that people can see is called "visible light", which occupies only a narrow band in the entire electromagnetic spectrum.

In the 1920s, when people used this principle to observe distant galaxies, they expected to find as many red-shifted and blue-shifted spectra, because the galaxies were thought to be randomly moving. Surprisingly, however, when observing other galaxies outside the Milky Way, it was discovered that except for a few galaxies that are close to us, all other extragalactic galaxies showed redshifts and they were leaving us; and the further away the galaxies, the faster they leave us.

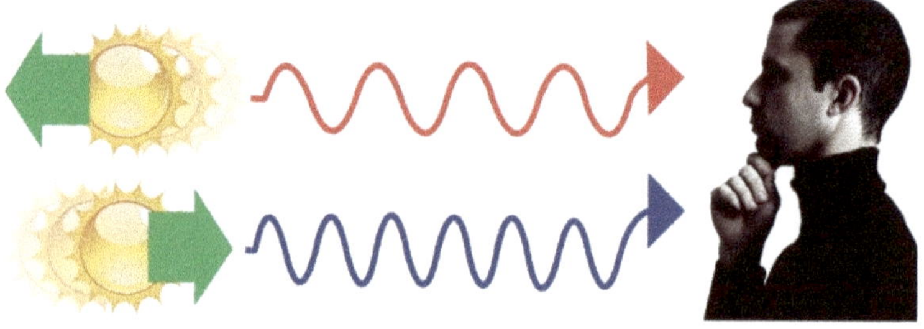

If the star that emits light moves in a direction away from us, then the wavelength of the light we receive will become longer, the spectrum will move to

the red end, and vice versa. So, by observing the spectrum of the star's rays, you can determine whether it is moving close to us or away from us, and you can determine their speed based on the degree of red or blue shift.

Based on the observations, people have come up with the possibility that the universe is not only limited but also in constant expansion. This idea subverts people's previous perceptions of the universe.

When we conducted a more in-depth study of this phenomenon, people came up with an incredible idea: If the universe is always in expansion, then look at this process in the reverse direction, does it mean that the universe started from an infinitesimal point at the beginning? Perhaps it was this kind of thinking that gave birth to the Big Bang theory.

The Big Bang theory describes the process of the making of the universe: the universe was born in a "big bang" a long time ago, and it has always been expanding, like a balloon that has been blown up from then on.

Such an incredible idea, of course, would not be believed at first, but, incredibly, there was more and more evidence to support this idea. The Big Bang theory predicts that the aftermath of the big bang at the time of the birth of the universe should still reverberate in the universe. As a result, the American astronomers Penzias and Wilson discovered microwave radiation in the cosmic background in 1964, confirming this statement. This discovery provides strong support for the Big Bang theory.

Later, more facts were found to support the Big Bang theory, and cosmologists had to face the reality and gradually accepted this strange idea. This theory shows that the universe was born about 13.7 billion years ago. It is not boundless but limited; it has a beginning, and very likely an end, and it is not an eternal existence.

The Big Bang Theory has brought a lot of confusion to people. The space inside the balloon is limited. We can easily understand this because the balloon has a film that separates the spaces inside and outside of the balloon. But the universe is limited. How do you understand this? Is there a membrane in our universe that separates the space inside and outside the universe? If so, what is there outside the universe? If there is no separation membrane and most of the space in the universe is a vacuum, then what is the difference between the spaces inside and outside the universe?

Why is there a big bang? The original Big Bang theory said that the big bang began with a "singularity", which is a point of infinitely small volume, infinite density, and infinitely high temperature. The idea is actually that all things now existing in the universe were infinitely compressed and existed in the form of energy at "the singularity."

Later, people further suspected that the world was born entirely in the void. The whole universe, including time, space, and matter, started from the Big Bang. Before the Big Bang, nothing existed. The creation of the universe is like what is said in the Bible: "God says that there is light, and there is light." It is a process of everything out of nothing. The American physicist Alan Guth once described this as: "The universe is a free lunch."

As soon as the Big Bang theory suggests that there was a day when the universe was created, we could no longer be indifferent to its existence. The universe cannot be born out of anything and for no reason. There must be some stories before this, and there must be something beyond it.

This is *the supernormal phenomenon* of the existence of the universe. The question we have to ask is: Why was the universe born? Why was it created out of a void? Who made the universe? What was there before the birth of the universe? What is outside the universe?

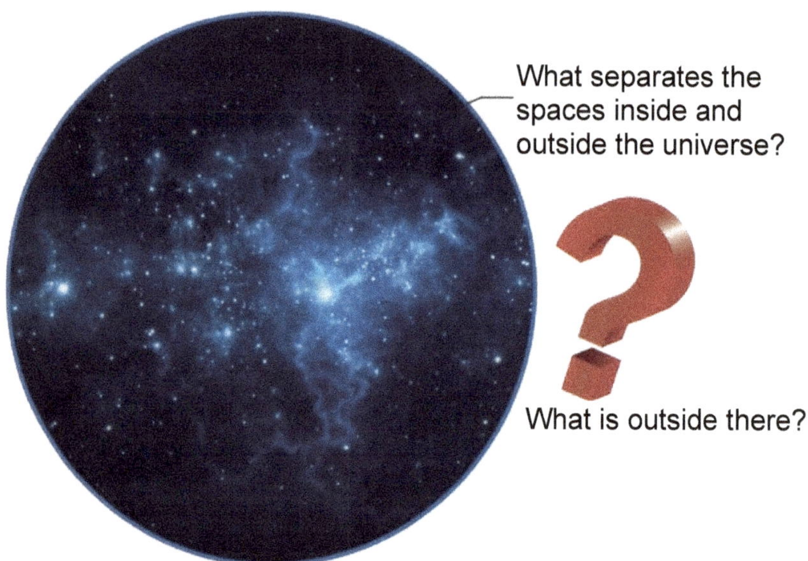

n addition to the Hubble red shift, and the cosmic microwave background radiation, the main evidence supporting the Big Bang theory is the abundance ratio of light elements in the universe. The Big Bang theory believes that in the first few minutes after the birth of the universe, nuclear fusion reactions took place in the universe. Its final products are mainly hydrogen atoms and helium atoms. This process is called " primeval nuclear synthesis." According to calculations, if the theory of the Big Bang is correct, then the matter in the universe should consist mainly of 25% helium and 75% hydrogen. This inference was later confirmed by observations.

But no matter how powerful the evidence is, objectively speaking, it is not enough to prove the Big Bang theory. There are too many problems in the Big Bang theory that cannot be explained. I would like to know, if the universe is limited, then what is outside the universe?

What is the Doppler Effect?

The Doppler Effect refers to the fact that the wavelength and frequency of the object's radiation changes due to the relative motion of the wave source and the observer. This phenomenon was first discovered by the Austrian physicist Christian John Doppler in 1842.

It is said that one day Doppler passed the railway crossing when he saw a train passing by. He found that when the train came from a distance, the whistle sounded and the tone was sharpening; and when the train drove from his side to the distance, the whistle sounded weaker, and the pitch was lower.

He put himself into the study and found that the reason is the change in the frequency of the sound wave (which can also be said to be the wavelength because the frequency is inversely proportional to the wavelength). The tone of the sound that people hear is determined by the frequency of the sound wave. The pitch is high when the frequency is high, and the pitch is low when the frequency is low.

If we and the sound source don't move, then the sound wave we receive will be the same as it was when it was sent, and the tone will not change. But if the sound source is approaching us, then the sound waves we receive, the wavelength, will be compressed and shortened, the frequency will be increased, the pitch will be sharpened, and vice versa.

The Doppler Effect was discovered in the study of sound waves, but it is not only applicable to sound waves but also to all other types of waves, including electromagnetic waves. The faster the wave source moves, the greater the change in wavelength and frequency. This principle is often used by traffic police to measure the speed of vehicles and is also used by astronomers to measure the speed of movement of distant objects.

The Big Bang Theory and Space Expansion

Before the Big Bang theory, people thought that space itself was stable, and there was a relative movement between the stars in the universe. Like in a big house, people in the house will walk around, but the size of the house itself will not change. No one ever thought that the space itself was in the midst of change and the house would be blown up like a balloon.

Strictly speaking, what people usually call "the expansion of the universe" is not very accurate. This expansion is not the overall expansion of the universe; it is only the expansion of the space of the universe, and the objects in the space have not become larger. As shown in the figure, the space becomes larger and the distance between the stars becomes larger, but the star does not become larger.

The development process of the Big Bang theory is rough as follows. In 1924, the Russian physicist Alexander Friedman first elaborated on the idea of the expanding universe based on the gravitational field equation of general relativity; in 1927, the Belgian cosmologist Le Mete had the same discovery and proposed that the universe originated from a "primeval atom"; in 1948, the Russian physicist George Gamoff and others published the "Hot Bomb Cosmology Model", which believed that the universe first began with the original material at a high temperature and a high density; and then as the universe expanded, the temperature gradually declined, and slowly formed the celestial bodies such as the current galaxies. According to this theory, they predicted the existence of cosmic microwave background radiation.

The earliest evidence supporting this theory is the observations of the universe. In 1914, the American astronomer Visto Sriver discovered that most galaxies were red-shifted. Later, the American astronomer Edwin Hubble conducted similar observations and discovered more red-shifted galaxies. In 1929 he published a further analysis of the observations to determine the degree of the redshift of the galaxies, that is, the linear speed that they are traveling away. The linear speed is roughly proportional to the distance between them and us. This is Hubble's Law.

The phenomenon of the red shift of the galaxy may suggest that the galaxies are moving in the direction away from us. But if this is the case, we can't explain why only the distant galaxies are showing redshifts; and some galaxies close to us, such as the Andromeda galaxy, will also exhibit a blue shift.

After excluding this possibility, the most reasonable explanation for the redshift of the galaxy is that the space itself is expanding, and the spacing between any two points in the background space is getting larger. According to Hubble's law, the farther away the space is, the more obvious the space expansion is. It can offset the relative motion between the galaxies, so those distant galaxies show redshifts. The spatial expansion rate between the nearby galaxies is small, and it is impossible to completely cancel their mutual movement. Therefore, there may be a red shift or a blue shift.

What Is the Universe's Microwave Background Radiation?

According to the theory of the Big Bang, in the high-temperature and high-density state at the beginning of the universe, space was filled with high-energy radiation, and the radiation produced pairs of particles, which were quickly annihilated in collisions and became radiation again. Later, as the universe continued to expand and cool, the temperature was reduced to a certain extent, and the radiation could no longer continue to produce particles, but the high temperature was still enough to separate the electrons from the nucleus. At this time, space was filled with free electrons, which hindered the propagation of radiation, so the universe was not transparent.

Until 380,000 years after the Big Bang, when the universe cooled to 3000 degrees, electrons could no longer escape the capture of the nucleus, and the original atoms were produced. The newly formed atoms are no longer filled with free electrons, the space becomes empty, the universe becomes transparent at once, and the radiation can pass through the universe without hindrance. Until today, after 13.7 billion years, we can still observe the radiation left at that time. In the long process of propagation, the space in which it travels has been continually expanding; and the redshift phenomenon makes its wavelength become longer and longer, and it eventually becomes a microwave, which is the "the universe's microwave background radiation" predicted by Gamow.

This type of radiation is nearly uniform, so theoretically it should be observed at any point in the universe and has nearly the same energy density in all directions. In 1964, Penzias and Wilson established a very sensitive angular antenna receiving system to improve satellite communications. They received an extra noise when they tested the system. Initially, they thought that the noise was caused by the antenna system itself, but after eliminating all possible faults, even after the bird droppings on the antenna were removed, the noise still existed, and no matter which direction the antenna pointed, the noise remained constant without any change of volume. As a result, they inadvertently discovered "the universe's microwave background radiation", and it is precisely because of this discovery that people began to accept the Big Bang theory.

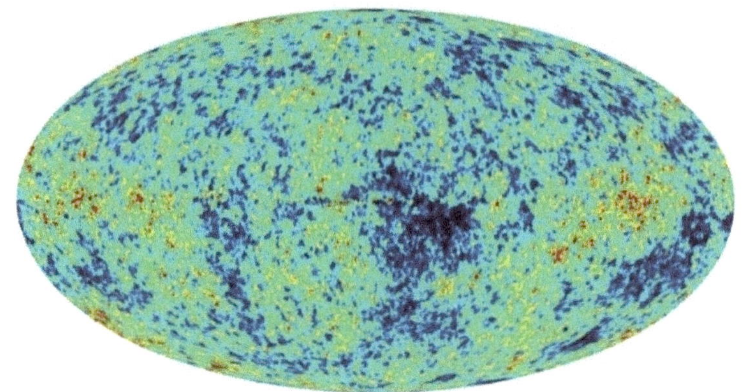

The above picture is an image reflecting the fluctuation of the cosmic temperature of 13.7 billion years ago, based on the observation of the cosmic microwave background radiation by the Wilkinson Microwave Anisotropy Detector launched by the United States. It is a "cosmic egg" in its infant period.

Inertial Thinking Embodied in Singularity

The vast universe originated from a small singularity, which is already a breakthrough in people's conception. It is generally agreed that time and space do not exist before the singularity, but in the understanding of the singularity itself, there are many different opinions, and it is difficult to form a unified opinion. Many people insist that singularity is a real point. Its volume is infinitely small but contains almost infinite energy. They think so because their inertial thinking is at work; they can't accept in any way that such a vast universe is born from nothing.

Such a way of thinking suggests to us a long-ignored fact: people are easily bound by established thoughts, and those inherent concepts are hard to change. As early as the 4th century BC, the Greek philosopher Plato understood that inertial thinking was too strong. He spoke of a famous "cave fable": a group of people lived in caves, they were tied from birth, they couldn't turn their heads, and they could only look at the wall in the cave forever. Behind them, a group of people walked around with torches every day, and their figures were cast onto the wall, which is the only thing those cave people can see. He asked: "Will these cave people regard the shadow on the wall as a real image of the world?" One day, a caveman accidentally gained freedom, walked out of the cave, and saw the real world. But when he went back and talked about the scene he saw, no one believed him at all. They all said, "Are our eyes blind? Can you only see it?"

Plato's statement has been repeatedly verified in history. Whenever someone puts forward a new concept for understanding the world, it will always be rejected by people, and that person even has to pay for it. Copernicus dared to publish the "solar center theory" only when he was dying. Bruno was burned at stakes in the square. Galileo had no choice but to sign the "repentance". These are all good proofs. Regrettably, people are taunting history while making the same mistakes.

Can You Get Something from Nothing?

The idea of creating out of nothing is not uncommon in the creation stories of mythology. For example, in Christianity, the creation of God requires neither material nor tools, and language alone is enough to produce the whole world. St. Augustine of the Roman times wrote in the 4th century AD in Confessions: "You are not holding any tools in your hands to create the heavens and the earth. Where do these tools come from that are not created but used by you for creating other tools? What kind of things come into existence not because of your existence? You give birth to everything, you use your 'way' -- words to create everything."

After the rise of science, for a long time, people did not believe that something could be born out of nothing. However, in the process of gradual acceptance of the Big Bang theory, some people began to suspect that since time and space start from singularity before they all exist, why can't material and energy be in the same way? Why do you have to believe that the universe was born in a singularity of high temperature and high density, rather than being completely born from nothing?

In the late 1960s, some people began to analyze the possibility that the universe was born from nothingness. They believe that the energy of gravity is negative, so when the universe was born, a gravitational field was formed between the material and energy appearing out of nowhere. The negative energy of this gravitational field can just cancel out the material and energy itself. From a technical point of view, it is possible to create a universe out of nothing without violating the law of conservation.

In 1973, the American physicist Edward Trian proposed the idea that the universe was born from nothingness. He believed that the universe was created by chance due to quantum fluctuations in the vacuum. In 1980, Alan Guth proposed the "inflation theory", saying that the universe did not expand from the singularity at a relatively fixed expansion speed, but it immediately formed a vast expansive universe after the Big Bang, then the universe expanded at a slower pace until now.

The theory of Guth solved some problems that the original Big Bang theory could not explain. As can be seen from the figure, the speed of the expansion of the universe is generally flat. According to this speed, in 13.7 billion years, the universe cannot expand as large as it is now. But if it has experienced a period of skyrocketing and a large universe is created in an instant, then this is a good explanation.

According to the inflation theory, the universe is formed in an instant. Just as the balloon was not blown up a little bit by bit, but suddenly there was a big balloon in the air, and then it was slowly blown even bigger. When we combine this scene with the mechanism of creating a gravitational field to create biomass, it is easy to think that the universe may have been suddenly born from nothingness, and there is no real singularity. So, Gus often refers it to as "the free lunch".

The British physicist Paul Davis said: "According to this unusual theory of cosmic creation, the whole universe is completely born out of nothing, and its creation process conforms to the laws of quantum physics. Such a universe in the process of its growth, created all matter and all energy, thus building the universe we are now seeing. Thus, this theory illustrates the creation of all physical things (including time and space). The model does not specify an unknowable singularity to give to the beginning of the universe."

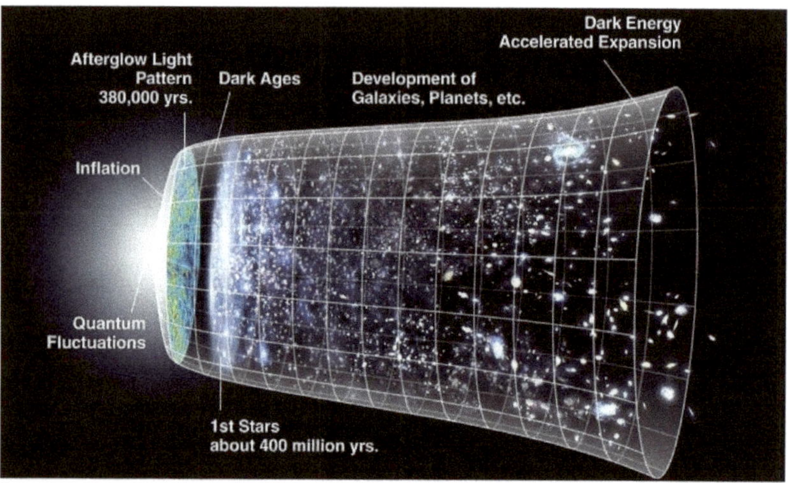

The universe is completely born from nothingness, and the degree of acceptance of this idea is not as high as that of the Big Bang theory. Because many people always think that creation needs raw materials, even if it is just a little something. The Japanese physicist Kako Michio once said: "In fact, to create a universe like ours, we may only need a very small net mass, maybe as small as 1 ounce."

The true meaning behind the birth of the universe out of nothing is still poorly understood. There are some confusing questions in Guth's inflation theory: Why did the universe suddenly become so big? Why did it suddenly stop this rapid expansion and turn into a slow expansion? What drives the skyrocketing expansion, and who is stopping it?

Chapter 4

What is Real?
Is the World in Front of You Real?
Don't Trust Your Eyes Too Much!

Compared with *the existence of the universe*, there is a deeper *supernormal phenomenon* that most people are not aware of, that is, *the authenticity of the world.*

I remembered when I was very young, I went to see the drama *The Fifteen Strings of Coins*. There was a murder scene in the play. When I saw the actor falling to the ground, I had a thought in my mind: "If in every play an actor will die, then how many actors are going to die?"

Looking back now, I feel that it was particularly naive and ridiculous at that time. But at the time, I thought so, because at that time I was still small, and there was no concept of "truth" and "falsehood" in my mind. I didn't know what had happened in the play was fake.

But don't laugh at me first, because in the face of the real world, you are actually like me, and the concept of "true" or "false" is also missing in your mind. We often say: "Seeing is believing". Of course, the world that the eyes see is taken as real. We never think about whether the world in front of us is also a play, or whether it is not real.

There are of course exceptions. Buddha Jodhpur Siddhartha has a different idea. In *the Heart Sutra*, he said: "Color is empty, empty is color." The "color" here refers to the world in our eyes. "Color is empty" means that the world we see is virtually illusory. In *the Diamond Sutra*, he also said: "All the truths are illusory." He thinks that everything we see in our eyes is illusory.

Some philosophers have similar views. In the 17th century, the French philosopher Descartes believed that the world was only a phantom in our hearts, not a real existence. But he also believed that everyone, their existence should be certain because if you don't even exist, then who is thinking and doubting? This is the origin of the philosophical famous saying "I think so I am."

If the world is illusory, why do *I* exist? If *I* do not exist, who is thinking about this problem? On the one hand, Descartes said that the world is illusory. On the other hand, he said that the existence of *I* is certain. It seems to be self-contradictory. It implies an inference that the spirit is more real than the substance.

This kind of view of negating the authenticity of the world is often called "idealism," and it is not recognized today because currently "materialism," another theory corresponding to this one, is in the dominant position.

According to materialism, the world is a real existence made up of matter. This kind of thinking has been in existence for a long time. The ancient "five elements theory" in ancient China believed that the world is composed of five basic elements of *gold, wood, water, fire, and earth*. Many philosophers in ancient Greece also had primitive materialistic thoughts. Heraclitus believed that fire is the source of all things, and the whole world is a group of eternal living fires. Thales believed that everything is composed of water. Anaksimini thought that gas is the origin of all things.

The influence of ancient materialism is not great, but it has become a mainstream thought in modern times. This change is closely related to new scientific discoveries, especially the law of conservation of mass.

A long time ago someone had conceived the idea of matter being constant. In the 5th century BC, the ancient Greek philosopher Democritus said: "Nothing that exists can disappear." Wang Fuzhi, a thinker in the late Ming and early Qing dynasties, said: "The changes of gathering and dispersion do not affect the basic body." But at the time this was just an idea, no one could prove it was right.

Scientific development has given this vision a chance to be proven. In 1620, the British philosopher Francis Bacon put forward the concept of *mass* and used it to measure the amount of matter contained in an object. This concept lays the foundation for the quantitative analysis of the matter.

In the 18th century, the Russian scientist Lomonosov first proposed the concept of *conservation of mass*. In his letter to Leonard Euler, he said: "Everything that happens in nature goes like this: how much is lost in one thing, and how much is gained in another. Therefore, if an object has added some substance, another object must have some substance disappear." He calcined a piece of tin in a closed container to form a white tin oxide. After measurement, the total mass of the material in the container was found to be unchanged before and after calcination. So, he proposed that the mass of matter in the chemical reaction is conserved. But at that time this statement did not attract the attention of the scientific community.

Later, in the study of oxygen, Lavoisier found that the increased mass of the burning object is exactly equal to the mass of oxygen reduction. He then conducted a series of precise quantitative experiments to prove that although the object changes its shape in the chemical reaction, the total mass of the object participating in the reaction does not change. Therefore, Lavoisier proved *the law of conservation of mass* by chemical experiments, and this law has been widely accepted since then.

This law holds that the total mass of everything in the world is constant and cannot be increased or decreased. Therefore, it is not difficult for people to come up with the idea that since the total amount of matter is constant and will never be lost, and then it should be an eternal existence, so the law of conservation of mass is also called the law of material immortality. With the support of this law, materialism has become popular. And by the 19th century, it has occupied a dominant position in the scientific community.

Under the influence of materialism, people think that the world is composed of a lot of real materials, and consciousness is only a highly developed material system--the function of the human brain is the subjective reflection of the objective world in the human brain. Therefore, consciousness is illusory. In this way, the authenticity of the world seems to have been proved, and there is no need to have any doubts.

Interestingly, scientific discoveries have caused the popularity of materialism; however, now more scientific discoveries are increasingly detrimental to this theory.

After entering the 20th century, materialism began to encounter serious challenges, and its cornerstone *the law of conservation of mass* was overthrown. It has been found that this law applies only to chemical reactions and is not a universal law of the world. Einstein's theory of relativity shows that the mass of an object is not constant, and the mass of an object increases with speed as it moves at high speeds. Later, in the particle accelerator, it was observed that when the speed of electrons and protons is increased to near the speed of light, the quality would increase by dozens of times or more, which proves that Einstein is right.

The European Nuclear Research Organization, located in the suburbs of Geneva, Switzerland, owns the world's largest particle accelerator, the "European Large Hadron Collider." It was installed in a circular tunnel of 27 kilometers at a depth of 100 meters underground and was officially put into operation on September 10, 2008. It is a high-energy physical device that can accelerate protons and let them collide, where protons can be accelerated to near the speed of light.

As the speed increases, the mass increases. The increase is just the measured mass of the existing matter. The matters are still those matters. But what is even more surprising is that it turns out that we can make new things. In the laboratory, two high-energy protons collide with each other at a very fast speed. Instead, they are not a pile of fragments, but three protons, one antineutron, and several π mesons. The total mass of these particles is greater than that before the collision. The mass of protons has indeed increased.

Since we can make matter, then the law of conservation of mass is finished. And materialism has a big problem: Since matter can be produced out of thin air, how can it be *the origin of the world*?

Fortunately, Einstein's *Equation of Mass and Energy* gave it a chance to justify it. According to Einstein's theory, under certain conditions, mass and energy can be transformed into each other. Those newly formed substances are not coming out of thin air. They come from the energy contained in high-energy protons, so that conservation of mass becomes conservation of mass and energy.

Then some people put energy into the category of matter, saying that energy is also a substance. As long as it is objective and practical, it is a substance. The common saying is that "material is an objective reality that does not depend on but can be reflected by human consciousness." If such a small change is made to this equation, materialism will not be overthrown.

But what does "reality" mean here? Is it "physical existence" or "real existence"? At first, people thought that matter is a "physical existence," which can be measured by the size of the master s. But, after discovering that the physical material and the intangible energy can be transformed into each other, one has to only modify the understanding of "reality" into "real existence."

The problem is that energy is intangible, and consciousness is invisible;

energy is real, doesn't consciousness exist? Every normal person is conscious, which is not what we imagined. Energy can matter. Why can't consciousness be her?

Some people may explain that energy can produce physical effects between other substances, so energy is a substance; there is no physical interaction between consciousness and matter, so consciousness is not a substance. But this is not necessarily true! As we will discuss in detail later, quantum theory has proved that consciousness can have a physical effect on the matter!

With the emergence of new scientific discoveries, the concept of *the materiality of the world* has long been made unrecognizable. If you are not a professional, you will feel that many things are too outrageous to be imagined.

Can you think of some particles in the world that are of no mass? Indeed, "photons" and "gluons" are particles of no mass. It can be seen from the words *light steam* that people originally thought that light is continuous, but it consists of photons. But photons have no static mass, so light can only exist in motion. Once it stops, it will disappear without a trace.

At first, Bacon put forward the concept of *mass* as a measure of the amount of matter. From this definition, the size of mass represents the amount of matter, and the absence of mass means no substance. But Bacon will never think that there are particles of no mass in the world.

In the face of numerous new scientific discoveries, materialism has long been turbulent, and it is difficult to protect itself, let alone use it to prove the authenticity of the world.

This result is not difficult to predict. If true material is the origin of the world, then in addition to pursuing material enjoyment, what else can we pursue in our life? But, in our lives, materials are only a part of it, otherwise, life is too boring. If the world is just a simple pile of materials, what is the significance of the splendid culture created by mankind—history, religion, literature, and art?

Materialism is going to collapse. If this fact only makes you doubt the authenticity of the world, then another scientific discovery may further consolidate your thinking. It is the Big Bang theory that I mentioned earlier.

The Big Bang theory says that the universe was born entirely in nothingness, which is actually enough to deny the authenticity of the universe. You can imagine, if you have the opportunity to observe outside the universe, when you see the universe born from nothingness, like a holographic image suddenly popping out in front of your eyes, do you still think it is real? Or ask from another angle, the real thing, can it be changed out of thin air?

Compared with our analysis, some people may be more willing to believe their eyes. He will say: "This world is of course real; it is what I saw with my own eyes!"

But is what we see really what it is? Scientists will say to you: you are wrong! You see the red flowers, just because the flowers absorb the light of other colors and only reflect the red light into your eyes. In other words, you see the red flower, not because it is red, but just because it can't absorb the red light. What is its true color? Only God knows.

So don't think "real" is too simple, and don't trust your eyes too much!

About the supernormal phenomenon of the authenticity of the world, the question we have to ask is: What is real for us? Is the world real? Or is it just a play?

I heard a friend talk about his experience at the Shanghai World Expo. In a certain hall, when he entered, he saw a lecturer standing in the middle of the field giving a wonderful commentary, but the wonderful thing was that after the commentary, the person suddenly disappeared. He was very surprised and stood there waiting for the next scene to find out what was going on. When the second scene began the speaker popped up again in an empty place. He immediately realized that it was a holographic image, not a real person.

Imagine if the friend watched the whole process from the beginning to the end for the first time and saw the scenes of the sudden appearance of the speaker. Would he still be deceived? On the issue of the authenticity of the world, the truth is the same. When we were born with our eyes open, we saw the world in front of us, so it is natural to think that it is real. If you have ever seen the birth of the world from scratch and the complete evolutionary process, would you still think so confidently?

Is the Basket Full of Fruit?

If you want to know what's in the basket, it's best to take a look inside and make a judgment.

Initially, you took out pears, bananas, mangoes, grapes, and apples from the basket... You found these are all fruits, so you summed up the "fruit-only theory": the baskets are all fruits. What has come out at this stage has indeed confirmed your judgment.

Then you continued to take out, and suddenly you picked out a cabbage, the "fruit-only" is challenged! But at this time, this concept has become ingrained in your mind and turned into a kind of inertial thinking, so your reaction is not "I am wrong", but "the cabbage is also a fruit!"

Later, you took out a book, a makeup box, a roll of paper from the basket... Are these all fruits? At this time your brain is completely messed up! But for you, the concept of "fruit-only theory" has been difficult to erase, so you simply stipulate: "All things in the basket are called fruits!"

This is the case with materialism. As early as the 5th century BC, Democritus of Greece believed that the world was composed of atoms and voids. This is typical materialism. The essence of the world is a pile of matter in space. The material mentioned here obviously refers to an entity like an atom. Later, many people accepted this idea. Newton often uses the "quantity of matter" to refer to mass. His claim is actually to treat matter as a substance and to think that mass is the ultimate measure of matter.

According to the *Law of Conservation of Mass*, people recognize that the world is material, and the concept of matter is clear to them. But then it was discovered that there are particles of no mass, and the physical matter can be transformed with an intangible energy. How can this be explained? Time, space, laws of nature, social structure, etc. are also all part of the world. If the world is only a simple pile of matter, then what are they? At this time, people's thinking has become chaotic. Some people simply say that everything that exists, in reality, is called matter.

Do you agree with this logic? Why do we have to hold on to the idea that the "world is material"? Can we simply recognize that there are not only fruits but also other things in the basket? This is the case with religion. Religion once thought that its teachings were correct and could not be changed. And it was only completely defeated by science. Do we want to repeat the same mistakes?

How the Visual Organ Works

Among the various sensory organs of human beings, vision is undoubtedly the most important one. It can be a kind of remote sensing, which enables us to receive information from a distant place without having to contact directly like touch and taste.

The formation of vision requires information, which is contained in the light we receive, so we can't see things in the dark where there is no light. Then to perceive the information in the light, we need a detector that responds to the light, which is the *retina*. As the light passes through the *lens* of the eye, the image is reversed and then focused onto the retina on the posterior surface of the eye.

The retina is both a signal receiver and an information converter. The innermost layer is composed of millions of photoreceptor cells. Each photoreceptor cell contains a light-sensitive molecule called *the photosensitive pigment*. When exposed to light, these photo pigments become unstable and decompose, in a process that changes the flow of current around the photoreceptor cells, triggering the action potentials of downstream neurons. In this way, the photoreceptor cells convert the external light stimulus into an internal neural signal that the brain can understand.

Next is the transmission of information. The efferent channel of retina information is the ganglion cells. The axons of this cell form a bundle of nerves called the optic nerve. The visual information is transmitted to the brain's central nervous system through the optic nerve.

Interestingly, there are about 260 million photoreceptors on the retina, but only 2 million ganglion cells and the cells receiving information are far more than the cells that transmit information. This illustrates the problem that the retina compresses the information before it is transmitted. This compression is so efficient that it is enough to dwarf the compression software currently on the market. At the same time, this phenomenon also shows that the visual center located in the brain is an efficient processor, and the level of decompression is also first-class so that the important details of the visual image can be recovered from this highly compressed information.

Then the brain acts as the processor that restores the information to an image. The principle is more complicated. People haven't mastered the details until now, only knowing that it is doing very well. In life, you should have the experience that the picture taken by the camera during rapid shaking will be much shaken, making it difficult to distinguish the image, but the image seen by humans in motion is still clear. The brain knows how to automatically eliminate the effects of sloshing when processing signals and its intelligence is far beyond our imagination.

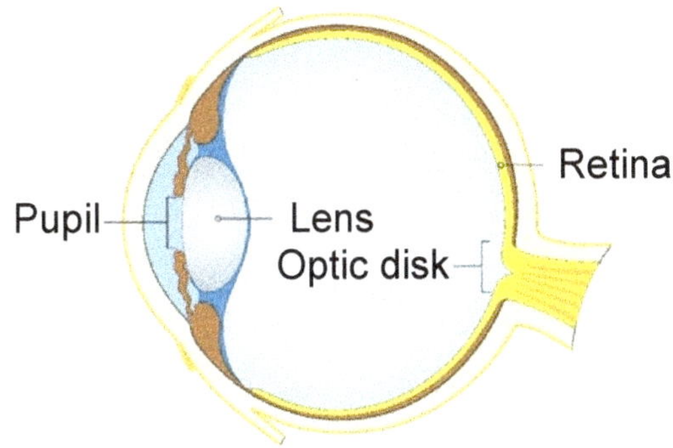

As can be seen from the above process of vision formation, what we see is highly dependent on the information received and the patterns that the brain employs to process this information. Once there is a problem with these links, we will have vision impairments. Some people lack the sensitizing pigments that are sensitive to medium or long waves in the retina, and they become red-green blind; some people lack short-wave sensitizing pigments and become yellow-blue blind. There is also a kind of person with visual cone cells that do not work properly, who is unable to recognize color by nature. For these people, the world they live in is a black-and-white world.

Logically, we see what kind of information is entered by the visual sense, and the same is true for other sensory organs. So, in a strict sense, we don't perceive the world. What we perceive are just the signal inputs.

Chapter 5

The Evolutionary Myth:
Are the Species Evolved?
Is There Any Other Possibility?

Some supernormal phenomena are created by humans themselves. Some of the most influential scientific theories were once doubted when they were first proposed, but later they were gradually accepted, as people slowly became accustomed to them and took their existence for granted. The theory of evolution is a case in point.

In the history of science, the theory of evolution is undoubtedly one of the most controversial theories, but its influence is unparalleled. The contest between science and religion delivers a fatal blow to the Church and causes the collapse of the Christian doctrine system.

Darwin studied theology at Cambridge University. He was expected to be a pastor. Instead, he became a champion who challenged the Christian doctrine, which is quite contradictory to his original purpose. In 1831, he boarded the royal warship *HMS Beagle* as a naturalist and began a five-year global scientific expedition. This journey opened his mind, casting his doubts on the origin of life held by the Church. In 1859, he published *The Origin of Species*. At the beginning of the book, he pointed out: "Species are not created by God, but are evolved from other species, just like variants." In this book, Darwin proposed *the evolution theory* opposite to the popular *creation theory* at that time, which profoundly impacted later generations.

According to the theory of evolution, organisms generally have variability, and many mutations are inheritable. There are survival competitions within and between populations, and competition can preserve favorable mutations and eliminate harmful ones. This is the process of natural selection of "the survival of the fittest, the elimination of the unfit". The result of natural selection leads to the evolution of living things, and the existing creatures on the earth gradually evolved from common ancestors by this mechanism.

Or we can sum it up in a simple sentence. The existing species on the earth are naturally formed by natural selection through the accumulation of random mutations.

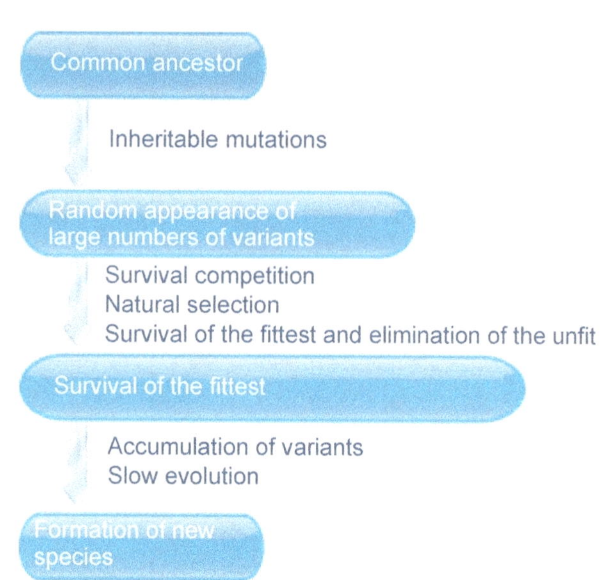

The publication of the theory of evolution caused a tremendous uproar at the time, and the controversy has not subsided until today. The Christians have never stopped attacking it. But in the scientific world, evolution theory has now basically dominated the thinking and become an unshakable pillar theory.

In those days, in such a social environment, I believe, Darwin had been hesitant about whether to disclose his findings for a long time, because the church was still very powerful, and such action took a lot of risks. But what's interesting is that today, if a person engaged in scientific research wants to put forward an idea negating evolution, he is also taking risks. This is because the existence of evolution has become a *supernormal phenomenon* created by man, and any theory that negates evolution can lead to hostility and even siege from the scientific community. You are likely to be marginalized, and even to be banished by the scientific community.

Even so, I still want to point out here, that there are many doubts about the theory of evolution, and it is hard to say how much of it is correct.

From the point of common sense, the theory of evolution is doubtful. The second law of thermodynamics shows that unless there is external force interference, an isolated system will always develop in a disorderly direction. It is easy to observe that in the natural state if it is not regulated, the disorder of things will continue to increase. Just as if you don't clean up the house, it will become more and more of a mess. But the situation in the biological world is exactly the opposite. It not only maintains an orderly state but also is still moving in an increasingly complex direction. The theory of evolution says that such a trend occurs naturally and that no matter how complex the ecosystem is and how delicate the biological structure is, they are just a series of accidental superimpositions. Don't you think this is contrary to common sense?

If the power of chance is so big, why can't the natural world accidentally generate a watch or a plane?

Darwin is not unaware of the flaws in his theory, nor does he cover up the problem. This is the reason why he is a respectable person. In his book, he frankly pointed out that there are some problems in evolution that are difficult to explain. This is not a problem in itself. Many theories have defects at the beginning, and they have been gradually improved. But what is worse is, that more than a hundred years have passed, most of these problems remain unresolved, and even the hope of resolution is not seen at all. This cannot but make us doubt. Could Darwin be wrong? Could the evolution theory be wrong?

The first unexplained problem in the evolution theory is if species evolve through subtle gradual changes, why couldn't we see a large number of transitional types? Why are species in nature different in such an obvious way that they are never confused?

Let me explain this problem. According to the evolution theory, the evolution

of species is the result of the accumulation of random variation through natural selection, and the change should be continuous in general. To give a simple example, people now think that birds evolved from dinosaurs. According to the logic of evolution, the process must be like this: dinosaurs become a bit like birds; they become like birds; they eventually become birds. In this way, in the long process of evolution, there will be countless transitional species between dinosaurs and birds, which are more like birds than dinosaurs or more like dinosaurs than birds. And because variation is continually occurring, the number and variety of intermediate transition species should be much greater than those for dinosaurs and birds themselves.

How are the huge differences between dinosaurs and birds eliminated? Where have those intermediate transitional species gone?

But in fact, there are no transitional species in the real natural world. Darwin explains that transitional species must exist, but they are extinct under the influence of natural selection. At the same time, he believes that the lack of fossil evidence of their existence is caused by the adequacy of geological records and that later, with the advancement of technology, the existence of transitional species will eventually be proved after more geological data is discovered.

However, the world often does not go as one might wish, and the development of the situation is beyond Darwin's expectations. Now that technology is quite developed, there are enough geological data, but there are still no traces of transitional species.

Don't you think that the evolution theory may be wrong?

The second unexplained question in the evolution theory is: Can the generation of complex organs like the eye also be explained by natural selection?

Darwin thinks it can, and he hopes that there will be more evidence to support his point of view. But now we can conclude through simple logical judgment that complex organs cannot be naturally generated.

The defense organ of *the farting insect* is a good example. The fart bug has a simple defense system that, when threatened, ejects a hot, toxic solution from the tail to kill natural enemies. This defensive organ consists of hydrogen peroxide and hydroquinone, an enzyme catalyst, a reservoir, a sphincter, an expander, and an efflux catheter. It works by storing a mixture of hydrogen peroxide and hydroquinone in the reservoir. When a threat is discovered, the sphincter opens like a control valve, feeds the mixture into the expander, and then injects the enzyme catalyst to cause an explosion. After the explosion, the mixture is ejected from the rear discharge tube and sprayed precisely onto the unfortunate enemy's face.

This defensive organ is a complete system and cannot work properly without any one of its components. If it is evolved, what component is the one that first evolved? From a practical point of view, it should evolve the chemical weapons that are conducive to survival, but which of hydrogen peroxide, hydroquinone, and enzyme catalyst first appears? The three of them mix together and only one does not work, so it doesn't matter which appears first. Even if the three chemicals can appear at the same time, if there is no sphincter blockage, the fart bug will blow itself into pieces, which is impossible, so you need to have a control switch first. But before the chemical weapons, will the fart bug evolve into a switch? If it does, it can only show that this evolution is purposeful and not random.

No matter which part of the defense system is developed first for the fart bug, it will not work alone and will not help the survival of the bug, and it will become a cumbersome burden. According to the evolutionary point of view, this variant will only be eliminated, and it is impossible to add more appendages on this basis until all the appendages are combined to form a complete defense system.

The defense organ of *the farting insect* is a good example. The fart bug has a simple defense system that, when threatened, ejects a hot, toxic solution from the tail to kill natural enemies. This defensive organ consists of an enzyme catalyst, a sphincter, an expander, and an efflux catheter. It works by storing a mixture of hydrogen peroxide and hydroquinone in the reservoir. When a threat is discovered, opens like a control valve, to cause a violent explosion. After the explosion, the Mixture Is Ejected From The Rear Discharge Tube And Sprayed Precisely Onto The Unfortunate Enemy's Face.

A reservoir
Mixture of hydrogen peroxide and hydroquinone
Control valve
Sphincter
Expander
Feeds the mixture into, and then ejects the enzyme catalyst
Explosion and ejaculation
Duct to outside

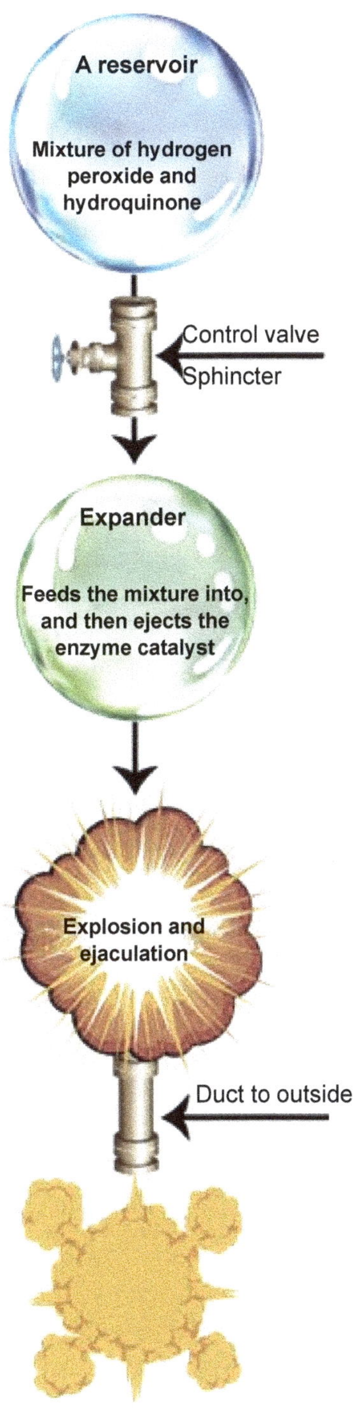

41

Even such a simple organ is logically impossible to form naturally, let alone those more complicated organs. Bats and dolphins have a sonar system with an echolocation function. They need to have a high-pitched throat and a high-pitched ear. They can use three-dimensional echoing depiction techniques in their brain to form a 3D image based on the acoustic waveforms. The complexity of this system is beyond imagination. The human eye can automatically adjust the focus according to the distance of the object and the intensity of light and can correct spherical aberration and color deviation. Such a color imaging system is much more complicated than the defense organs of the fart insect. How could they be naturally formed?

The reproductive organ is another type of organ which is more difficult to explain with the evolution theory. It is well known that male genitals are associated with female genitalia, and they must be present at the same time to function. Otherwise, this evolution is meaningless. How can you convince me and make me believe that the male reproductive organ just evolves at the same time as the female reproductive organ evolves and that the two types of organs match each other perfectly and can interact and produce appropriate responses?

Modern molecular genetics points out that the growth and normal functioning of biological organisms are under the control of the genetic genes inside their cells. The exquisite and ingenious operation mechanism of these genes is far beyond imagination. The complexity of the eye is not worth mentioning, compared with it. Some even said that if Darwin had understood molecular genetics, he would never have published his theory of evolution again.

Don't you think that evolution is really wrong?

The third unexplained question in evolution is how an extremely complex instinct like a bee nesting can be acquired and changed by natural selection.

Instinct is the innate ability of animals and does not need to be learned. I can't imagine how the formation of animal instinct is explained by evolution. From common sense, the variation of the body may be inherited, but the acquired abilities could not be inherited. The artist cannot pass the skills of painting onto the child so that he can understand painting without learning. So how do the bees obtain the ability to build so complex nests, and how are they passed on to the next generation?

Evolution cannot explain this phenomenon at all.

There is still a fourth unexplained problem in evolution. It is not only confusing but also has some mystery, that is, the sudden emergence of clusters of related species mentioned in *The Origin of Species.*

Darwin believes that evolution is the result of natural selection of randomly generated mutations. To form such a complex biological structure, the number of random variants used for selection is of an astronomical order. The best explanation for producing so many variants is that the variation is continuous and long enough. Therefore, Darwin believes that biology should evolve gradually. *There is no leap in nature.*

From current knowledge, we know the earth was born about 4.6 billion years ago and the earliest signs of life that have been discovered date back to 3.8 billion years ago. This is good news for evolution. It seems that it can produce enough variants in such a long time. According to Darwin, the ideal situation is that in the following time the creatures are constantly evolving in equilibrium. But the fossil evidence does not support his wishes.

The fossil evidence that has been discovered so far shows that organisms have been slowly evolving until the Cambrian period more than 500 million years ago. In the long period of more than 3 billion years, almost all of life was still in the stage of single-celled creatures. In this period, the earth was quiet. However, after entering the Cambrian, the evolution of life made a rapid leap forward. In just a few million years, almost all major biological groups suddenly emerged. This *is the Cambrian explosion*.

This is a magnificent bloom of life, and its scale is beyond imagination. Simply put, the variety of creatures at that time was much more than it is now. Almost all the biological categories we see now can be found in the Cambrian period, and as many as 20 phyla of species existing at that time have become extinct now!

Such a large number of biological species emerged in a short period, and this phenomenon cannot be explained by evolution theory anyway. This is not only a leap in the natural world but also a gorgeous collective jump of the lineup. It is more like a wild experiment of nature. It is more like the intense drop of the species by the creator. Most of them are unsuccessful test items. They are extinct shortly, and only a few survive and become the ancestors of all later species.

Stephen Jay Gould, an American paleontologist who has studied the Cambrian life explosion, wrote in *The Wonderful Life*: "Life history is a massive elimination, and then a few surviving varieties are divided. The story of life, unlike what is usually thought, is a story of constant optimization, complication, and diversification."

From this point of view, the theory of evolution is completely wrong in the direction of the evolution of life.

The problem is not limited to these. A few days ago, I watched the documentary *Killer Instinct*. When the scene that the crocodile preying on the prey appeared on TV, the commentary sounded: "This evolution that was completed before the prehistoric period is still very successful today!" This passage reminded me that the crocodile appeared in the biosphere 200 million years ago, sharks existed 400 million years ago, and there has been little change in the last 100 million years. This phenomenon is very abnormal. According to the evolutionary point of view, variation is random, and evolution should be endless. But the shark has stopped evolving. What has it done in the long years of these 100 million years?

Under careful scrutiny, the theory of evolution is full of so many loopholes that it is difficult to justify it. American mathematician Cohen wrote in *Darwin's Wrong: A Study of Probability*: "All the concepts put forward by evolution are just imagination, and the reliable scientific facts from microbiology, fossils, and mathematical probabilities do not support these concepts. Darwin is wrong."

About the *supernormal phenomenon* of *evolution*, the question we have to ask is: given so many flaws, can evolution be correct? What is the truth about the evolution of life?

Can the System Structure Be Naturally Generated?

When we describe a group of people's lack of organization, we usually say that it is "a loose pile of sand." This term illustrates the problem that there is a loose relationship between each grain of sand in the pile; taking off a few grains of sand, or adding a few grains of sand, the sand pile is still a sand pile, and it does not show any significant changes. This simple accumulation of things is easily generated automatically under natural action. The sand pile you see in front of you is likely to be formed entirely under the influence of the wind. A few grains of sand are blown to the pile every day, which is slowly formed over time.

Evolutionists believe that species are naturally formed, and the logic behind this is exactly the same. They believe that a little bit of inheritable variation slowly accumulates, and as long as the time is long enough, it can naturally generate a colorful world of organisms.

But when people make such logical derivation, they ignore a very important fact: the pile of sand is just a simple pile, but the organism is a system structure, and there is a big difference between them.

The various components of the system structure are closely related, and they can only play their respective roles under the premise of cooperation. They are not in a simple relationship of "1 plus 1 equals 2". Therefore, removing a few grains of sand from the sand pile makes little difference. But, if a component is missing from the system structure, the whole system may be affected, and even more seriously the system function may be completely lost. Just as you remove the hands of the watch, it does not play the role of indicating time; if you remove the clockwork, it will not run completely.

The existence of holism makes the system appear as a structural form with significant functions and strong purposes. It is not like simple stacking, which can be automatically generated by accumulation over time. The system structure can only be consciously made. Natural effects can generate sand piles, but it is impossible to automatically generate a watch. The system structure like a watch can only be artificial.

Naturally, given that a simple watch can't be automatically generated, how can the biological organs of much more complicated structures be automatically generated?

Darwin had long realized that the evolution theory was flawed. In *The Origin of Species*, he wrote: "If it can be proved that any complex organ cannot be formed by a large number of continuous and subtle improvements, then my theory will be completely shattered."

Maybe he is right in saying so.

What is the Cambrian Explosion?

The geological time of the earth is usually divided into different stages in terms of eon, epoch, period, and age. It is divided into the Archaeozoic eon (2.5 billion years ago), the Proterozoic eon (2.5 billion to 570 million years ago), and the Phanerozoic eon (570 million years ago to present). The Phanerozoic eon is further divided into the Paleozoic era, the Mesozoic era, and the Neozoic era. The Cambrian period is the first period of the Paleozoic era, which began about 570 million years ago and ended 510 million years ago.

The Cambrian Explosion is known as the large unsolved case of paleontology and geology and has long been intriguing to biologists. It refers to the emergence of a large variety of animals in a short time on the earth during the Cambrian period. They quickly originated in great numbers. Arthropods, brachiopods, creeps, sponges, and chordates all appeared on the earth. They cover almost all animal species that now live on Earth. The earth has suddenly changed from a sterile desert to a lively bazaar of life.

The concentrated emergence of the Cambrian creatures made the evolution idea of a *common ancestor* very embarrassing. If all living things gradually evolved from a common ancestor, then they must have emerged in a long history. How can they concentrate in such a short period?

Darwin was greatly puzzled by this phenomenon of the *sudden emergence of clusters of related species*. He believes that this phenomenon should be an illusion. A large number of Cambrian animals must have evolved from the Precambrian animals over a long period. The sudden appearance of Cambrian fossils and the lack of fossils of Precambrian animals are due to incomplete geological records or the inundation of old strata in the ocean.

This is entirely something taken for granted. In the era of Darwin, because fossils were scarce, people's understanding of the early and middle Cambrian organisms was still very simple. Darwin simply did not know the phenomenon of *this sudden appearance of species*. Even in 1948, when Preston Kraus solemnly proposed *the Cambrian explosion* hypothesis, fossils, although rich in many, are still in the normal range. It was not until 1973 that the famous *Burges shale* was rediscovered by Conway Morris and others that people realized how magnificent this bloom of life was!

Over the past one and a half-century, the evidence of biological fossils has increased, but it has become increasingly unfavorable to evolution. Although the Ediacaran fauna was discovered in 1947, which proved that mollusks appeared shortly before the Cambrian, they were far less in quantity than the Cambrian biota; and the morphologies were too different to be the likely ancestors of modern biota. The Burkins biota in Canada and the Keili biota in Guizhou, especially the Chengjiang biota in Yunnan discovered in 1984, indisputably suggest that there is a sudden outbreak of life in the Cambrian period.

Many doubts are hanging over the theory of evolution, and the truth about the evolution of life is still buried in the clouds of mystery.

Chapter 6

An Intelligent Design:
The Laws of the Universe Look Like
Exquisite Designs for Human Existence.

The far-reaching influence of the theory of evolution is that it is far more than a biological theory and it also contains profound philosophical connotations. Its logical and philosophical thinking has penetrated the entire scientific community as well as human society at large, and it has influenced many people's philosophies of life.

Some people apply the logic of the *Survival of the Fittest* to human society and form the theory of *Social Darwinism*. They believe that the natural elimination caused by competition for survival is also a common phenomenon in human society. In their view, social inequality, racial discrimination, and imperialism all have reasons for their existence. The underprivileged groups are not worthy of sympathy, and it is unnecessary to help the poor, for *the survival of the fittest* is a natural law, and the weak should be eliminated.

Some people take as their philosophy of life the idea that *the strongest survive and the weakest is eliminated and believe in the jungle law of the winner takes all.* They unscrupulously strive to become stronger to gain what they think is success, even if they have to tramp on others.

That's why I am very respectful of Darwin on the one hand but extremely disgusted with his theory of evolution on the other hand. Of course, this is not the point that we want to discuss. We will focus on the following issues.

Some people have extended the logic of *species being naturally formed* from the field of biology to the field of cosmology, saying that the universe is also naturally formed. Evolution believes that the role of natural selection eliminates countless random variations, and the last thing that we see is the species we see in front of us. The current most popular theory in the field of cosmology uses the same logic and states that when the universe was born there was not only one universe but countless universes. Their physical laws are different. Most of the universes have become dead universes or waste universes because the laws of physics there do not meet the requirements of life. But there must be one universe, whose laws of physics are suitable for the existence of life, and that universe is the one in front of us; otherwise, we will not exist.

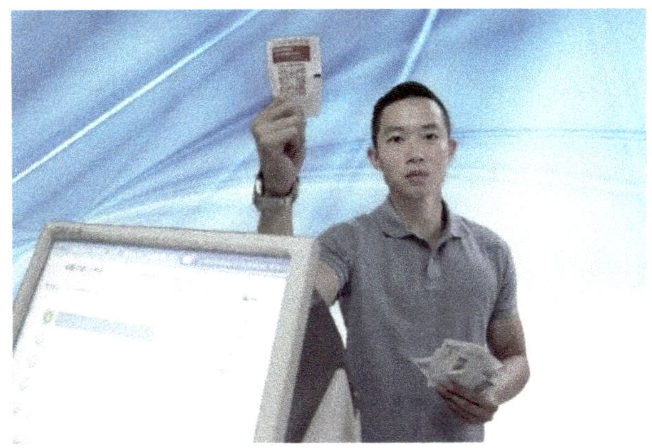

Lottery ticket buyer: "I want to buy all the lottery numbers. There must be a grand prize for one of them!"
Vendor: "If there were a few more such fools, I would make my fortune..."

The universe is formed naturally by chance. Because of the great influence of evolution, it has been widely recognized by the scientific community and has become a *supernormal phenomenon* in the eyes of scientific circles.

However, if you use philosophical thinking to look into the new discoveries in modern science, you will find a lot of questions. Our universe does not look like a natural creation; instead, it is more like a well-designed one.

This idea is not a novel one and its root can be traced back at least to the era of Plato. Plato believes that there is a physical model behind the world. The world before us is just a replica of this eternal model. Everything has its cycle of life, but the model is eternal. Although these models are numerous in number, they are not in a mess and without an order. They together constitute an interconnected organic whole, a well-organized orderly universe.

Newton also believes that the world is designed. He believes that the world is not "generated only from the turbidity by the laws of nature;" and that the order of the universe "was originally created by God, and the same state and conditions were preserved by Him to this day."

In 1973, the British astrophysicist Brandon Carter pointed out: "Humans are in a special position in the universe to some extent." This view is called *the principle of choice*. It theorizes that the laws of nature exist as they are just because they are designed to facilitate the emergence of human beings.

Was the universe formed by chance naturally, or was it carefully designed? Let's analyze this.

The first question to think about is that as the universe is so complicated but orderly, can it be generated by chance?

Let's take a look at some of the fragments of the Earth's life-forming process to see how far this complexity has reached.

The emergence of life, first of all, requires producing organic substances such as amino acids, which is relatively simple. But the next step is to string together the amino acids to make protein, which is very troublesome.

If protein is accidentally generated, then, according to the law of probability, to make collagen, it is necessary to select the appropriate kinds from the 20 amino acid molecules and perform 1055 times of arrangement in absolutely correct orders. We are currently playing a 15 to 5 lottery game, and we only need to choose 5 out of the 15 numbers to win the grand prize. However, if you refer to the collagen production process to formulate the lottery winning rules, you need to select the correct number 1055 times in 20 numbers to have the right one to get the bonus. This desperate gameplay will surely make all the lottery stations close their doors.

How many possibilities are there in this arrangement? It is 201055. Maybe you don't know how big the number is, but I can tell you that if nature starts to make collagen in a natural way from the moment the universe is born, try one of the possibilities every millisecond, then by now it has just tried 4.32×1020 times.

Some people may say that in different parts of the universe, perhaps collagen is being made at the same time, so more than one possibility is tried every millisecond. But I can tell you that the number of all atoms in the universe is estimated to be on the order of 1080. Even if every atom in the universe is involved in making collagen, it still doesn't make such a big number.

The probability of the natural generation of simple collagen molecules is almost zero. Some people think that the possibility of happening of this kind of thing is equivalent to that of the various raw materials in your kitchen that can somehow be put together and baked into a cake.

Only one kind of collagen is not enough to be able to make life appear; there may be around 1 million kinds of protein in the human body. The generation of one type of protein is virtually impossible according to the principle of probability, let alone generating so many kinds.

The next step is the formation of cells by proteins and more complex DNA, as well as other life elements, which are more complex structures. Even if you make a basic yeast cell, you need as many parts as for a Boeing 777 jet airliner, and you have to assemble them in spheres that are only 5 microns in diameter.

A single organism is already complicated beyond imagination, but compared to the Earth's ecosystem, it is nothing. The ecosystem is a perfect system. Let's take just the food chain as an example. Plants make use of the nutrients from the soil through photosynthesis for their growth; herbivores eat plants, large carnivores eat small carnivores and herbivores; dead animals return to dust through decomposition by scavengers or microorganisms. This is a perfect and complete cycle.

The formation of the Earth's ecosystem is just a piece of cake compared to the evolution of the entire universe. Such a grand system, such a complex evolution, is it possible to be created just by a random process, rather than a pre-designed program?

This reminds me of a performance at the opening ceremony of the Beijing Olympics. In the beautiful piano music, 1000 actors in green walked back and forth on the field, forming sometimes a dove and starlight pattern and sometimes a green nest. The whole process is as smooth as flowing. Do you think that such a beautiful picture does not require design and rehearsal? Can the performers form such a pattern by random walks?

The second questionable phenomenon is that the laws of physics of the universe are so precise that they seem to be more like a sophisticated design than accidentally formed, no matter how we look at them.

Martin Rees, the astronomer, and former chairman of the Royal Society believes that the universe seems to be dominated by six numbers, each of which has a very precise value as if it had been carefully debugged. Even if they were subtly changed, the world would not be what it is today, and life could not exist. If gravity is a little stronger, then the universe will collapse like an unsupported tent; if it is a little weaker, then nothing will come together, and the universe will always be monotonous, scattered, and empty. If the nuclear force changes by 4%, carbon cannot be formed on the star, and life-based on it cannot occur.

Hawking once said: "The laws of nature form an extremely delicate system. The possibility is very small that the laws of physics can be changed without destroying the possibilities of life that we know. If not for a series of surprising coincidences of precise details of the laws of physics, humans and similar forms of life seem never to have been formed."

It is also a coincidence that a planet suitable for life can be found in the universe. In the solar system, there are very few places where life can exist, and the earth is just inside such a *buttercup area*. If the earth is farther away from the sun, then the water will be frozen into solid, and without a liquid ocean, life will not be possible; and if the earth is a little closer to the sun, then it is likely to become a *greenhouse planet* like Venus, where the temperature may rise as high as 500 °C, which is terrible like hell.

There are quite a lot of such contingencies. If there was no moon, or if the size of the moon was not enough to stabilize the Earth's orbit, then the earth would shake like a pendulum, and the resulting dramatic climate change would make life's existence a luxury. If there were no giant planets such as Jupiter in the solar system, which uses its gravity to throw the asteroids into outer space and clean up the comets and asteroid fragments left over from the formation of the solar system in the past 1 billion years, then the earth would often be attacked by them and there could be no relatively stable environmental conditions to support the emergence of life.

American paleontologist Peter Ward and astronomer Donald Brownlee also cite a series of astounding facts about many other features of the Earth, such as oceans, plate tectonics, oxygen content, heat content, and Earth's axis angle, etc., which are just right for creating intelligent life. If the Earth is not just in the realm of such a small area, then humanity cannot occur.

As the buttercup has a thin and long peduncle, physicists have called the narrow parameter band that makes the emergence of intelligent life possible in the buttercup area. At present, dozens of such buttercup areas have been discovered based on the physical constants of the universe and the characteristics of the earth. It is precise because of the existence of such a narrow and slender parameter band that the chemical substances that constitute intelligent life in the universe could emerge, which makes the emergence of life on earth possible.

"Looking up at the full bright moon, one could not help thinking of his hometown". The moon in the sky has evoked the homesickness of countless

wanderers. But I believe most people will not know that the existence of the moon is not to make you feel homesick, it is a "must" for the birth of life on earth.

Is it just an accident that so many coincidences take place? Who can believe that these very precise systems are naturally formed, rather than from carefully modulated designs?

The third questionable phenomenon is that there are striking similarities between different regions of the universe. If the universe is naturally formed, it would be difficult to get a reasonable explanation for this.

Astronomical observations show that no matter which direction we look at, the universe seems to be the same, with the same types of galaxies, and distributed almost in exactly the same pattern.

This fact is puzzling. The two galaxies in opposite directions are 9 billion light-years away from us, and the distance between them is 18 billion light-years. At present, the most commonly accepted age of the universe is 13.7 billion years. There is not enough time even for light to travel from one galaxy to the other galaxy, and it is obviously impossible to pass on any information between them.

As there is no way to communicate with each other, they can't meet to discuss the issue of how to maintain consistency in the direction of evolution. If they are naturally generated, how can the two galaxies be so similar? How can the differences between them be eliminated?

Some people think that this phenomenon can be explained by the inflation theory: before the skyrocketing inflation, the universe was so small that it was possible to exchange information between various parts. We don't think this explanation is enough because it only shows that at the end of the inflation, perhaps the various parts of the universe will be similar, but not enough to explain why the universe is still so similar in all directions when it has evolved to this day.

The most plausible explanation for this phenomenon is that the entire universe evolves according to the same course designed in advance, rather than completely naturally as people have taken for granted.

The fourth questionable phenomenon is that the universe has incredible similarities in the structures of different scales, which reflect the same design style.

The universe has many unexplained repetitive structures on different scales. The atomic model proposed by the New Zealand physicist Ernest Rutherford in the early 20th century is known as *the planetary model* because from this model it can be seen that the structure of the atom looks very similar to that of the solar system. More than 99% of the atom's mass is concentrated in the very small nucleus, and the quality of the solar system is also concentrated in the sun as the core. Both of them only occupy a very small volume in the whole system but have the vast majority of the mass. An electron revolves around the nucleus, just like a planet orbiting around the sun. There are striking similarities between the atom and the solar system, which are apparently two systems of completely different scales.

Not only that. If you compare the atom with the Milky Way and the neutron star, you will find that they are very similar in many aspects such as radius, period, vibration, etc. As long as the atom is scaled up, it is like a galaxy or a neutron star. *Fractional Cosmology* thus even believes that in every particle in our universe there is a complete universe, which is composed of a multitude of smaller particles, in which there will be other even smaller universes, and this process is repeated like this indefinitely.

The Russian doll sets are the most common fractal structures. When you open a big doll set you will see that there is a small doll set inside, but the scale is reduced. Then, when you open this small doll set, you will find there is a still smaller doll set inside. This process can be repeated a few times.

Why does the universe show such striking similarities in the structures of such a disparity? If the world is naturally formed, this phenomenon is difficult to explain. But if the world is designed, it could be easily understood. Everyone who had renovated a house knew that designers often have their own styles. In *the Mediterranean style* design, arc-shaped elements such as arches will be used repeatedly. Therefore, the repetitive structure between different scales of the universe may simply reflect the unique design style of the designer.

There are many more examples to suggest and support that the world is carefully designed, and some of them are almost irrefutable evidence, such as the existence of genetic language.

Hawking said this in The *Great Design*: "the precise form and nature of the basic laws of physics cannot be explained as mere luck and chance..., and they must have much deeper physical and philosophical implications. Our universe and its laws seem to be a design, both of which are custom-tailored to sustain us."

In recent years, the idea of smart design is circulating among American universities, which believe that the world is designed.

For the notion *that the universe is naturally generated*, we have to ask the question: Is the universe likely to be naturally generated? Why does it look more like a carefully designed one?

How Big is the Number in Geometric Progression?

The ancient Indian king Sherhan was very playful, so his Prime Minister Daier invented chess for him. The king was very happy. To reward his intelligent prime minister, he promised to meet one of his requirements. Daier pointed at the chessboard and said, "Your Majesty, please give me some wheat as my reward. There are 64 grids on the chessboard in total. Please just put 1 grain of wheat in the first grid, 2 grains in the second grid, and 4 grains in the third grid; and for each latter grid, the number of grains will be doubled. In this way, please fill all 64 grids with grains of wheat!"

When the king heard it, he felt that such a small request was really nothing, and he agreed to it. However, when he asked someone to fetch a bag of wheat to fulfill the promise, he knew that he was being fooled. He never imagined that this number, which is increasing in geometric progression, would be so terribly large. According to the calculation, the king will have to give the prime minister 264^1 grains of wheat, which is about 4.6262×10^{18} grains, which is about 1.822 billion tons according to the conversion rate of one kilogram of wheat containing 25380 grains. In 2004, the world's total wheat production was about 627 million tons. That is to say, even if the world's people help the king with their wheat, in the present-day agricultural production capacity it will take 290 years to pay off!

A number that is incremented in the geometric progression is generally expressed in terms of an exponent. It looks inconspicuous but is tremendous. As long as you understand this, you will understand that life is a natural form of formation and is completely untenable in terms of probability.

Genetics is a Language

Protein is the material basis of life. It is a polymer compound composed of peptide chains, and the peptide chain is composed of 20 basic amino acids arranged in a certain order. According to Darwin's logic, the proteins in nature should be accidentally generated.

But in fact, nature uses another method. The amino acid sequence of the protein is precisely controlled by the genetic information of the gene. Its generation is completely a process of an assembly according to design drawings.

Genes are usually found on chromosomes in the nucleus. The chromosome is mainly composed of "nucleic acid" and protein. It is cylindrical or rod-shaped under a microscope, and it is easily stained with a basic dye, so it is called a chromosome.

Nucleic acids have three basic components: phosphoric acid, ribose or deoxyribose, and bases. A ribose-containing nucleic acid is called RNA, and a deoxyribose-containing nucleic acid is called DNA. There are four kinds of bases in RNA, which are represented by G, C, A, and U respectively. There are also four kinds of bases in DNA, three of which are identical to RNA, and only one is different. They are represented by G, C, A, and T respectively.

The genetic information of an organism is contained in the genes. But how is the genetic information in the genes expressed? How can we read their contents?

We can make an analogy to the English language to illustrate how it works. There are 26 letters such as A, B, C, and D in English. Several letters can be combined to form a word like home. Words are organized according to a certain grammatical structure and become an article that can express complete information.

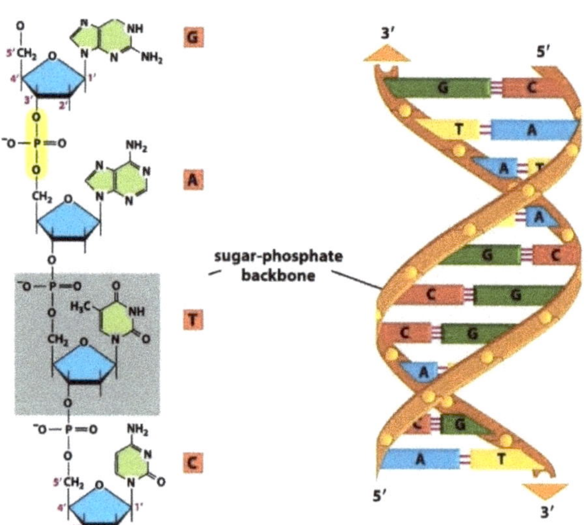

The expression of genetic information is more or less the same. There are 5 bases in DNA and RNA, which are equivalent to 5 letters; each of 3 letters are joined together to form a word, which corresponds to one of the 20 basic amino acids; for example, ACC corresponds to *threonine*, TCC corresponds to *serine*, and TTC corresponds to *phenylalanine*. These words are organized in a complex grammatical structure and become the human genome, *the code of God*.

Of the 64 words of the genetic code of E. coli, only 60 correspond to amino acids, one is indicative of the start of protein synthesis, and three are indicative of the termination of protein synthesis, reflecting a simple grammatical structure. With the further deepening of genetic research, it has been found that the grammatical structure of these *codes of God* is much more complicated than the human language.

The process by which cells produce protein is simple. It simply interprets each word according to grammar, then finds the corresponding amino acid molecules and assembles them in order.

From the above introduction, it should be easy to see that the genetic code is a language like English, with letters, words, and grammatical structures. But it is more like a programming language, for there are many conditional control statements like *operators, inhibitors, and promoters.*

We know that language is a special phenomenon of advanced life. There is no language in the natural world without life, and low-level life cannot produce a complex language. The symbol dog is used to represent a creature dog. This is obviously a kind of thinking activity, and only intelligent life has the mind to know how to create language.

So, we have to ask, if nature is unconscious, if life is naturally formed by unconscious nature, how should the existence of this genetic language be explained? How can nature, without thinking ability, know that the symbol *TCC* represents the real thing *serine*? How do cells know that three letters make up a single word, which corresponds to a specific amino acid?

We have every reason to believe that the emergence of life is not an accident at all, but a design.

Chapter 7

Climbing Steps: The World is Just Like a Mountain Road with Steps, and Quantum is the Step.

The existence of some scientific theories is an abnormal *supernormal phenomenon* in itself, such as the theory of evolution; while some other scientific theories, though we have not found any problems with them, have problematic phenomena, such as the quantum theory.

The quantum theory is one of the two pillar theories of modern physics, describing the physical phenomena of the particle world. For the ordinary reader, this is probably a very strange field, and it is very difficult to understand. But if you want to understand the deep mysteries of this world, quantum theory is very important. It can be said to be a key that you can't do without.

If one wants to learn about quantum theory, the first thing that one should figure out is the concept of *quantum*. We again use everyday life as an example to make it easier to understand what is called *quantum*.

When we decorate a house, there are generally two ways to do the wall. For the living room and the bedrooms, most of them are brushed with cement paint. The brush goes all the way across the wall and the whole wall becomes a white one. This kind of decoration can be called *the holistic style*. For the kitchen and the bathroom, because the walls are very likely to be sprayed with water, they are usually covered with pieces of tiles. Sometimes people deliberately make the tiles small, and the whole wall is like a collage of small pieces. This type of decoration can be called *the mosaic style*.

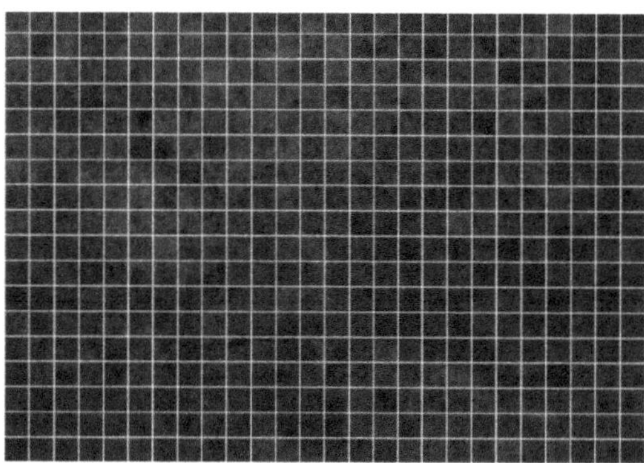

The mosaic style of decoration deliberately divides the complete wall into small pieces.

Corresponding to the two styles of decoration, there exist two different views on the composition of this world since ancient times.

One view is that the world is *holistic*. Matter, time and space are all continuous, and thus can be divided infinitely. In *Zhuangzi: The World, this is said: "For a rod of one foot long, if a half is cut off it a day, it will not be exhausted in infinite time."* Explaining this sentence in mathematical language means that you can cut a one-foot-long stick into halves innumerable times. The first half of the first cut is 0.5 feet long; the second is 0.25 feet; the third is 0.125 feet. This process can be carried out infinitely.

In the 4th century BC, the Greek philosopher Aristotle also believed that the world is holistic, the material is continuous, people can divide it indefinitely, and we will never get the smallest particle that cannot be further divided.

Another view is that the world is a mosaic. The Greek philosopher Democritus, born earlier than Plato, believed that there exists the smallest particle in the matter. He called the particle atom and believed that all matter is composed of atoms. According to him, an atom is an impenetrable and inseparable entity. All atoms have the same nature but differ in shape, size, weight, arrangement, and position. Everything is born and destroyed, but the atoms that make up things will not be destroyed but will only be transferred from dead objects to new ones. All the matter in space is made up of atomic particles that cannot be further divided.

And who is right and who is wrong in these two views? For a long time in antiquity, people tended to lean toward the first view, because in our perception the world is continuous, not look like being made up of small particles. Just like when you look at a mirror, you will only see a smooth surface and you won't find any gaps in it.

The answer to this question was not revealed until the birth of *the quantum theory*. The concept of quantum is the final answer to this question.

The discovery of the quantum theory was very dramatic. In 1900, when the German physicist Planck studied *black body radiation*, he proposed a formula whose calculation results were tested by various experiments. But what's interesting is that this formula was completely patched out by Planck's experience. Even he couldn't tell why this formula was like this and how could it be derived. Nor did he know what significance this formula would bring to physics.

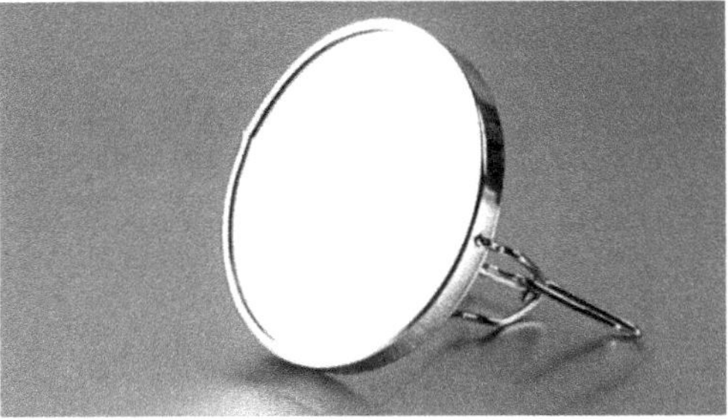

After a period of research, Planck found that this formula contains a strange premise: in the past, we usually premise that the transmission of energy is continuous, just as the temperature rises continuously from 0 ° C to 1 ° C. The continuous process can be mathematically divided into an infinite number of states, but this formula requires that the transfer of energy cannot be continuous but can only be transmitted one part by one part, although each one is extremely small, small enough to almost ignore it so that you can approximate it as a continuous process.

More generally, Planck found an amazing secret, that is, the world is not "*holistic*", but a "*mosaic.*" The transfer of energy in nature is not a continuous process but is transmitted intermittently, and the amount of each transfer cannot be less than a certain minimum value. This means that during the temperature rise from 0 ° C to 1 ° C, its value does not have an infinite number of possibilities, but only a limited number of states can occur.

This phenomenon can be understood by the example of mountain climbing. An ordinary mountain trail is usually an inclined soil slope. It is easy to slip on rainy days and is not easy to climb. This ordinary mountain trail can be regarded as a continuous state. To make traveling easier, mountain trails in many places have built stone steps, and these stepped mountain trails are no longer in a continuous state. In this discontinuous state, in theory, in the process from the foot of the mountain to the top of the mountain, the person climbing the mountain passes through an infinite number of altitudes, but he actually can only stay at a limited number of altitudes.

Why would you say this? Let's take a look at the difference between walking stone steps and walking slopes when climbing a mountain. If you are climbing a continuous slope, then your footsteps can stay in any position, so in theory, you can be in an infinite number of states. But if you take the stone steps, then the situation is completely different, and the position where your footsteps can stay is limited. If each stone step is 12 cm high, which is a basic unit, now you stand at an altitude of 300 meters, as long as you take the next step, the position becomes 300.12 meters high. You can't stop anywhere between 300 meters and 300.12 meters because there are no steps in between.

Planck called the most basic unit *quantum*, and *quantum theory* was born. It tells us unambiguously that the world is not "*holistic*," but "*mosaic*" and "*quantum*" refers to the smallest block of tiles.

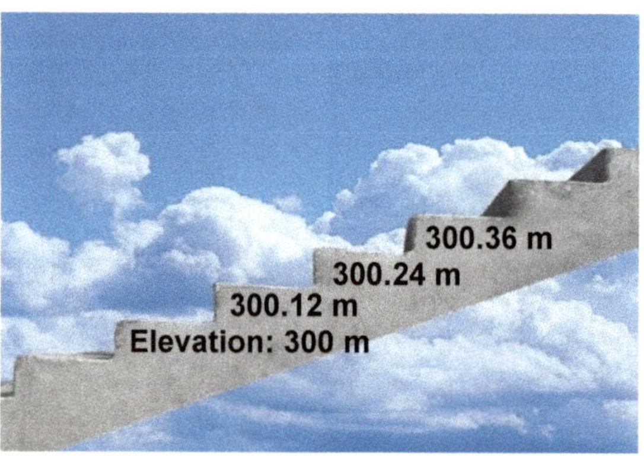

When you walk down the slope, your steps can be put in any position. But if

you are walking on the steps, then you can only step on the steps, and you can't step on the gap between the two steps. At this time, your steps are not continuous. Each step must cross at least 12cm. Of course, you can also cross two or three steps at the same time, but you can't cross 0.1 or 0.2 steps. This concept is just the physical meaning represented by quantum. The transfer of energy between objects and the transfer of objects in space must not be less than a certain minimum amount each time, so they are not continuously changing but in a leaping process.

The quantum theory introduces people to a mysterious world, just like a wizard chanting a spell. A door suddenly opened on the originally unremarkable stone wall, and behind the door, there was a new world that people had never seen before. The rules of the quantum world are completely different from those of the macro world that we are familiar with. Many of the experiences we have accumulated in our daily lives are useless here. In the quantum world, we need to change the original way of thinking and use quantum thinking to think about problems.

Let's take the following as an example. It was known in the early 20th century that when light hits a metal, electrons are struck out of its surface. This phenomenon is called *the photoelectric effect*. But what puzzles people is that for a particular metal, whether light can produce electrons or not is only related to its frequency and has nothing to do with its intensity.

In terms of traditional thinking, this is a very strange phenomenon. Light is a wave, and the intensity of a wave represents the magnitude of its energy, just as the strength of an army represents the magnitude of its combat power. The light from the searchlight is much stronger than the light from the flashlight; just like the combat power of an army of one million soldiers is much stronger than that of a hundred-strong army. According to traditional thinking, whether it is possible to produce electrons from a metal surface depends on the intensity of light, just like whether an army can defeat an enemy depends on its combat power.

But this is not the truth. Whether light can produce electrons is only related to the nature of light and has nothing to do with intensity. High-frequency light, such as ultraviolet light, can emit electrons even when the intensity is weaker. Light with low frequency, such as red light and yellow light, can hardly produce electrons even if the intensity is strong. Just like an army, whether it can win or not has nothing to do with the number of soldiers but is only related to the ethnicity of the soldiers of this army.

How should this phenomenon be explained? It is impossible to explain it in traditional thinking. In the end, Einstein explained this phenomenon perfectly with quantum thinking.

Einstein said that the light beam we see seems to be a continuous line, but it is not like that. It is made up of many "*photons of light*" (now commonly called *photons*). The magnitude of energy of a single photon is determined by its frequency, and the intensity of a beam of light is not only related to the energy of a single photon, but also the number of photons. The intensity of the light may be large, but the energy of a single photon is small, and the intensity is large only because of the large number of photons.

Whether a beam of light can strike electrons out of the metal surface depends on the strength of the collision of a single photon with an electron, which depends on the frequency of the light. In other words, this is only related to the energy of a single photon and has nothing to do with the intensity.

If the two armies fight in accordance with the quantum rules, then it is not a group fight, but a one-on-one contest. At this time, winning or losing has nothing to do with the number of soldiers, only related to the combat effectiveness of individual soldiers. If an army has a strong personal combat capability, even if it has only one soldier, it can still destroy another army with weak individual combat capabilities, even if the army has a million troops

As a famous Chinese saying goes, "The thin thread will saw the wood and the water drops will wear the stone." It means that the subtle effect will produce a very powerful effect if it lasts for a long time. Just like using a scoop of water to pour stones, you won't see any change in the stone, but the smooth pebbles in the river are formed by the long-term flushing of the weak water. When this kind of accumulation is too much, *the quantity change* will become *the quality change*. One thing that many people understand but often ignore, is, that for the subtle effects to accumulate over time to reach an obvious effect, there must be such a premise: the actions must be continuous and can be accumulated.

In a group fight, the group with more people will have an advantage, because each person's role can produce a superposition effect; but if the fight changes to a one-on-one fight and the fight cannot be conducted continuously, then the number of fighters is irrelevant, and winning or losing will only be determined by the strength of the individual fighter. This is an important difference between the existence of physical phenomena in a continuous macroscopic world and a discontinuous quantum world.

There is an interesting situation in the history of science that this discovery of Einstein is so significant that even the famous relativity theory has not brought Einstein a Nobel Prize. Instead, the paper that uses quantum concepts to explain the photoelectric effect won him the award. Einstein became one of the founders of quantum theory.

The quantum world is a new field of science, and its weirdness is far beyond your imagination. In a physical sense, quantum theory profoundly reveals the problem that the world we live in, in the usual way, seems to make people feel smooth and continuous, just like looking at the road up the mountain from a long distance, it is a smooth slope; but once it is enlarged to the particle level, the situation is completely changed, and it becomes no longer continuous and smooth, just like when you walk to the front of the mountain, it is no longer a slope, but flights of steps.

From our intuition, the world is a completely integrated continuity, but now quantum theory tells us that this is not the case. Our world is like a whole of building blocks. It is made up of some basic units, and there are gaps between them.

The physics theory before the 20th century, whether it is Newton's classical mechanics or Maxwell's electromagnetic theory, is based on the belief that the world is smooth and continuous. In Newton's view, when you push an object with a force of 5 kilograms, the force is a whole, acting continuously, rather than being pieced together by the tiny forces of many basic units, as quantum theory believes. So, quantum theory completely subverts people's original cognition. Together with the theory of relativity, it overthrew the entire theoretical system of classical physics.

The atom that Democritus referred to is the smallest particle, the basic unit of matter, but the atom we are talking about now does not have such a property. So, what exactly is the smallest particle? No one knows this at present. But basically, the world must certainly have a minimum unit. When the world is enlarged to the level of particles, the concept of smooth and continuous has no market. Here the world shows obvious quantum properties, not only in matter but also in time and space. If there is no minimum unit in the world, then there is no way for a quantum phenomenon to be reasonably explained.

The big bang theory says that the world originated from a singularity and there was nothing before the singularity. So how can the matter be compressed into nothing in the world with the smallest unit? It stands to reason that even if the compression is the smallest, it can't be smaller than the basic unit. Some people may say that according to Einstein's equation of mass and energy, matter can be transformed into energy, and all matter may be converted into intangible energy at the singularity. But this kind of statement is definitely wrong because there is nothing at the singularity, not only without matter but also without energy. And more importantly, the energy itself is also quantized!

When the world was born, why wasn't it a continuous smooth world? Why do quantum properties appear in the world? When climbing the mountain, we can climb the slopes without steps and why do we need steps? We know that the appearance of the steps is made by man. The hillsides in nature have no such steps!

If you read the relevant books, you can find the story of how people discovered the quantum theory, but never see anyone question why it exists. People seem to be too familiar with this problem and become accustomed to it. They don't feel anything abnormal about it.

The magnificence of nature and the order of the biological world make me believe that the Creator likes perfection. But the problem now is that a smooth continuous picture will obviously feel more beautiful and more perfect than an intermittent image. The kitchen and the bathroom are designed to be waterproof, so the tiles are used, and the mosaic decoration style is subsequently incurred. Except for these uses, it is rare to see someone filling the living room and bedroom with mosaics. But when the Creator created the world, he did not choose the overall style but adopted the mosaic method. Why is this?

About the *supernormal phenomenon* that "the world is quantized", we have to ask the question: Why does quantum exist? Why is our world a mosaic style?

What is Black Body Radiation?

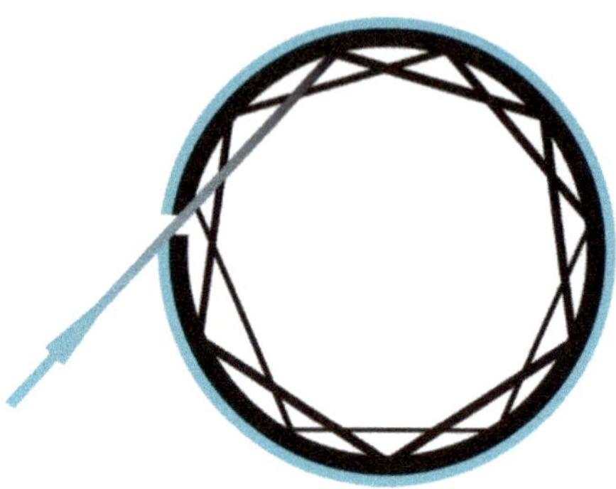

Everything in nature, including you and me, emits electromagnetic waves because of the temperature. This kind of electromagnetic wave is also called *thermal radiation*. There is an *infrared night vision scope* that uses this principle to see things.

This radiation is related to the temperature of the object. The higher the temperature, the higher the power of radiation and the farther the intensity distribution shifts to the short wave on the spectrum. For example, if a piece of iron pliers is heated continuously, it will first turn dark red and then turn orange. The higher the temperature, the brighter it will become.

Obviously, there should be a certain functional relationship between the energy of the object's thermal radiation and the wavelength and temperature.

But this radiation is also related to the characteristics of the object itself. If one pot and a pair of iron tongs are heated at the same time, the conditions they display will be different. Therefore, to determine the relationship between radiant energy and wavelength, and temperature, we must first eliminate the influence of the characteristics of the object, so physicists have imagined an ideal object - *the black body*, which is used as a standard object in thermal radiation research.

A black body refers to an object that can completely absorb external radiation. Under certain temperature conditions, the black body is also the largest object of radiation, called *the complete radiator*. The thermal radiation emitted by the black body is called *Black Body Radiation*, which emits the maximum amount of radiation at a specific temperature and wavelength, regardless of the characteristics of the object itself.

In this way, the influence of the characteristics of the object itself is eliminated. The distribution of the radiant energy of the black body is only related to temperature, and there is a correspondence between them. For example, *the cosmic microwave background radiation* we observed corresponds to a black body radiation of about 3K, so *the cosmic microwave background radiation is also called the 3K background radiation*.

The black body is just an imaginary object that does not exist in reality. It is usually described approximately in this way: it is a hollow sphere, the inner wall is coated with radiation-absorbing paint, a small hole is formed in the outer wall, and the light into the small hole is not reflected, so the small hole is close to the black body.

Planck discovered the concept of *quantum* by accident when he studied the formula of the law of black body radiation energy distribution, which opened the prelude of quantum theory to shock the physics world of the 20th century. But this was only an accidental discovery. Planck himself was not mentally prepared beforehand, and even after a long time he was even not inclined to accept it. This is like a fisherman who originally intended to catch a turtle but pulled up a big shark. This scared him.

Chapter 8

God's Dice!
Everything in the Quantum World is Uncertain.
God is Rolling the Dice.

Understanding *the photoelectric effect* requires only a change in the way of thinking but understanding the other weird phenomena in quantum theory that we will talk about next requires a change in the whole worldview.

Let's talk about an interesting topic first, that is, *destiny*. Do you believe in the existence of fate? Whether it is self-sufficient in the midst of it, no matter how hard we work, everyone must obey the arrangements of fate, let himself be at the mercy of it, and have no resistance at all.

There is a kind of thinking called fatalism which says life and death are decided by destiny, wealth is in the hands of heaven, everything has been arranged in heaven, how many years you can live, how much money you earn, everything is fixed.

Nowadays people rarely believe in fate. They generally believe that it is the law of nature that dominates the world. With the help of science and technology, human beings can master their destiny by grasping the laws of nature.

What they don't necessarily know, however, is that for a long time, there was a dominant ideology in the scientific world called *determinism*, which, like fatalism, believed that everything in the world was destined beforehand.

Where does deterministic thinking come from?

When you are learning middle school physics, you will often encounter such a problem, telling you the initial position of a projectile, the initial speed and angle of shooting when leaving the cannon, and letting you calculate where the projectile will appear at some point of time and where the final landing point is, without considering the air resistance.

Solving this question reflects the understanding of the world by classical mechanics, which believes that any event has a cause, and this causal relationship can be described by scientific laws. As long as we know the initial conditions, we can predict the course of events and the results according to scientific laws and equations. By the same token, as long as we determine the current state of affairs, we can infer the previous situation according to the laws.

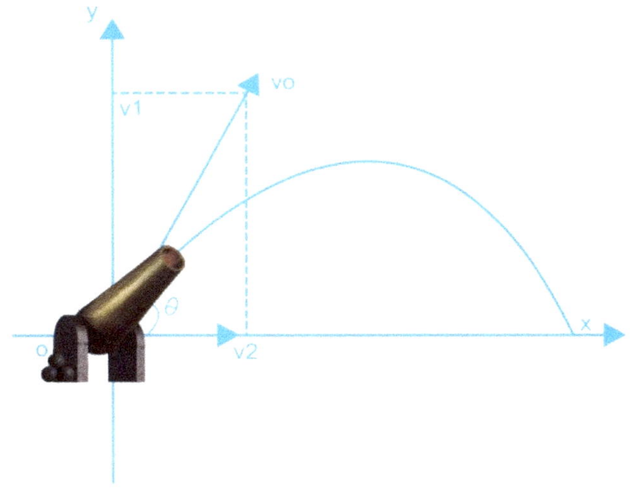

This view seems to have been proven in reality. We can predict the trajectory of the projectile and its landing point. We can know in advance when the eclipse will occur and can send the satellite into the predetermined orbit, based on the understanding of this causal relationship. We can know what happened before the birth of human beings, be able to measure the age of the earth and be able to arrive at the big bang theory through the phenomenon of the expansion of the universe based on this law of causality.

Following this logic will lead us to an astonishing conclusion. We know that from the moment the universe was born, the initial conditions of the evolution of the whole world were determined, the laws of nature are fixed, and things are evolving according to their causal relationships so that we can seem to make a judgment: from the moment of the birth of the universe, it is determined how it will evolve and what the final result will be.

According to this inference, if we can figure out all the initial states of the universe, master all the laws of nature, and have enough powerful computing power, then we can predict the evolution of the entire universe until the end of the world. It can also be said that we are currently unable to grasp the evolutionary trajectory and final outcome of all things in the world, just because humans have insufficient levels of understanding and computing power. The process and results of the evolution of the universe have already been determined.

This kind of thinking is *determinism*.

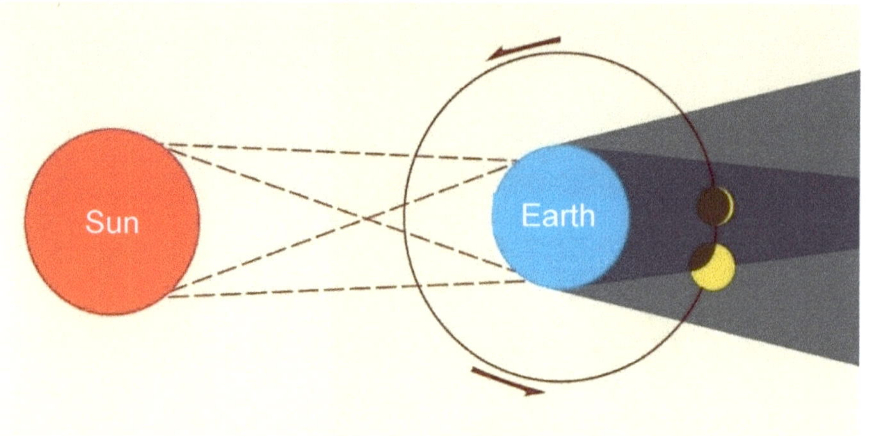

According to the respective orbits of the Earth and the Moon, the time when the eclipse will appear can be calculated. That is to say, the eclipse that will appear in the future is an event that was determined before it happened. It has already been destined to happen.

Determinism was born with classical physics theories. Newton is a determinist. He thinks that the universe is like a huge clock. The springs of the clock are relaxed in a predetermined way, without fail. Everything has been prescribed by the laws of physics, and even one single detail cannot be changed. Even the trajectory of each atom was determined at the beginning of the universe. The past and the future are all like already-written scripts. The development of the universe can only be rolled out in strict accordance with this script.

The 18th-century French astronomer Laplace, who had served as a teacher of Napoleon, also believed that if he could know the position and movement of each particle in the universe at a certain moment, he would have mastered all the details. And he could calculate the whole past and future of the universe.

Determinism is somewhat horrifying, but its influence on science is beyond imagination. Scientists have believed in determinism for a long time, and even Einstein is a staunch advocate.

Is the world just a grand movie going on like what determinism says? The plot has not yet begun, but the outcome is already doomed. Emotionally, no one likes cold-blood determinism. Believing that everything has been determined means that all our efforts are just meaningless struggles.

During the period that classical physics dominated, it was difficult for people to break free from determinism. But fortunately, after the emergence of quantum theory, the situation has changed completely.

Quantum theory is the theory of physics in the world of particles. The particle world is a very abstract field for ordinary people because even with the most efficient *scanning tunneling microscope*, we can only see things at the atomic level, and there is no way to see particles smaller than atoms. Therefore, in this extremely microscopic world, we can only understand through indirect methods, and there is no way to directly see their real situation.

When people discovered the atom, they thought they found the smallest inseparable particle that the Greeks said about, but the British physicist J.J. Thomson discovered the existence of electrons in the atom when studying the cathode ray, which indicates that the atom also has its own internal structure. Thomson imagined the atom as a positively charged sphere, with negatively charged electrons embedded in it. This kind of imagination is intuitive. People subconsciously think that the tiny particles that make up the real thing should be solid.

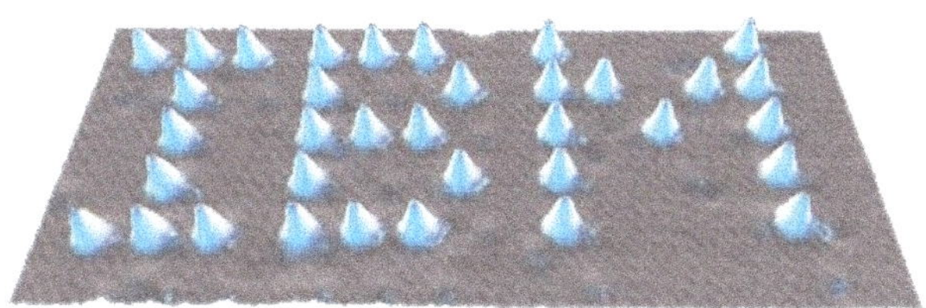

The picture shows the arrangement of 35 helium atoms into "IBM" by two scientists from IBM in the United States through a scanning tunneling microscope. A scanning tunneling microscope is a microscope made by the effect of quantum tunneling to generate a tunneling current. Its resolution is up to the atomic level, and atomic-level images can be observed. The atomic level is already the most microscopic level that humans can see today. We can't directly see anything smaller than an atom. Therefore, electrons, protons, neutrons, quarks, etc. are indirectly speculated based on experimental results. In fact, no one has actually seen them.

When people discovered atoms, they thought they had found the smallest indivisible particles so called by the Greeks. But when British physicist J. J. Thomson was studying cathode rays, he discovered the existence of electrons in the atom, which showed that the atom also has its own internal structure. Thomson imagined the atom as a positively charged sphere, with negatively charged electrons embedded in the sphere. This kind of imagination accords with intuition. People subconsciously think that the tiny particles that make up the real object should be solid.

In 1858, the German physicist J. Prick discovered cathode rays while conducting research on low-pressure gas discharges, but no one knew what these kinds of rays were, until 1897 when J. J. Thomson proved with experiments that this kind of ray is a stream of negatively charged particles, measured the particle's charge-to-mass ratio, and determined that its mass is about one-two thousandth of that of a hydrogen atom. Only then was it confirmed that it was a new kind of particle, and people called it an "electron." Before J. J. Thomson, the British chemist John Dalton, who proposed the atom theory in 1803, once believed that the atom is an indivisible solid ball. In 1903, Thomson proposed a new atomic structure model based on the discovery of electrons. In line with conventional thinking, he also believed that the atom is a solid sphere and electrons are embedded in this sphere like raisins, which people vividly dubbed "the plum pudding" model.

Later, Thomson's student Rutherford discovered through experiments that there is a core in the atom. This core is positively charged, and its radius is less than one ten thousandths of the atomic radius. This discovery completely subverts our intuition. The tiny atom is not solid. It is like our solar system. Most of the places are empty! On this basis, Rutherford proposed his own atomic model, which is *the planet model*.

However, in theory, Rutherford's atomic system is unstable. According to the classical electromagnetic theory, it will release radiant energy and cause collapse. If there is such an atom, in reality, it will soon disintegrate itself.

How to solve this problem? A Danish physicist Bohr thought of quantum thinking. He found that the different orbits of the electrons inside the atom have different energy levels. An electron can only absorb the energy equivalent to the energy level difference between the two orbits, jumping from the lower energy level orbit to the higher energy level; or in a reverse way, it releases the same amount of energy, falling back from the higher energy level to the lower energy level. It cannot continuously absorb or release energy as the classical theory assumes.

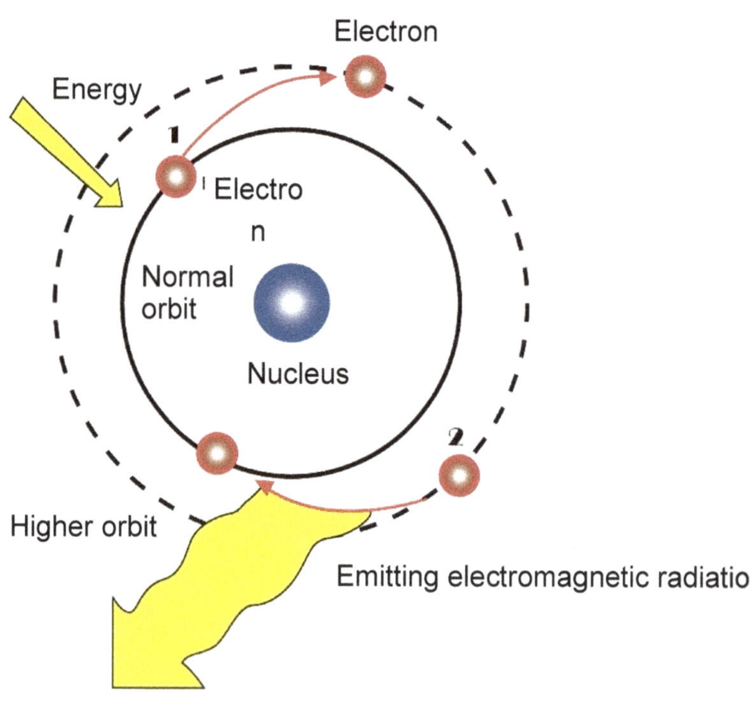

There is a difference in energy levels between the atomic structures of Bohr and Rutherford, but there is a common feature that electrons have a fixed orbit, rotating around the nucleus, just like a planet orbiting the sun. Obviously, this is a kind of inertial thinking. At that time, it was difficult for people to get rid of the classical mechanical thinking of electrons moving in orbits.

Bohr's atomic theory can explain the spectroscopy of hydrogen atoms, but it can't explain the intensity and fine structure of the hydrogen atom spectrum, nor can it explain the slightly more complex helium atom spectrum, as well as other more complex atomic spectra, so it is only correct for 13 years before it was overthrown.

Until Bohr, everything is still within the normal thinking range, but normal thinking can't solve the problem. Finally, in 1925, the German physicist Heisenberg published matrix mechanics. In 1926, the Austrian physicist Schrödinger published the wave equation, which solved the problem of the movement of electrons inside the atom. Their findings are so weird, that not only did they send a shock wave to the physics of the 20th century, but also subvert our worldview philosophically.

In classical physics, the world is certain, and everything has a certain state. The real things in front of us, a basketball in a game as an example, at each moment of time its state is certain; there are certain positions and certain speeds for this object, which can be accurately measured.

But in quantum theory, the seemingly simple question of the world's *certainty* has become complicated. In 1927, Heisenberg derived an unacceptable conclusion from matrix mechanics: for an electron, we can only determine one of them, its position or velocity (usually momentum), and the two can never be known at the same time. This is the famous *principle of uncertainty*. It shows that for an electron, we can't know its position and speed of a moment at the same time as we do for a basketball.

People initially had a bias in understanding this principle and called it the principle of immeasurability. The implication is that we can't simultaneously determine the position and speed of the electrons because the electronics are too small. With our current technology, as long as it is measured, its state will change. And we have no way to measure it without disturbing it. Just like when we want to weigh the fish on the market. When it is fished out of the water, it is disturbed and jumps on the weighing pan, so it is impossible to weigh exactly how much it weighs.

But then people realized that things were more complicated than imagined. We can't know the state of the electron at a certain moment, not because of the measurement, but because it is not sure! This is like the fish that I said before. We don't know how much it is, not because it is not accurate, but because its weight itself is uncertain!

Heisenberg's principle of uncertainty reveals the fact that the macro world in our eyes is a certain world, but the particle world that constitutes this macro world is completely another scene. Everything there is uncertain!

Schrödinger's wave equation also contains the same unreasonable content. There is a wave function ψ in the equation, but he does not even know himself what physical meaning this function has. He once thought it represented the spatial distribution of electronic charges, but the German physicist Bonn later pointed out that things are far from simple. Bonn believes that ψ represents randomness, a probability that the square of ψ corresponds to the probability of an electron appearing in a certain place.

It turns out that the movement of electrons does not have a certain trajectory as classical mechanics says. Where it will appear as just a probability phenomenon!

How do you understand this? Simply put, for a projectile moving in accordance with the classical laws of mechanics, at the moment it is launched, the initial state is determined, and it has a certain initial velocity, a determined initial position, and a determined initial angle of incidence. Next, under the influence of gravity, it falls down as it rushes forward, and the entire trajectory is also determined. We can calculate where it will fall down.

But if the shell is moving like an electron, then there will be big trouble. First of all, you can't know its initial velocity and initial position at the same time. Its initial state is completely uncertain. Secondly, its landing point is not a certain point. There are many possibilities. At which point it will fall is a completely random process, its probability is like a wave, strictly distributed in accordance with the distribution of ψ. This means that we can't determine where the shell will fall down, but only know the probability that it will fall at a certain point. Whether the shell can fall on the enemy's head is only a matter of luck. When the luck is bad, it may even fall on your own head.

Bonn gave the wave function the nickname *the dice*. Every time we throw a die, we can't know in advance what points will appear on its face side, but we know that the probability of each point is 1/6. So, Bonn means that when you want to know where the electrons will appear the calculation is useless because you can only calculate the probability, so it is better to simply throw the dice!

Determinism based on classical mechanics believes that the initial state of the world is deterministic, and the process of evolution is completely determined by the laws of physics. The result of evolution is determined in advance. It was originally taken for granted by people, but now this logic cannot work.

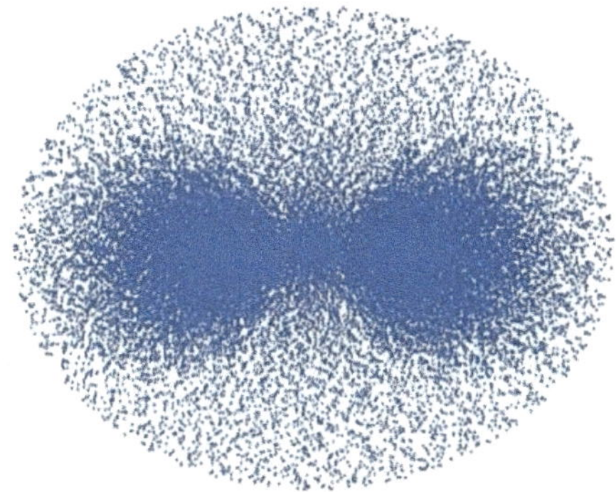

The high-speed motions made by an electron are different from those of objects in the macro world. It has no defined orbit, but it is diffused in space in the form of waves. Since it does not have a certain position and speed at some point, it is impossible to draw its trajectory.

In this way, how should the movement of an electron be described? One way people think of it is to express its trajectory with the probability that the electron appears everywhere. As shown in the figure, the density near a certain point represents the opportunity for the electron to appear there. Where there is a high density, there is a higher opportunity for the electron to appear in a unit volume; in places with a low density, there is a lower opportunity for the electron to appear. The electron movement image drawn in this way looks like a cloud of negatively charged, which is often called an electron cloud.

First, Heisenberg said that we can't know the initial state of electrons, because electrons have no definite initial state at all; then Bonn said that we can't predict the behavior of electrons according to the laws of physics, and what we can determine is probabilities. In this way, where the electrons will eventually appear is completely random, and there is no strict causal relationship with its initial state and process. In the subatomic world, the logical chain of determinism has completely collapsed.

There is a deeper philosophical meaning behind this matter, and it is our worldview that collapses with determinism. We have unreservedly believed that the world at hand is a real, certain world, but we now find that the world is uncertain. Then, can it be true?

Perhaps because of this, many people can't accept this result anyway, especially Einstein. In the letter written to Bonn in 1926, Einstein said: "Quantum mechanics is impressive, but an inner voice tells me that it is not true... I believe without reservation that God does create this world by throwing the dice. "

Later, Einstein launched many debates with Bohr. He did not believe till his death that the particle world that constitutes the macro world was uncertain. Regrettably, however, more and more experiments have denied his views, and it turns out that God is indeed rolling the dice.

In our daily life, a certain degree of certainty must exist; otherwise, our life cannot go on. Let's take saving money in a bank as an example. If you originally had 50,000 dollars in your checkbook, and now you deposit another 100,000, then you will have 150,000 dollars in your checkbook. This is certain. There is a strict causal relationship between the initial state, the process, and the outcome of the whole thing. If there is a certain amount of money in your account, and it has nothing to do with the initial deposit of tens of thousands of dollars and a further deposit of a certain amount; instead, it is all decided by the bank by rolling a dice. In the end, it may be 150,000 dollars, or it may still be 50,000 yuan, or it may even become 20,000 dollars, all depending on probability. Do you dare to put your money in the bank?

The existence of uncertainty allows us to conclude that the world is not just, as a determinist said, a film that was shot in accordance with the set script, with the outcome having been doomed from the beginning.

"Being in a room of orchid for a long time one will not smell its fragrance anymore and being in the market of abalone for a long time one will not smell the foul smell." People have become accustomed to the existence of uncertainty over time. It becomes a *supernormal phenomenon*. If we think carefully, we will see that Einstein's question is not unreasonable. This is really abnormal. Einstein is right in being skeptical about determinism, but he took the wrong direction. He has been skeptical about the phenomenon but has not gone further to explore the truth behind it.

What I want to ask is: Why should the creator design a system that is full of randomness?

The Interior of the Atom is an Empty Arena

In 1909, Rutherford made the famous alpha particle scattering experiment, originally intending to use it to verify Thomson's atomic model, but it had completely unexpected results. This experiment uses the alpha particles emitted from natural radioactive materials to bombard the gold foil. Most of the alpha particles went through unimpeded, but very few particles have been deflected at a large angle, and some have even been bounced back.

If calculated according to the Thomson model, the angle of deflection of the alpha particles from the original direction after passing through the gold foil should be small. Because the mass of alpha particles is much larger than that of electrons, it hits electrons like flying bullets hitting dust and does not change direction significantly. On the other hand, the positive charges of the atoms are evenly distributed, and the repulsions received by the alpha particles will cancel each other out, so there should be no large deflections.

However, things that should not happen have happened. Rutherford later recalled the situation at the time and said: "This is the most incredible thing I have encountered in my life. It is like you fired shells at a piece of paper, and some shells bounced back and hit you."

After analyzing the experimental results, Rutherford believed that there is only one explanation for this phenomenon, that is, almost all the mass and positive charge in the atom is concentrated in a small space of the atomic center, while most other spaces are all empty. Because the interior of atoms is empty, most alpha particles pass through the atoms without any obstacles; and because there is a dense core in the middle when a very small number of alpha particles hit it, they deflect at a large angle and even bounce back.

Now we know that his idea is correct. The nucleus is really small. If the atom is compared to a closed football stadium, the nucleus is just as big as an ant.

When you touch the surface of the steel plate with your hand, you may be thinking that this thing can't be pierced even with a needle, and it must be very dense. Naturally, you will have the idea that the world is made up of physical matter. So, when people first discovered an atom, the first reaction was that it should be a dense solid ball. But now we know that the atom is not a solid ball, but an empty arena!

Fractal cosmology holds that our universe is a large particle, and each particle in the universe is a small universe. Now maybe you won't laugh at the absurdity of this theory, because if you are living as big as an electron in an atom, then for you, the atom is really like a small universe. When we compare the nucleus with the atom, it is like an ant in a football stadium; but if you compare it with electrons, then the situation is completely reversed. At this time, the atomic nucleus is like the arena, and the electrons are like the ants!

The size of the sun in relation to that of the solar system is of the same order of magnitude as the atomic nucleus in relation to the atom, so fractal cosmology is really a very vivid description of the universe.

Chapter 9

The Flower in the Mirror:

Does Quantum Theory Imply that the World is Only an Illusion like a Flower in the Mirror or a Moon on the Water?

Quantum theory, one of the two pillars of physics in the 20th century, has triggered more technological revolutions than any other theory in history. The widely used technologies such as nuclear energy, information technology, laser, and semiconductor are inseparable from quantum theory.

But what's interesting is that the success of quantum theory in applications in the field of technology has been achieved without a clear knowledge of the principles and theories. Just as the ancients did not know the existence of the Earth's magnetic field, but still able to invent and use the compass. Although quantum theory has found wide applications, the physics community has not figured out what its principles are until now.

What is going on here? The following is an experiment to illustrate this.

In 1807 Thomas Young published a famous experiment, the double-slit interference of light. He put a candle in front of a piece of paper with a small hole in it, forming a point source of light, then placed another piece of paper with two parallel slits in it behind this piece of paper, and then placed a projection screen behind the second piece of paper. It was found that the light emitted from the small hole was cast through the two slits onto the screen, forming a series of alternating stripes of light and dark.

 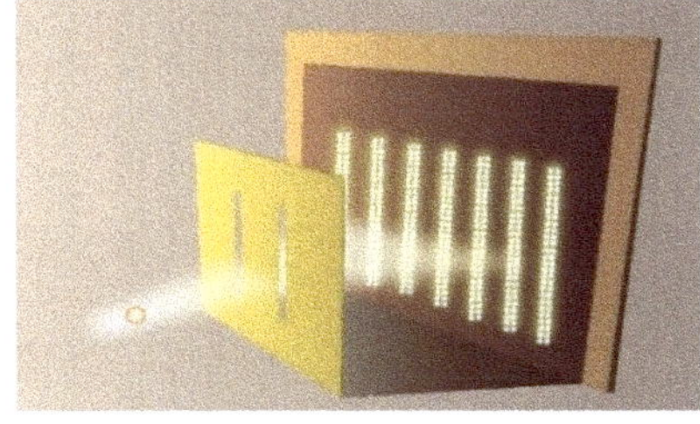

Obviously, these stripes are due to interference. As interference is a characteristic of waves, this experiment proves that light is a kind of wave. The two beams of light passing through the two slits form an interference phenomenon. In places where peaks meet peaks they will reinforce each other, so there are bright stripes on the corresponding positions on the screen; in places where peaks meet troughs, they will cancel each other out, so there are dark stripes.

Later, this classic experiment became an important experiment for quantum theory after being modified. People used electrons instead of point sources of light to do this experiment. The result was surprising, and interference fringes appeared on the screen. This phenomenon is quite challenging for people's nerves because only waves can produce interference. According to the usual understanding, electrons are the internal structures of atoms. It is obviously a kind of particle. How can interference occur between particles?

More interesting things are following. We know that there will be interference between two waves. If there is only one wave, interference will not happen. Later, someone modified the experiment a little, trying to control the number of electrons, only one electron was emitted at a time so that each time it could only emit a small bright spot on the back of the screen. Surprisingly, when people strike the electrons one by one on the photographic screen, as the bright spots slowly increase, the interference fringes gradually become visible. With more and more bright spots appearing, the stripes become more and more clear.

How should these phenomena be explained? Is the electron a particle or a wave? Diffraction and interference are the characteristics of waves. If electrons are particles, why do they create interference-like waves when they pass through double slits? But a wave is not a solid entity. If an electron is a wave, why does it produce a bright spot when it hits the screen, thus showing the physical characteristics of a particle?

The most difficult thing to explain is when electrons pass through double slits one by one, why is interference there? The generation of interference fringes requires two columns of mutually influencing waves at the same time in the two gaps. And an electron can only pass through a gap, that is to say, it can only produce one wave. How does it interfere with itself?

Strange things are more than these. In the process of emitting electrons, one by one as long as one of the double slits is closed, the latter electrons can immediately sense the change, and no interference fringes will appear on the screen. Even without closing the slit, as long as a detector is installed behind the double slit to measure which slit these electrons come through, the electrons will respond, and the interference fringes disappear immediately without a trace.

How does the electron quickly know that the other slit is closed at the moment before the electron passes through the slit? Compared with the size of the electron, the distance between the other slit and the electron is astronomical. How can the electron react in an instant? Unless it receives some kind of instantaneously transmitted signal. Who sent the signal to it? Why did the electrons change their behavior when a detector faces it?

As to how to explain the above phenomena, there was a fierce strife in the physics community. There are a lot of explanations, but none of them unify everyone's opinions. Here I would like to highlight the most influential version - *Copenhagen Interpretation*.

The contents of Copenhagen's explanation mainly consist of three parts. In addition to the aforementioned Heisenberg's *Principle of Uncertainty* and Bonn's *probability interpretation*, there is also the *Complementary Principle* proposed by

Bohr in 1927. The principle of complementarities is much bolder than the previous two theories. It actually thinks that the world is determined by consciousness.

The principle of complementarities says that in fact, electrons are both a kind of particle and a kind of wave. This is called the *Wave-Particle Duality*. But at every particular moment, electrons cannot be both particles and waves at the same time, and their state depends on whether someone is watching them. When no one observes it is a wave, in the form of a wave function in a superimposed state, diffusing throughout the space; and once observed, the wave function suddenly shrinks from space, concentrated at a point, so it becomes a particle. This miraculous change in the wave function is called *collapse*.

According to Bohr's explanation, in the previous experiment, the electron was originally a wave, and in some way passed through two slits at the same time and interfered with itself. At the moment of hitting the photographic screen, which is equivalent to someone observing it, it immediately becomes a particle and randomly hits a certain position on the screen according to the probability. When the detector is mounted behind the double slit, for the same reason, the observed electrons immediately become particles. As the particles do not interfere, the interference fringes disappear.

Waves are nothing but ethereal things, and they are not solids like the real points of particles. The principle of complementarities means that electrons are not real things when we don't look at them. They spread out like a ghost and float in space with the probability of waves. But as soon as you open your eyes, all the phantoms disappear immediately, and the wave function of the electrons collapses in an instant, turning into a real particle that appears randomly at a certain position so that you can see it.

This is more like a scene in *The Ghost Beauty*! When you looked at it, the ghost beauty Xiaoqian stood in front of you and smiled at you; but when you turned around, she immediately turned into a light smoke, disappearing without a trace.

Is this still a scientific theory? It is simply one of the ghost stories from the most famous Chinese ghost story book *Strange Tales of Liao-Zhai*.

To make the matter even worse, people use photons, mesons, and other subatomic particles, even with atoms, to do the same experiment and get exactly the same results as with electrons. It shows that this property is not unique to a certain particle, but a common phenomenon in the particle world.

The physical entities in our eyes are all composed of particles, so if each particle is real when it is observed, it is only an illusory wave when it is not observed, which means that the material world composed of it is also like this. What does this imply? Is it true that as Bishop George Berkeley of Ireland said in the 18th century, "existence is perceived?" Is matter determined by consciousness?

There was a widely circulated statement that described this explanation very well: "The moon does not exist when we don't look at it."

This is too scary. For a long time, we all believed that the world is objective, and it does not depend on the existence of human consciousness. The universe has evolved for 13.7 billion years, and the history of human beings has only been a few million years. How can the world not exist without observers? This is ridiculous, no matter how you look at it.

Copenhagen explained that electrons in the form of waves have many possible superposition states, and the wave function collapses into a particle only when it is observed. Does this mean that what happened to electrons in the past has become a reality after the influence of consciousness? If this is the case, then, in theory, we should have a chance to change it after things have happened before it becomes observable!

It is not easy to verify such an idea, but there are always a few wise men who can design a way to do it. In 1979, American physicist John Wheeler proposed the famous *delay experiment*, pointing out that we can really try to make the electron delay to decide. After it has actually passed the double slit, we choose whether it will go through a slit or two, and whether there appear interference fringes or not. To put it more simply, it is possible to decide or modify the way in which the electron passes through the double seams after the fact that the electron passes through the double seams.

The experiment designed by Wheeler is different in form from the double-slit experiment, but the principle is the same. It is equivalent to the way we can place or remove the detector before the electron passes through the double slit to determine whether the electron will pass a slit or two before it goes through the double slit in the front.

This is really an incredible idea! Five years after Wheeler's vision, Carroll Alley of the University of Maryland led a team to conduct a delayed experiment. The results really prove that we can decide how the electron passes through the double seams after it has passed the double seams.

We can really decide how it happened after things happen. What is going on? Wheeler later quoted Bohr as saying: "Any basic quantum phenomenon is a reality only after it has been recorded."

The evolution of the universe is like making a movie. The content of the film cannot be said to be certain until the release, and until then the director can edit it at any time. It is said that there have been such examples in the past. Some actresses were not willing to be taken advantage of. As a result, although they participated in the acting of the film, the parts of the scenes that involve them were all cut off, so they were irrelevant to the films when they are shown after editing!

Is the observer the equivalent of a movie audience? The film is only certain after it is shown to the audience. Does the history of the evolution of the universe only become reality after being observed? In this way, the evolutionary history of the universe for more than one billion years is only to become a reality afterlife has emerged as an observer.

It takes courage to accept the idea that "consciousness makes the world a reality." You may want to find comfort in other versions of the explanation, but the problem is that their interpretations are much crazier.

Ranked second is the multi-cosmic interpretation, which has many supporters. The most unacceptable part of Copenhagen's interpretation is the need for an observer to collapse the wave function in a superimposed state, thereby introducing consciousness into physics and drawing the conclusion that the mind can directly play a role in the material world. This is unacceptable to some people, and they try to remove the role of consciousness from physics. One attempt is the *Multi-Universe Interpretation*.

They think that the reason why consciousness is introduced is that the wave function has collapsed; that the reason why a collapse is determined is that the interference will disappear when the observation is made, and we only see that the electron passes through a slit and no one has ever observed that the electrons come out of the two seams at the same time. From this, they further infer that there is no collapse if the electrons actually pass two slits at the same time when we observe. Can we exclude the effect of consciousness in this way?

But why do we only see electrons passing through one seam? The multi-cosmic interpretation" says that because the electrons face choices in front of the double slits, our universe splits into two *parallel universes*. In one of the universes, electrons pass through the slit on the left, and in another universe, electrons pass through the slit on the right. We are only in one of the parallel universes, so we only see electrons passing through one slit, while in another universe we will see electrons passing through another slit.

This means that every possibility of the evolution of the universe corresponds to a parallel universe. In some universes, Liang Shanbo and Zhu Yingtai (the protagonists of a Chinese folk tale, known as Chinese Romeo and Juliet) eventually married, while in other universes, Jing Ke, an assassin in Qing Dynasty, killed the king of the Qin Empire.

The multi-universe interpretation does exclude the role of consciousness, but the cost is staggering. The boundless universe, because of a small choice of a small electron in a small laboratory on our little planet, must be split into two. God knows how many particles in the universe are facing choices every moment, and how many splits need to be done in our universe!

Are you willing to accept the Copenhagen interpretation that consciousness makes the world a reality, or are you willing to believe the multi-world interpretation" that an electronic choice can cause the universe to split? In comparison, I think it is better to accept Copenhagen's explanation, because this interpretation is a bit strange except for the introduction of consciousness, and other aspects are easy to understand. And for the multi-world interpretation, it is too weird to let the whole universe cater to an electronic behavior in order to eliminate the role of consciousness.

Copenhagen's interpretation introduced consciousness into physics, which is too challenging for people's nerves, so it has been accused, questioned, and attacked by all parties. What is surprising, however, is that it has withstood the test again and again, and all the experiments that tried to overthrow it have proved its correctness instead.

Einstein was extremely disgusted with this. He worked hard to deny this theory throughout his life. Schrödinger also held the same position. However, the fame and prestige of the scientists cannot prevail over the facts. In the end, physicists can only accept reality unwillingly, simply enjoy the benefits brought forward by quantum theory, and then ignore the astounding philosophical implications behind it.

Flowers in the mirror, the moon in water, although beautiful they look, they are just illusions. Doesn't the quantum theory tell us that this complicated and colorful world in front of us is just an illusion?

Is Practicality Equal to Correctness?

People in ancient China did not know the concept of the magnetic field but were able to invent the compass. This phenomenon gives us a hint, that is, the practicality of a theory does not need to rely on the integrity and correctness of the theory, and the two cannot be directly equated.

On the one hand, an incomplete or even vague theory may often have a high practical value. For example, people have used it to create a large number of high-tech products when the principles of quantum theory are still unclear.

On the other hand, theories that have proven to be useful are not necessarily correct. Newton's classic mechanics are still very useful now, and people still use them to calculate ballistic trajectories, but it has long been proved by the relativity theory to be limited in terms of correctness.

However, there is a tendency in people's habitual thinking that the practicality of a theory is often taken for granted as proof of its correctness. Just like when you see a monk using technological products, making phone calls with a mobile phone, for example, you will naturally make a new judgment in your heart on the supremacy of science over religion.

Paul Davis once said: "In many cases, the concept of religion is no more falsified by modern science than surpassed by modern science." Indeed, science far surpasses religion in practical terms, and this alone is enough to give it an upper hand in the contest with religion.

But as said before, practicality is not necessarily correct, and being incorrect is not necessarily unpractical. If you don't have a clear understanding of this, then your thoughts will be easily influenced by the phenomena in front of you and cast a thick layer of utilitarian color. This phenomenon has an ugly name in life: "She who has milk is a mother."

Wave and Its Reflection, Diffraction, and Interference

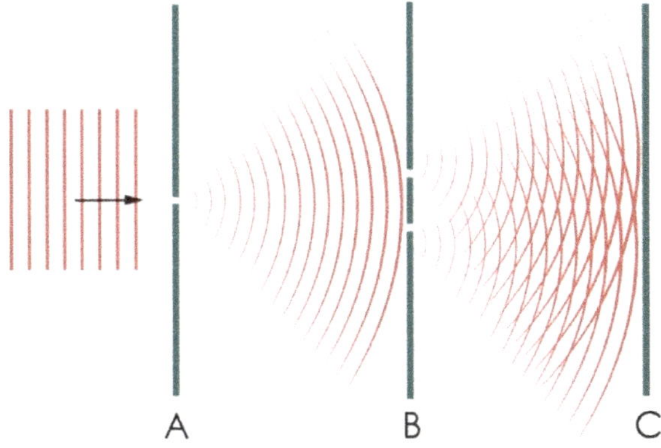

Fluctuation is a very common form of material movement in life. For example, if you drop a stone onto a calm water surface, it will ripple a wave of water. The water wave is transmitted through the water. What we say in the mouth will be transmitted to the ears of others in the form of sound waves. The sound waves are transmitted through the air. These waves are mechanical vibrations of elastic solid materials, so they are called mechanical waves.

For a long time, people thought that all waves are mechanical waves, and they need to pass through a medium to spread. For example, in space, we can't hear each other without the use of instruments. This is because sound waves cannot transmit in a vacuum.

Later, people discovered a wave that can propagate in a vacuum, the electromagnetic wave. In 1865, the British physicist Maxwell predicted the existence of electromagnetic waves, which are the propagation of varying electric fields and changing magnetic fields in space. He also inferred that the propagation speed of electromagnetic waves is equal to the speed of light, and that light is one kind of electromagnetic wave. In 1888, German physicist Hertz used experiments to verify the existence of electromagnetic waves.

Whether it is a mechanical or an electromagnetic wave, there are some common characteristics, such as reflection, diffraction, and interference. People often use these characteristics of waves to determine whether something is a wave.

When we shout into a valley, the echo produced was the reflection of the sound wave.

If a wave encounters a small obstacle while propagating, it will go around; if it encounters a large obstacle with gaps or holes in the middle that are equal to or slightly smaller than the wavelength, then it will pass through. In this process, the direction of wave propagation will change. It looks like the obstacle, a hole or a gap, is used as a wave source to form a new series of wavelets of the same frequency. This phenomenon is called the diffraction of waves.

If two waves of the same frequency overlap during the propagation process, then there will be the phenomenon that the vibration is strengthened where the peak meets the peak and the vibration is weakened where the peak and the valley meet, and the strengthened region and the weakened region are separated from each other. This phenomenon is called the interference of waves.

In the above figure, a wave passes through a small hole in the middle of obstacle A to form a diffraction, then it passes two small holes to obstacle B to form two rows of diffracted waves, and interference occurs between the two rows of waves.

Is the World Just a Fantasy?

What is a wave? Wave is just a phenomenon, not an entity. The "waves of people" on the stands in a football stadium are formed because the fans stand up and sit down one after another, forming a regular dynamic pattern. And there is no such thing as "human waves." The same is true for water waves, which are formed by the regular vibration of the water's surface. There is no such thing as "water waves" in the world.

Both human waves and water waves can be regarded as mechanical waves (of course, human waves are just an analogy; it is not a wave in the strictly physical sense). They are a kind of movement phenomenon of physical matter. It is important to point out that when the mechanical wave appears, the physical matter does not disappear, and turns into a wave of nothingness. Just as human waves appear, people still exist; when water waves appear, water still exists.

However, the wave-particle duality indicates that the particle property and the wave property of electrons cannot coexist at the same time. It can only switch between physical matter and ethereal waves. When it becomes a wave, the physical matter disappears in an instant; and when it becomes a real particle, the wave disappears in an instant. And the most surprising thing is that the reason for this conversion is just like what the Chinese singer Fei Wong sang in her song, "just because I happened to catch sight of you in the crowd."

An electron is sometimes a real particle, sometimes an ethereal wave; when we look at it, it is a particle, and when we don't look at it, it is a wave. Where does this illusory scene often appear? Yes, it appears in the fantasy depicted in fairy tales. Does the wave-particle duality feature of electrons also indicate that the world we are in is actually a fantasy?

Chapter 10
The Invisible Hand:
Telepathic Quantum Entanglement and the Invisible Hand Behind the World.

From a philosophical point of view, quantum theory is a very destructive theory. Although it did not help us to build a new world model, it has shattered the old view of the world. It undermines the certainty of the world and overturns *Determinism*; it undermines the authenticity of the world and causes people to begin to doubt *realism*; and what is more, it will also destroy the locality of the world and challenge Einstein's *relativity theory.*

Locality means that all causal relationships in the universe must be maintained within a specific area within a certain period of time, and there is no instantaneous action and transfer beyond time and space. This is the basis of relativity. The transmission of any information cannot exceed the upper limit of the speed of light. There is no possibility of over-distance interaction in the universe ignoring time and distance.

In our experience, any information transfer takes time. In ancient times, as communication tools were not developed, it often took several months for letters to arrive at the remote border outposts from the capital city, so there was a saying that "the family letter is worth a thousand gold coins". Now there are telegrams, telephones, and the Internet, but the transmission of information still takes time, and it is impossible to exceed the speed of light at the fastest. This leads us to believe that there is no two-way interaction in the world that is similar to telepathy—instantaneous information transmission with no consumption of time.

However, there is a new saying about this issue. There is a strange experiment in33 quantum theory called the "EPR experiment" involving the interaction of particles which makes physicists confused.

The EPR experiment was a thought experiment proposed by Einstein and two colleagues in 1935 to overthrow Copenhagen's interpretation.

Suppose there is a large particle with a spin of 0. It is unstable and decays into two small particles, A and B, which fly away to the opposite sides. The small particles have two kinds of spin modes, called *"upper spin"* and *"down spin"*. According to the Law of Conservation of Angular Momentum, if particle A is down-spin, then particle B must be up-spin, and vice versa.

According to Copenhagen's explanation, we can make the following inference: the initial spin states of two small particles are uncertain; when we observe particle A, it will randomly select a certain state, such as down spin; According to the Law of Conservation, particle B will necessarily be determined as of upper spin at the same time.

But the problem is, if the two small particles are very far apart, such as billions of light years away, then how does particle A pass information to particle B when the state of particle A is determined so that particle B can react to it at the same time?

If the spin directions of the small particles are uncertain before the observation, then at the moment when one of the particles is observed, according to the requirements of the Law of Conservation, the two particles will react at the same time regardless of how far apart they are and determine their respective directions of spin.

There are only two explanations for this situation. The first one may be there is an over-range effect similar to telepathy between the two small particles, that is, some kind of information transmission beyond the speed of light so that they can communicate instantly. The second possibility is that the two small particles are not as uncertain as Copenhagen explained; instead, their spin states have already been determined from the moment they are separated.

Einstein believes that the theory of relativity prescribes that the transmission of any information cannot exceed the speed of light. There is no over-range effect in the universe that does not require transmission time, so the first possibility does not exist. As such, there is only one other possibility. The states of the particles have already been determined, which proves that there is a problem with the interpretation of Copenhagen.

Einstein's attack made it difficult for Bohr to be able to fight back, and he was depressed for a while. Later, Bohr explained that there is actually no signal of superluminal speed between the two small particles. Before the two small particles are observed, they are still a whole, no matter how far away they are apart. So, as long as one of them is observed, the other one will inevitably respond accordingly.

Who is right the one here? The key to the test is to determine whether there is a correlation between the small particles that are far apart and whether there is *telepathy* or an over-range effect. If Bohr is right, then the small particles are still whole before they are observed, and there must be a certain correlation between particle A and particle B. If Einstein is right, then the two small particles become uncorrelated as soon as they are separated.

This thought experiment could not be tested under the technical conditions of the time. Bohr and Einstein did not know whether they were right or wrong. Later, the Northern Ireland physicist John Stewart Bell published "the Bell Inequality" in

1964, which cleared the way for testing EPR experiments. Bell is a supporter of Einstein. He believes that the experimental results will tell people that the telepathic association between particles is pure nonsense.

In 1982, the French physicist Alain Aspect led a team to do this experiment. The results of this experiment are so important that some people even call it "God's ruling." The result turned out to be Einstein's defeat. It turns out that the separated small particles do maintain a subtle and magical connection, similar to the telepathic transcendence of time and space. This association is called *quantum entanglement*.

After the publication of the experimental report, the scientists were silent and did not know what to say. Later, people introduced new methods to improve the reliability of the experiment. The experiment was repeated many times, but the results were all the same: no matter how far apart the two small particles are, there is still a mysterious relationship between them.

Now we are faced with two tough choices. If we believe what Bohr said that the two particles are still a whole before they are observed, no matter how far away apart, that means we need to give up the reality of the world and admit that the particles become reality only after being observed. The world is determined by consciousness. In addition, we have to accept the fact that there is indeed an over-range effect between the particles faster than the speed of light. In doing so, the cornerstone of relativity is shaken.

After the results of the Aspect experiment came out, eight experts on quantum theory were invited to an interview, including Aspect and Bell. The experts have a wide range of opinions. Aspect does not believe that there is a superluminal speed, preferring to give up the reality of the world in exchange for the locality. Bell was silent for a long time and finally preferred giving up locality to believe there is indeed an overreaching effect faster than the speed of light, to giving up the reality of the world to admit that the world is ethereal.

Like Einstein, Schrödinger is both a founder of and a staunch opponent of quantum theory. After the publication of the EPR experiment results, Schrödinger was very excited and thought that he had grasped the key points of Copenhagen's explanation. In order to make up for a shot, he published a famous thinking experiment – the cat experiment.

Suppose that a radioactive atom is packed into an opaque box and there is a clever and precise device in the box. As long as the radioactive atom decays and emits a neutron, it can trigger a chain reaction in the device, which will eventually break a poisonous gas cylinder in the box and kill a cat in the box.

Schrödinger said, since Copenhagen had explained that the states of the particles are uncertain before being observed and are in various possible mixed states, it means that as long as no observations are made, the radioactive atoms are in a state of ambiguity, and the decay is not certain.

The next question is coming. Before we open the box to observe, it is not certain whether the atom decays or not, which means that the life and death of the cat inside is also uncertain. This inference is unbelievable. Have the cats been in a mixed state of death and alive before?

Schrödinger's attack made the Copenhagen followers embarrassed. According to their theory, the cat was indeed both dead and alive before we observe. This conclusion is too shocking. You said that the state of the particle is uncertain. And you also said that a cat is in a mixed state of death and life. Is this not nonsense?

After we observe it, the life and death of the cat can be determined. Does this mean that our consciousness determines the life and death of the cat? If we have not observed, would the cat have never died? Moreover, the uncertainty mentioned here is not because we don't know the situation. This uncertainty is really an uncertain situation. That is to say, if the cat is self-conscious, even if it is self-conscious, it will not know if it is dead or alive.

The question raised by Schrödinger is really difficult to answer. Some people think of the *multi-cosmic interpretation*. They theorize that as there are so many parallel universes, the atoms in some universes have not decayed, and the cats are still alive; and in other universes, the atoms have decayed, and the cats are dead.

Do you believe in this? Anyway, I don't believe it.

But the EPR experiment, and the cat experiment are really puzzling. Why are the small particles separated by hundreds of millions of light years still a whole? What is it that connects them together? How can a living cat be in superimposed states of death and living?

In fact, as long as you understand a simple truth, perhaps all these problems can be solved, that is - there is supervision behind our world.

In citizen law education, we often hear the phrase: "To learn to protect yourself with the weapons of the law." In reality, some people have used legal means to safeguard their legitimate rights and interests. In this way, some people really regard the law as a weapon and think that it does have a powerful force. In fact, this is just an illusion.

As a kind of rule, the law itself has no power. What is really powerful is the state machine that enacts the law. The reason why the law is awesome is that there is a state machine behind its back. It is the state's coercive force to supervise the enforcement of the law and impose penalties on those who violate the law. For a country, only the legislature is not enough. The law will not automatically take effect when it is formulated. It also needs law enforcement to guarantee its implementation and supervise the public to observe the law. Once there is no support from the state machine, the law will be completely ineffective.

Some people are too superstitious about the law because they don't know this. In fact, in a society ruled by people, when you offend a person who is too powerful to offend, it is only futile to take legal weapons to protect yourself. At this point, you will find that without the backing of the state machine, the law becomes weak and useless and can no longer protect you.

Interestingly, such commonsense mistakes often occur in the scientific field. Most scientists believe that the laws of nature dominate the world, and the laws of science embody the laws of nature, so as long as they master the laws of science, they are equivalent to mastering powerful weapons capable of dominating the world. A widely circulated phrase shows this point: "Knowledge is power!"

After mastering the laws of science, people have had great success in using science and technology to transform the world. This seems to prove that the natural laws behind the laws of science are really a powerful force that dominates the world.

However, has it ever occurred to you that natural law is the same as human law? In fact, it is just a rule, and the rule itself has no power. Human law requires the support of the state machine and requires law enforcement agencies to supervise the implementation. Doesn't the law of nature require somebody to enforce it?

What is it that supervises the operations of the world in strict compliance with the laws of nature? This issue has never been raised before. Many people naively believe that the laws of nature can work by themselves. This is a strange idea. It is tantamount to believing that human law can be automatically activated as long as it is formulated, needing no one to implement it.

The power behind the laws of nature is the true master of our world. What is this power? Where does it come from? We are not clear, to be honest. But what we can be sure of is that there is some kind of supervision power behind this world, and it is this power that makes sure the laws of nature work well.

As long as you understand this point, the first two experiments are easy to explain. The mysterious connection between the two small particles, if there is a monitoring system behind the world in working, is not surprising, for the monitoring system can completely treat two separate small particles as a whole. The theory of relativity is only effective for the things that belong to our world. For the monitoring system behind this world, there is no binding force, and it can easily create a super-distance effect in our eyes.

Schrödinger's cat experiment is also very easy to explain. There are some problems with the understanding of uncertainty in Copenhagen's interpretation because uncertainty actually only appears in the initial state of the system and does not exist in the running process. Atomic decay is an event in the operation of the system. It must be recorded in the monitoring system. Therefore, whether Schrödinger's cat is dead or alive is certain for the monitoring system. There will never be the situation of a cat both dead and alive.

The operation of the macro world cannot be uncertain before observation and is always in a fuzzy state of superposition. The life and death of a cat will never be determined after human observation, and the universe will never become a reality only after the observers appear. Otherwise, how could the evolution of the universe before the existence of life be explained? How does something that did not exist evolve?

For the invisible hand behind the world, people are not unaware of its existence. In quantum theory, in addition to *the Copenhagen interpretation* and *multi-universe interpretation*, there is another interpretation version - the "hidden variable theory" of the American physicist David Bohm, which to some extent reflects the role of the monitoring system. The theory of hidden variables suggests that the unpredictability of electronic behavior is caused by hidden variables. These variables are hidden, and you cannot directly detect them.

The question we have to ask is: Do the EPR experiment, and the cat experiment mean that there is an invisible hand behind the world? If so, what is this hand?

Conservation and Non-conservation in the Universe

The Law of Conservation is a special kind of existence in the laws of nature, which shows that something in our world is eternal. There is an opposite spin of one of the two small particles, which is derived from the Law of Conservation *of Angular Momentum*.

A long time ago, people felt through experience that the world has been changing. The Greek philosopher Heraclitus in the 5th century BC said: "Man cannot enter the same river twice." He believes that things are in an eternal movement of change. When you walk into the river next time, everything is different.

There is a similar saying in Buddhism that Siddhartha called this phenomenon "impermanence."

Although life cannot be retained, people always hope that something can last forever, such as love. The lovers who are bathed in the river of love like to use the vows to strengthen their feelings, and hope that both parties can be loyal to each other till death. Some people have fulfilled their promises and have lived together for the rest of their lives, but it is not uncommon to find examples of betrayals and separations in marriages. The world is changing all the time. It is not easy to let one's heart not change!

The rise of natural science has made people see the hope of eternity. Early scientists discovered that there are really things in the universe that are eternal, such as mass, energy, momentum, angular momentum, and charge, so a number of conservation laws are raised. These laws say that certain things in the universe can exist forever, and they will neither increase nor decrease, and the total amount will remain the same.

The concept of *momentum* may be stranger to us than quality and energy. It refers to the mass of an object multiplied by speed. *Conservation of Momentum* means that the total amount of motion of objects in the universe does not change, and *Conservation of Angular Momentum* means that the total amount of rotational motion of an object in space is constant. The Law of Conservation of momentum and the Law of Conservation of angular momentum are the laws that are basically observed in the process of decay, collision, and transformation. In the EPR experiment, Einstein concluded that the spin directions of two small particles must be in opposite directions, and the basis for this assumption comes from this law.

However, after people discovered that mass and energy would transform into each other, the Law of Conservation of mass and the Law of Conservation of energy was broken, and the Law of Conservation of Mass and Energy took their place. This discovery is really disappointing. It seems that conservation is conditional. Even the Law of Conservation cannot be eternal. How can we expect even love to last forever?

Let's talk about a more interesting story of the failure of the Law of Conservation.

Let's start with *symmetry*. The concept of symmetry in the laws of physics is different from that in everyday life. It means that under certain circumstances, the laws of physics will not change after the conditions have changed. For example, in one inertial system, you derive a law of motion. After you change the inertia system to another one, the law of motion is still the same and there will be not any change in it. In 1918, the German mathematician Amy Nott proposed the famous "Nott theory," suggesting that every kind of symmetry in the universe corresponds to a conservation law, which set up a link between the two concepts of symmetry and conservation.

The basic particle has a very interesting symmetrical way called "parity", and its corresponding conservation law is called "parity conservation." *Parity* is also called bilateral symmetry, or mirror symmetry. When we look in the mirror, the people in the mirror are opposite us. No matter how we are doing, he is doing it. This is mirror symmetry. If the spin direction of one particle is *left-handed* and the spin direction of another particle is *right-handed*, then the two particles are mirror images of each other. It is reasonable to say that the physical representation of the mirrored particle should be exactly the same. This is called parity.

Under strong interaction and electromagnetic action, people have indeed observed the phenomenon of *parity conservation*. However, in 1956, the Chinese American scientists Yang Zhenning and Li Zhengdao proposed an astonishing prediction; that under weak interaction, *parity* is not conserved.

A few months later, Wu Jianxiong, another Chinese American scientist, did a beta decay experiment on polarized nuclear 60Co. Beta decay is a weak interaction. This experiment proves that in the process of weak interaction the parity is indeed not conserved. Just one year later, both Yang and Li won the Nobel Prize in Physics.

This seemingly reasonable law of conservation can also fail. How wonderful the universe is. We don't know which other laws of conservation are in danger of failing. What is certain, however, is that any laws of physics, including the Law of Conservation, will fail at a *singularity*. Is it true that in our world we should not expect anything to last forever?

Chapter 11

The Legend of Immortality:
"One Day in the Heavens Equals a Thousand Years of Time in our World of Life."
This Phenomenon Really Exists!

There are two pillar theories for modern physics. One is the quantum theory and the other is the relativity theory. If the quantum theory gives people the feeling of "being weird", then the theory of relativity gives people the feeling of "being magic."

There is such a saying in ancient Chinese mythology: "It is only one day in the heavens, but it has been a thousand years in the earthly world." The time flow rate between the heavens and the human world is different. The gods living in the heavens will never be old and can live forever with the heavens and the earth, and with the sun and the moon.

The flow rate of time can be slowed down or even stopped. We used to think that was just people's imagination, but now we know that this is really the case.

In the era of classic physics, people think that their time and space is "absolute time and space." What is absolute time and space? You can simply explain it as that at anytime, anywhere in the universe, the speed of time is constant, and the distance of space is fixed. Whether on the ground, on a plane, on a spaceship, or on Mars, the length of one hour should be the same, and the length of 1 meter should be the same.

This kind of understanding is in line with our experience, but this seemingly natural problem is now answered differently because of Einstein's theory of relativity.

The concept of time and space in classical physics is equivalent to treating the universe as a grand theater. It regards the heavens and the earth as actors

In the absolute space and time of classical physics, the motion state of an object is relative. Because according to classical physics theory, it is necessary to select a reference object to judge the motion state of any object in relation to it. For the same moving object, if the selected reference object is different, the result will be different.

For example, the *Mir* train travels from west to east at a speed of 50 kilometers per hour on the rails. This sentence implies a hypothesis -- using the earth as a reference. If the reference is replaced, the result will be different.

As long as you select different references, you will get different speeds of an object. Unless there is an absolute constant reference system, there is no absolute value for the speed of an object. According to this idea, we can speculate that the speed of light should be no exception. If a beam of light comes to you, the speed of light is C. When you move at the speed V toward the light source, then if you are the reference, the speed of light will become C+V; and when you move away from the light source, the speed of light in your eyes should be C-V.

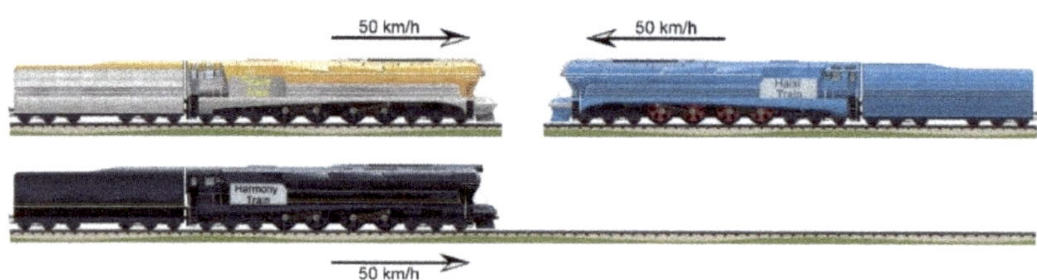

The answer to this question seems obvious. But in 1886, American physicists

Albert McGerson and Edward Morey discovered in the famous Michelson–Morley experiment that when the earth moved in different directions, the detected speed of light did not change at all. This means that our previous speculation is completely wrong, whether you are moving towards the light source, perpendicular to the light source, or even away from the light source, the speed of light you see is a constant speed C, and not C+V or C-V.

The physics community is thus in a state of disappointment. Regardless of what is used as a reference, the measured speed of light in a vacuum is a constant value, which is completely contrary to the common sense of classical physics.

But the reality is stronger than people's conviction. In the face of irrefutable facts, we can only try to find the cause. According to the classical physics formula, speed = distance/time, and speed is related to space and time. Since the speed of light is constant, then the changes must be from space and time.

In the end, Einstein published the *Special Theory of Relativity*, pointing out that the flow rate of time is changing.

According to the special theory of relativity, a high-speed moving object will have a slower time flow rate and its length will be shortened. The closer the speed of the object is to the speed of light, the more obvious this effect will be and the time will stop flowing after reaching the speed of light. If you are sitting in a spaceship with a speed of 0.99999 times the speed of light, then your hour will be different from one hour on Earth, and it will be equivalent to 250 hours on Earth. At the same time, your 1 meter will be different from the 1 meter on the earth. If you measure the length of the spacecraft to be 500 meters, then people on earth will only measure it to be 2 meters long!

The time flow rates of objects in different motion states are different. Classical physics studies low speed moving objects for which the time flow factor can be ignored. However, when studying high-speed moving objects, as their time flow rates are greatly different, this factor can no longer be ignored, and their speeds cannot be simply added and subtracted.

It is precise because of the flexibility of time and space that light always travels in a vacuum at a speed of about 300,000 kilometers per second, no matter where you are and from which direction light goes to you.

If you take a spacecraft to travel into space at a speed of 0.99999 times the speed of light, you will only be one year older when you return to Earth after one year, but it has been 250 years on earth since you left. Your childhood friend is already dead, and you may only see his descendants after 8 generations.

The special theory of relativity well explained the problem of the constant speed of light, which was later confirmed by more and more experiments, but Einstein himself was quickly dissatisfied with it. His dissatisfaction came from the word "special".

The attributive qualifier added to the "theory of relativity" in German and English is the word "special". Why is it "special"? The original special theory of relativity is based on two hypotheses: one is the principle of the constant speed of light, that is, the speed of light is constant, independent of whether the illuminator or the observer is moving; and the other is the principle of relativity, that is, the laws of physics are the same in all "inertial systems", and no matter which inertial system is chosen as a reference, there is not a slight influence. The special feature of special relativity is that it can only be applied to inertial systems, that is, objects that are stationary or do a uniform linear motion.

The problem is there is nothing in the world that is absolutely stationary or moving in a uniform linear motion. Is the trajectory really a straight line for a train that travels straight forward at a speed of 50 kilometers per hour? No, it isn't, for the earth's surface is actually a curved surface. Can it really maintain a speed of 50 kilometers per hour? No, it cannot. It is constantly accelerating or decelerating. Are the mountains standing quietly there really stationary? No, it is making circular motions along with the earth around the sun.

"According to Newton's gravitational theory at the time, gravity is a kind of over-range interaction. Every object in the universe must be subjected to forces in any spatial position, so there is no absolute inertial system at all. It turned out that for a long time Einstein only discovered a theory that was applicable to an ideal state. Of course, he was not happy with that.

How can we remove the word "special" and find a theory that is universally applicable in the real world?

Einstein was troubled by this issue. He thought about it over and over and eventually figured it out. He discovered "the equivalence principle". This principle suggests that acceleration and gravity are equivalent. In this way, for *the non-inertial system* under acceleration, according to the principle of equivalence, its acceleration can be treated as gravity. So, as long as the gravitational factor is added to the special theory of relativity, the statement that the laws of physics are the same in all inertial systems can be extended and rewrote into the statement that the laws of physics are the same in all systems, thus turning it into a universally applicable theory, the "general theory of relativity".

The equation for the general theory of relativity is much more complicated than that for the Special Theory of Relativity because the gravitational force is a quantity that changes at all times during the motion of the object, so the formula of general relativity is a differential equation. In order to get the gravitational field equation, Einstein deliberately went back to college for a year to make up for calculus.

Bank cards, shopping cards, and banknotes look different, but when you buy things, you can pay for anything with any one of them; this is because their roles

in this regard are equivalent. There are a lot of equivalent things in life. For example, in an elevator, when the elevator accelerates, there will be a feeling that the body sinks. It seems that the gravity of the earth is strengthened in an instant; when the elevator accelerates down, there will be a feeling of weightlessness in an instant, as if the gravity of the earth is weakened in an instant. In this way, although acceleration and gravity are different things, as the upward acceleration can enhance the effect of gravity, and the downward acceleration can offset the effect of gravity, they play equivalent roles.

The general theory of relativity, which is much more complicated than the special theory of relativity, is much more mysterious with its conclusions. According to this theory, Einstein concluded that "gravitation will bend time and space". The stronger the gravitation, the more space and time are bent.

The result of time-space bending is that the time flow rate is slowed. The stronger the gravitation, the slower the time flow rate. The earth's gravity on flat ground is larger than that on the mountain. Therefore, according to the principle of general relativity, the clock on flat ground will go slower than on the mountain. But, as the earth is spinning, the higher above the ground, the greater the linear speed of rotation. According to the principle of special relativity, the speed will be slower at a faster time, so the clock on the mountain goes slower than that on the ground.

Will the conclusions of the special theory of relativity and the general theory of relativity be contradictory? No. In fact, both effects are working at the same time. According to calculations, the effect of general relativity is more significant, so considering the two factors comprehensively, the clock on the flat ground is going to be slower, which was later proved by experiments.

Another implication of time and space bending is that around a massive celestial body, the space is no longer flat, but curved. You can imagine putting a heavy iron ball onto a stretched net, and a large depression will appear at the place where the iron ball is pressed. The space is like a big net. The celestial body is like an iron ball. The space around the celestial body will appear concave. This is space bending.

Einstein thus believes that gravity is not a real force, but a phenomenon of object movement caused by a space depression. Just as a glass playing ball rolls into a recessed place, it rolls around the iron ball round and round, looking like there is a force pulling it. Some time ago, scientists announced that they had observed the ripples of time and space caused by the merger of two black holes - "gravitational waves". It seems that Einstein is right.

The degree of curvature of time and space is determined by the distribution of the energy density and momentum density of the mass in space and time. If the mass of the celestial body is small, such as the Earth, then it is only possible to push out and make a dent in space. But if the mass of the celestial body is very large, the volume is very small, and the density is large enough, then it will no longer make a dent, but a deep hole. Anything that is close enough to the hole will fall into the hole, and even the light can't escape from the hole. This is the "black hole."

Space curvature and depression proposed by Einstein are really unimaginable. According to our normal thinking, space is empty. How can empty space be bent and how can it sag? Does this prove that space is not actually "void"?

There are even more amazing things. Einstein found that, in theory, if two holes are just connected as buttock to buttock, then a channel can be formed that can connect different regions of the universe. It's a bit like a bug that digs a hole in the apple and connects the upper and lower sides of the apple. People visually call this fast-track tunnel that connects different regions of the universe, "the wormhole." Of course, if the two holes are black holes that nothing can come out of, then the existence of the wormhole is meaningless. So, people imagine that one of the two holes is a "black hole" that only devours things, and the other one will be a "white hole" that spits out things.

The theory of relativity has aroused a big discussion about time travel. According to the special theory of relativity, the faster the speed, the slower the flow rate of time will be, and time will stop flowing after reaching the speed of light. Do many people wonder what will happen if the speed of light is exceeded? Is it possible that time will fly back?

It was Einstein who shattered people's dreams. He said that the faster the speed, the slower the flow rate of time will be, but the mass of the object will become larger. The closer the speed of an object is to the speed of light, the closer its mass will be to infinity. Since you can't find an infinite amount of energy to accelerate an object of infinite mass, so as long as it has a static mass, it can never run as fast as light. Photons can travel at the speed of light because it has no static mass.

The "wormhole", also known as the "Einstein-Rosen Bridge", was conjured by Einstein and Nathan Rosen in the study of the gravitational field equation in the 1930s. It is a narrow tunnel that may exist in the universe connecting two different times and spaces. Future people may be able to make some instantaneous space transfer or time travel through the wormhole in some way. People have found some black holes in indirect ways, but until now there is still no evidence that there is a "wormhole" in the universe. And it is still more science fiction.

But in general relativity, time travel is theoretically possible. Time and space can be bent. If the degree of bending is large enough, it is possible to bend back to the past. How big is "big enough"? According to calculations, it should be as big as the black hole, so the black hole is very likely to be the only channel for people to travel in time.

Einstein also has another amazing point of view. He said that if we do not regard the world we live in as a three-dimension time-space, but as a four-dimension time-space, then the speeds of all things in the four-dimension time-space are the speed of light C.

You can imagine a Cartesian coordinate system where the axis X represents the velocity of motion of an object and the axis Y represents the flow rate of time. The motions of all objects can be expressed by the line section of the same length in the sector between the X-axis and the Y-axis. The length of each line section is equal to C.

When light travels on the axis X, because its speed of motion is C, but the flow rate of time is zero, the light will never grow old. The light from the distant galaxies we see now is exactly the same as when it came out from an ancient star more than one billion years ago. From this point of view, light seems to be born to let us see things, and it can guarantee that what we see is what it was.

If something is absolutely static, it will be on the axis Y, with the highest flow rate of time, its life consumption is the fastest, but the speed of motion is zero. The closer the line segment of other objects is to the axis X, the faster the speed of motion and the slower the time flow rate; similarly, the closer the line segment of other objects is to the axis Y, the slower the motion speed and the faster the time flow rate.

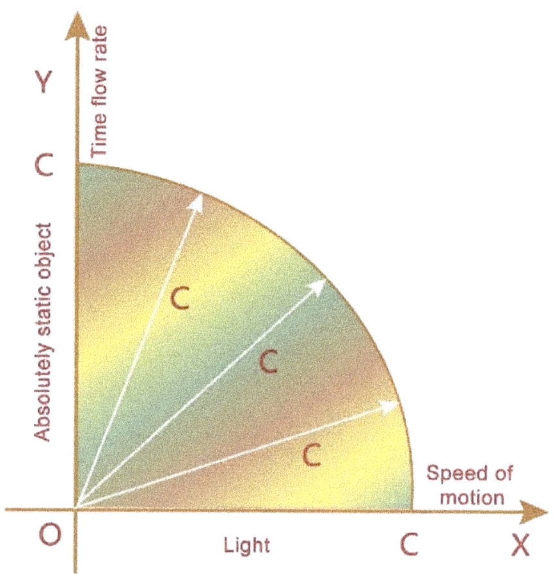

Compared to the speed of light, our speed of movement is as slow as a snail, so it is basically equivalent to traveling on the axis Y.

From this perspective, the world revealed by relativity is just the opposite of that by classical physics. Classical physics believes that time and space are absolute, and movement is relative; whereas relativity theory proves that time and space are relative, but the movement is absolute.

Now we have to ask the question: What is time? Why does its flow rate change? Does it mean the eternity of life when it stops flowing?

The Michelson–Morley Experiment and the Not Void Space

The Michelson–Morley experiment is often used as an example of *the special theory of relativity* in popular science books about relativity, but in fact, Einstein did not know much about this experiment when he published his paper in 1905. The original intention of Michaelson and Morey to perform the experiment was not to prove that "the speed of light is constant", but to measure the speed of the earth in the "*ether*" to prove the existence of the *ether*.

What is ether? It is a substance conjured by the ancient Greek philosopher Aristotle and later introduced into physics by Descartes. In Descartes' view, all the forces between objects must be transmitted through an intermediate medium. There is no possibility of over-range action, so space cannot be really "empty". It should be filled with some kind of medium matter. The substance is called "ether." Descartes believes that although ether cannot be perceived by the senses of human beings, it can transmit the action of force.

The 17th-century Dutch physicist Christian Huygens also believed that the reason why light can travel in a vacuum is that the vacuum is filled with ether, and it works as a medium to transmit light. And so is the transfer of gravity.

Maxwell also believed that the ether exists, and he believed that it is the medium that transmits electromagnetic waves in a vacuum. According to Maxwell's equations, the propagation speed of an electromagnetic wave is calculated to be the same as the speed of light, so Maxwell concluded that light is an electromagnetic wave. But there is a question here. What is the reference system of the speed? If there is no fixed reference object, why can you say that the speed of light has a certain value? The earth is obviously not suitable as a reference for light, because it is moving by itself. But there is one thing that is appropriate, and that is ether. According to people's assumptions at the time, the universe is full of ether. There is no better reference standard than this one, for it makes up an absolutely static cosmic background

In such a case, if a beam of light travels at a speed of C in relation to the propagation speed of the ether, the earth moves in the direction of the light source at a speed of movement relative to the ether V, then the speed of light seen by the person on the earth should be C+V; when the direction of motion of the earth is perpendicular to the direction of the light source, the speed of light seen by people on the earth should be C; when the earth moves in the direction of away from the light source, the speed of light seen should be C-V.

According to this reasoning, as shown in the following figure, the earth travels through the ether around the sun, and the speed of light measured when the earth is moving in the direction of the light source should be greater than the speed of light measured when the light source is perpendicular to the direction of motion of the earth. The purpose of the experiment of Michelson and Morey is to observe this speed difference so as to determine the existence of the ether.

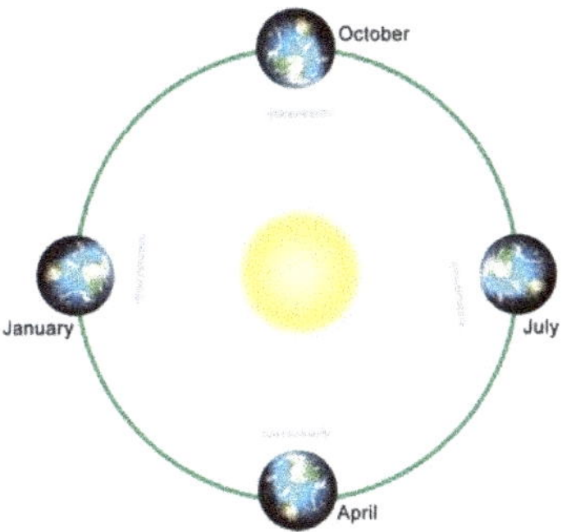

As a result, the experiment "failed" and they did not observe the slightest difference. Later, Einstein explained that as long as the concept of absolute time is abandoned, it can be determined that light is constant for any reference object. And the concept of ether is superfluous. Since then, the existence of the ether has gradually been denied by people, and few people would mention it now.

However, if we reason carefully, we will find that Einstein's theory of relativity only shows that the problem of the constant speed of light does not need to be explained by the ether. It does not prove whether the ether exists or not. Therefore, people cannot take it for granted that the ether does not exist. In fact, there is no such evidence.

We need to consider: Is space really "void"? Doesn't the ether really exist?

What is the *Inertial System*?

Newton's first law says that an object will remain stationary or in constant linear motion when it is not subjected to a force unless the force acting on it forces it to change its state of motion. The property of the object that maintains the original motion state is called *"inertia."* So, Newton's first law is also called *The Inertia Law*, which shows that force is not the cause of the object's state of motion, but the cause of the object's change of state of motion.

The Law of Inertia also raises the question of a reference system. The state of motion of any object is relative to the reference object, so what is the reference system to which the inertia to maintain the stationary or uniform linear state of motion is relative?

Practical experience tells us that Newton's first law is not true for every reference system. We refer to the reference system that Newton's first law holds true as the "inertial system". The reference system in which Newton's first law is not applicable is called the "non-inertial system."

The earth seems to be static, so people often use it as a reference system for inertia. For example, if a car is driving on the highway and brakes suddenly, passengers who are not prepared for it will be thrown forward. This phenomenon is well explained by the ground as a reference system. Passengers have inertia and must maintain a constant speed relative to the ground. The speed of the car relative to the ground is declining, so the passengers are moving forward relative to the car.

In general, a system that is stationary or moving in a uniform linear state of motion can be said to be an inertial system. If the car is always moving forward at a constant speed, then the passengers in the car will maintain the original state of motion, and the phenomenon of dumping out forward will not occur. At this time, it is an inertial system. Once it suddenly accelerates, decelerates, or makes a sharp turn, although the passengers are not pushed by any external force, they are pushed forward, pulled backward, or pulled to the side, and they have to change their states of motion relative to the car. The phenomenon of going backward or going to the side shows that Newton's first law does not hold true in the system inside the car, so it is no longer an inertial system.

We usually regard the ground as an inertial system. But is it really true? No, the earth is actually rotating around the sun while spinning, so it is not a strictly inertial system. We can think about the balls that are spinning rapidly. The water droplets on it will be thrown away. How could it be an inertial system? Fortunately, our earth only rotates one round a day. It is this slow speed that makes the ground an approximate inertial system. Otherwise, we will have been thrown away into outer space like a passenger in a car.

Is there anything in the universe that is really stationary or doing a uniform linear motion? The big tree that seems to stand silently on the wasteland is actually rotating around the sun, and the sun is rotating around the center of the Milky Way. So, it is not easy to find an absolute inertial system in the universe!

Chapter 12

The Genesis Program:
The World is Like a Game.
It is Born After the Program *Tao* is Run.

The so-called "supernormal phenomena" and the unsolved mysteries of modern science are just to tell you the fact that our views on the world need to be fundamentally changed.

I still remember a scene in *The Matrix* more than a decade ago. In the hands that Morpheus opened, there were two small pills, a red one and a blue one. If you choose to eat the blue one, nothing will happen, the sun will rise as usual tomorrow; if you choose to eat the red one, you will understand all the truth.

It's time to take the pills, the red one or the blue one.

After he hesitated for a moment, Neo picked up the red pill. He finally chose to face the truth bravely. With the help of Morpheus, he returned to the real world, only to know that he had been living in the virtual world before. It turned out that in the real world the artificial intelligence robots invented by human beings had been rebellious. Human beings had to block the entire sky to cut off the solar energy source of the robots. As a result, the robots developed bioenergy and used genetic engineering to manufacture human beings. Then they connected the humans to the Matrix and let their consciousness live in the virtual world where their bodies were used as bio-batteries.

There are two different options now in front of you. You can choose to close this book, forget all the previous questions, and continue your life in the past; or you can also choose to continue to read on and understand the truth of the world. If you choose the second option, please make sure that your mind is fully prepared.

What I want to tell you is that *The Matrix* is not completely fictional, and the philosophical thinking embodied in the film just holds a key to the answer to the ultimate question.

Why can't scientists still answer the ultimate problem of the world even when the development of science is advanced? The main reason is that the *Reductionist Theory Thinking* still dominates current scientific research. The boundaries between the disciplines are so clear-cut each field only narrowly focuses on its own issues with barriers being set up between them. Few people could consider the problem by integrating insights from different disciplines.

As scientists delve deeper into their disciplines, the classification of modern disciplines becomes more and more detailed, and people's horizons become narrower and narrower. Like the frog in the well, the deeper you go down, the smaller the sky at the wellhead you can see. So, if you can't dismantle the fence between disciplines and go out of the single discipline of your own research, you can never see the whole world.

It seems that the world could not be divided into small pieces for us to study and put back together to restore its overall appearance, as the reductionist theory believes. In fact, many of the mysteries of the world at the overall level can only be discovered through holistic research.

Philosophy is the study of the world as a whole. Early philosophers such as Lao Tze, Confucius, Gautama Siddhartha, Plato, Aristotle, etc., have all achieved brilliant achievements, and their insights still shine with wisdom. Compared with these great minds, the current philosophical researchers have gone astray, just playing games of words and concepts.

But in any case, to answer the ultimate question, we must combine philosophy with science, and we must not leave philosophy aside.

It's a coincidence that makes a difference. By chance, I found that from the ancient philosophies and religions, I was able to find the answer to the ultimate question, and I could use it to solve the mysteries that are difficult to solve in modern science.

My inspiration came from the *Tao Te Ching*, the mysterious classic of ancient Chinese philosophy written by Lao Tze in *the Spring and Autumn Period.* Though only a short essay of about 5,000 words, it is extremely philosophical and esoteric, especially its core concept *Tao*. No one really knows what it is.

Lao Tze describes *the Tao* as follows: "There is something chaotic, born before the heavens and the earth. As a loner, it exists without change and cycles without dying. It can be the mother of the world. As I don't know its name, I call it "*the Tao*". From the meaning of this passage, *Tao* is not something in our world, because it is generated earlier than the heavens and the earth; but it is closely related to our world. It can generate everything in the world. It is independent and never changes; it goes cyclically and never stops or dies. What is it that is able to have all these characteristics?

"The snow-white towel has three stripes, but we could hardly strike a talk even when we see each other every day." This northern Shaanxi folk song depicts the scene that due to the deep gullies on the Loess Plateau, two people on the two sides of the gully could not meet even when they are just dozens of

meters away. The current situation in the scientific field is like this. There is a huge gap between science and humanity that is difficult to cross. There are invisible walls built between different disciplines. Even researchers in different areas of the same discipline can't figure out what people in other areas are doing. The entire scientific community is like a loess plateau separated by many gullies.

The academic community believes that *the Tao* refers to "the ontology, the dynamics, and the laws of operation of the world." After reading this explanation, do you understand what *the Tao* is? Anyway, I didn't understand it. I don't understand what "the ontology of the world" is.

Many scholars either don't understand what the *Tao* is or don't think it is concrete. When Liang Qichao talked about *Tao*, he said that it is *"indescribable"*, so it is not clear to us. Other scholars such as Hu Shi (胡适), Feng Youlan (冯友兰), and Chen Guying (陈鼓应) simply said that it is a concept of Lao Tze's fiction. In fact, there is no such thing in reality.

Is the truth really like this? I once wrote book reviews online. To improve the quality of the articles, I began to read the *Tao Te Ching*. In this process, an incredible thing happened, and I actually gained an understanding of what Lao Tze meant by *Tao*. This revelation is so significant. It is not only the key to unlocking such a "Book of Heavens" as the *Tao Te Ching* but also allows me to understand how the whole world works.

Lao Tze's ideas were indeed too advanced. I can fully understand this point: due to the scarce knowledge and simple vocabulary of the people living in his lifetime, Lao Tze could not explain his thoughts to the world in words. This has led to it being incomprehensible and misleading for more than two thousand years.

But now, as people have accumulated great amounts of knowledge and their levels of understanding have been greatly improved, it is no longer difficult to explain the meaning of *the Tao* clearly. In the process of trying to figure out Lao Tze's thoughts, I was surprised to find that if we could use computer games to make an analogy, it would be much easy to make it clear what Lao Tze wants to say.

In fact, *the Tao* that Lao Tze said is actually not so mysterious, and it is not a fictional concept. It is so simple that it can be expressed in two words, that is, the "creation program".

It is really hard to believe that, more than 2,500 years ago, at the low level of people's understanding at that time, how could there appear a wise man like Lao Tze who knows the cause of the universe?

Following Lao Tze's line of thinking, we could easily draw the analogy that the birth of the universe is much more likely to be the same as the generation of the game world in the computer by running a program. If we can understand the seemingly incomprehensible words from the *Tao Te Ching* in line with the Big Bang theory and the generation of the game world, we could appreciate the amazing wisdom and insights of Lao Tze.

First of all, Lao Tze said: "There is a beginning in the world, and it is the mother of the world." He affirmed that the universe has a beginning. This understanding happens to agree with the Big Bang theory. But what is clearer than the Big Bang theory is that he further pointed out that the birth of the universe cannot be unreasonable and out of thin air. The universe should have its own "mother."

Who is the "mother" of the universe? Who generated this vast universe? Lao Tze said: "There is something mixed, born innately before the heavens and the earth." Before the birth of the universe, one thing had already been created; "I don't know its name, so I try my best to use the word *Tao* to name it." He does not know how to call this kind of thing. He calls it "Tao." Lao Tze believes that the *Tao* he does not know how to call "the mother of the universe," so it is said that "it can be the mother of the world."

In the game world, there is a game program first, and the game world will appear after the program runs. According to Lao Tze's point of view, the same is true also with the real world. It is due to the first program of *Tao* that there arises the universe of heaven and earth.

On this point, *the Tao* exactly matches the characteristics of the game program.

Secondly, everything in the game world is generated by the game program. Lao Tze believes that the real world we live in is the same. After the operation of the Tao, one after another, everything in the world is created. This is said as "the Tao creates one, one creates two, two create three, and three create all the things."

The running of the game program will make various things like tools and characters appear constantly in the game. In the same way, Lao Tze said that as long as *the Tao* works, everything in the world will continue to emerge and endure. From this point of view, *the Tao* is like the womb of a great mother, the root of the heavens and the earth, and its role will never be exhausted. This is expressed as "The goddess of fertility will not be dead; it is the supreme mother; the womb of the supreme mother is the root of heavens and earth. It exists in eternity and will not be exhausted."

In this respect, *The Tao* is similar to the game program.

Thirdly, the computer game program can be run, and its running cannot be stopped. Once the computer program is stopped, the game is gone. The same is true of *the Tao*. It can be run, and it can't stop running. Once we stop, our world will be gone. So, we say that it works "cyclically and eternally."

The game program runs independently and does not change as the game progresses. The same is true of *the Tao*. It always operates independently and does not change during the evolution of the world, so it is said to be "independent and not changed".

In this respect, *The Tao* is also similar to the game program.

Fourthly, the game world is completely created from a state of nothing. Creating it does not require any material. Just having a game program is enough. According to Lao Tze's point of view, the real world is also created in the same way. After *the Tao* runs, the world is born of the void. He said: "*Nothingness* is the name of the beginning of heaven and earth; *having* is the name of the mother of all things," and "Everything in the world is born of *having* and *having* is born of *nothingness*." Earlier when we said that the world was born from nothingness, many people would wonder how it could be possible. But as long as you think of the scene of the birth of the game world, you should suddenly understand this.

The Tao and the game program are also the same in this respect.

Fifthly, the Big Bang theory says that the universe has been inflating, and in many computer games the game maps are also constantly in the process of expansion. Lao Tze also had a surprising understanding of the expansion of the universe. He used such phrases to describe the expansion of the universe: "Greatness means flying away, flying away means moving to distance, and moving to distance means moving toward the opposite ".

The word "opposite" here seems to imply that the universe will shrink when it expands to the extreme. I really don't know where Lao Tze's judgments came from. Maybe he derived it from a law of nature that things are always in a cyclical evolution, and they will reverse when they reach their extremes. I have some doubts about this. In the current online games, the game world will generally continue to expand, and it will never shrink.

However, there is a saying in astronomy that after the universe expands to the end, it may reverse to contraction. Hawking once predicted that there may be a "cosmetic implosion".

In any way, what is certain is that Lao Tze knows very well about the entire process of the world being made out of nothing. The scene he depicted is very close to that suggested by the Big Bang theory and the creation of the game world.

The Tao that Lao Tze spoke of is equivalent to the "creation program" of our world. From this point of view, we can easily explain several issues of the Big Bang theory clearly.

The first one is *Singularity*. The Big Bang theory says that the universe begins with a singularity; but unlike some people think, there is really not an infinitesimal point where matter has an infinite density and from which the whole world was born. The so-called singularity is actually only a boundary, not a concrete object. It refers to the moment when the creation process of *the Tao* started. Just like a newly developed game that was officially put into operation from 10:00 on July 1, 2016. This time is the singularity of the game world.

The moment at which the game starts running is its singularity.

The second issue is cosmic inflation. Guth's inflation theory holds that after the Big Bang there was an extremely short period of rapid expansion. The universe suddenly expanded rapidly to a fairly large expanse before returning to a relatively stable expansion rate until today. This is hard to imagine, but it is easy to understand against the game world's generation process. When the game program starts running, there is a sudden large map. Then the map expands slowly with the progress of the game.

The third issue is why there is a Big Bang. This is also very simple to explain with an analogy with the games. As long as the game program is clicked and run, the virtual world in the game will suddenly appear; for the same reason, when the creation program starts, the universe will suddenly be born in an instant.

The game map is generated in an instant and then slowly extended outward.

Some people may ask if the world was born from nothingness and there was no substance in the void, how could it explode? In fact, this is a misunderstanding of *the Big Bang theory*.

When the world was born, a map appeared suddenly in an explosive way out of the explosion. The word "explosion" was used here to describe its suddenness and speed. The speed of expansion of this map can no longer be described by ordinary nouns. It is even far faster than the speed of light, so the words "the Big Bang" were used to describe it. It was not really something that was ignited when the universe was born. It's bursting. In fact, the term *the Big Bang* was not originally proposed by the founder of this theory, but by its opponent, the British astronomer Fred Hoyle, in a mocking tone.

The American astrophysicist Evelyn Gates said: "Although the name sounds scary, the Big Bang is not an explosion in space, but a starting point for time and space -- or more accurately, the closest place to the starting point that our current human knowledge of physics can bring us to."

The Big Bang theory can well be explained by Lao Tze's thoughts; and at the same time, many of the questions we raised earlier can be answered.

The first question is why there are natural laws. In the game world, there ought to be rules of the game, and these rules are contained in the game program. The same is true with the real world; the creation program contains the rules of the world, and the evolution of everything will show regularities, and they are the laws of nature. Lao Tze said that as long as we master the laws of nature, we can derive the previous situations of things or predict the possible changes that may occur in the future. This is expressed as " To know the way of the ancient is vital to governing the present things; to know how things happened in the ancient times is to know "the rules of the Tso". "The rules of the Tao" refers to the laws of nature.

The second question is why the world is like a well-designed one. The creation program must be the brainchild of some super intelligence, and it is a carefully designed work. The world created by it will inevitably show the characteristics of logical thinking– delicate and complex, and with a unified style. So, the amazing complexity in the biological structure of nature, the puzzling similarities in distant star structures, and the repetitive nature of the universe at different scales are all easily understood.

The third question is why the physics laws and parameters of the universe are so precise and optimal for the creation of the "golden phoenix area" where life could be possible to occur. This is also easy to explain. The creation program must have been carefully debugged during the design process, so it is normal that you will see that these parameters match superbly with those required for the emergence of life. From this point of view, the "human choice theory" is correct. The laws of physics are designed for the emergence of life.

Are you shocked when you first see this? Some people may even begin to doubt the meaning of life and have a strong sense of emptiness in their hearts. Don't worry; the curtain has just been opened and the great show is about to begin.

You will find the magic of the world is far beyond your imagination.

The Merits and Demerits of Reductionism

In our life, many people have the experience that the whole thing can be split into parts, and the parts can be put back into one whole. For example, you can dismantle a machine into a bunch of parts. When it is reassembled, it becomes the complete machine again. Modern industrial production is very much based on this concept, consisting mostly of assembly operations with each task job only responsible for manufacturing or installing one component.

This is the logical basis of *reductionism,* which is sometimes translated into "divisionism" and "segmentationism." This theory holds that various phenomena in the world can be broken down into basic elements that are independent of each other and can be studied separately. When you have studied these separate elements well, you can put them together to restore the overall phenomenon. In short, you can infer the whole by grasping the parts.

The method of reductionism has far-reaching influence on the history of science. For example, the current classification of disciplines is the embodiment of this kind of thinking. In ancient times, people understood nature in general, so there was only one discipline of philosophy and no other discipline. Later, based on the theory of reductionism, people's knowledge of nature was divided into many disciplines such as physics, chemistry, biology, etc., and this division is still carried on into smaller and smaller areas.

In Western medicine, the human body is divided into different parts according to the theory of reductionism, so there are different departments such as internal medicine, surgery, ENT, orthopedics, and neurology in the hospital, while in traditional Chinese medicine the human body is not divided into different parts in this way.

Based on the theory of reductionism, people further believe that the whole is based on the various components, so the basic laws can be used to explain the overall phenomenon. For example, between the disciplines, a hierarchy of "physics - chemistry - biology -psychology - sociology" has been proposed. It is believed that life phenomena can be explained by chemical reactions, and chemical reactions can be explained by the physical motions of particles. And physics, as the most basic science, can explain everything in the world.

It is based on this understanding that physicists often have an inexplicable sense of superiority in front of people studying other disciplines. It is said that the Austrian physicist Wolfgang Pauli when he learned that his ex-wife had married a chemist, shook his head and said, "Why a chemist?"

Reductionism is the soul of Western scientific thought. The developments of science in recent centuries have benefited much from its widespread applications. Reductionism is indeed very practical. As human intelligence is limited, it is impossible for them to grasp the myriad of things in the world and the relationships between them. Therefore, by dividing complex objects into small pieces and separating them from the whole, it is possible to make complex problems simpler and thus easier to study.

This segmentation method has achieved great success. The small-scale specialized research has helped scientific research reach an unprecedented depth in many fields. People's understanding of the world has thus entered onto a subtle and refined level that was previously unimaginable.

However, the success of reductionism cannot conceal its defects from birth. The world is an organic whole, and each component is not isolated. So now people have become more and more aware that the mechanical method of reductionism not only cannot help us to see the true colors of the world but also may mislead humans to destroy their living environment at will and cause disastrous consequences in the name of transforming the world. It can be said that human beings have already been facing many survival problems that are difficult to tackle. To search for the reason why humans have gone to such an extent along this road of damage, reductionism is one to blame.

Chapter 13

The Heavens is Above:

As in Games, There is a Monitoring and Control System Behind Our World. We Call It *Lord Heavens.*

In most of the history of human civilization, it is widely believed that the world is under supervision. Who is fulfilling the duties of the supervisor? Usually, people think it is "the god(s)." In many cultures, there is a god or gods that dominate the world, but they have different names and different images. The Westerners generally refer to him as "God," while the Chinese usually call it "the Heavens" or more popularly, "Lord Heavens."

The ancient Chinese believed that *Lord Heavens* is ubiquitous and monitors everything in the world all the time, and nothing that happens in the world could escape its eyes. *The Chronicles of the Latter Han Dynasty* records such a story. Yang Zhen of the Eastern Han Dynasty once recommended a person named Wang Mi to be a county magistrate. Later, when he passed the county town, Wang Mi came to his residence at night and wanted to give him ten pounds of gold to show his gratitude. Yang Zhen did not accept it. Wang Mi further pressed and said: "Do not worry, nobody will know this!" Yang Zhen said angrily: "Of course, you are wrong. How could nobody know this? The heavens know this, the gods know this, I know, and you know this.

This story tells us that people are in awe of this supervision from heaven. This invisible deterrence is beneficial. The person driving the car will have to perk up when passing through the monitored roads so as not to be punished for unintentional violations of traffic rules. This monitoring from Lord Heavens will also make people behave themselves. We often warn others not to do bad things: "People are doing, and Lord Heavens is watching you."

The driver is not afraid of the traffic lights, but of the electronic monitoring. This is because running red light itself does not hurt you and you will only be subject to

Those who believe in karma believe that Lord Heaven is not only watching but also can't help but pick you up if he finds what you are doing is vicious. There is a saying like this: "There is a sure reward for any good and evil, and the heavens ran in a cycle of cause and effect; if you have any doubt about this, just look around you, who can escape his rein?"

In the West, God plays a role similar to Lord Heaven, and his skill is no smaller than Lord Heaven. He is the omnipresent, omniscient, and omnipotent supreme god. He is omnipresent and omniscient, which means that we are under his supervision anytime and anywhere, and we have nowhere to hide.

No one likes to be monitored, for it only makes people feel not free, even with the supervision of the god(s). So, when Darwin first subverted the idea of God's creation and then denied the existence of God, the awe that people had long held for the god(s) was falling, and slowly lost control of people's spirits. Many people cheered for this and thought that they were finally freed.

Human beings liberated from the relentless mercy of God suddenly felt that they became so powerful and great by virtue of the science and technology they had mastered. So, humans began to have the courage to challenge themselves. They wanted to challenge nature. They wanted to transform and conquer it and eventually dominate the world.

In the absence of road monitoring, people often ignore traffic rules and drive as they wish, causing chaos in the traffic order until it eventually collapses. Similarly, after losing their awe of nature and the gods, under the influence of such concepts as *human rights* and *freedom*, human beings are free to enjoy the benefits provided by nature but do not care about the impacts of their behaviors on natural ecology. Due to lack of supervision humans will become unscrupulous and irresponsible. This is the reason why humans have inflicted more damage on nature in recent centuries than the total damage that they had done for all the other periods in history.

Is it really without any supervision? Can humans control their future and destiny?   No, there is something that is always supervising us. And anything that

Human rights and freedom are the mainstream values of the modern West, which originated in the Renaissance period. From the perspective of dealing with

relationships between people, advocacy of these notions may be an improvement. But if these notions are infinitely magnified to emphasize people's orientation in dealing with the relations change to hip between man and nature, humans will disregard nature's ability to bear and restore and incur tremendous destruction to it. This unscrupulous destruction of the ecological environment by human beings began with the Renaissance which advocated the notion of human awakening.

What are the conditions for the emergence of the game world? After the programmer has developed the game program, what will he do next? That's right, it's running this program. So where should the program run? You need a computer to work as a server at this time. Then, where does the creation program *Tao* run? There should be something behind our world that can play the role of the server. I call it "the Creation Host".

There is indeed monitoring in our world, but the supervisor is not necessarily a personified God. It may well be a creation host. It is precisely this creation host that supervises the strict operation of the creation program to generate a universe similar to the vast game world and to let it evolve in an orderly manner according to the procedures and paths specified by the program. We can recall Newton's words: "The order of the universe was created by God, and He preserves the same state and condition till now." The situation is very similar to what he said. The rules are contained in the creation program. These rules have been running in the creation host until today, maintaining the evolution paths set originally by the program.

The existence of the creation host, if any, will give a simple answer to many of the questions raised earlier. Why does the law of nature take force? What is the power to supervise the world meticulously to let it operate in strict accordance with the laws of nature? It turned out to be the creation host. In the double-slit experiment, why can the electrons sense that the double seam becomes a single slit and reacts? This is very simple. It's not that an electron can sense, but the creation host is constantly monitoring everything in the world. It can immediately know the changes and control the electron to follow the new mode of motion.

Why is there still an action between two small particles separated by thousands of miles? Bohr said that they are still a whole, which was hard to imagine then but is easy to explain now. They are all in the same host. In our eyes, although they are far apart, there is no distance problem for the creation host. As long as the creation host sees them as a whole, they are still a whole; and as long as the creation host keeps them in touch, they will remain in touch.

Einstein's theory of relativity states that the transmission of any information cannot exceed the speed of light, and there is no over-range action in the universe. But now we know that this rule is only valid for things that exist in our world, and it does not work for the creation host. As the creation host does not belong in our world at all, there is no need for it to abide by the rules of our world, and it is precisely the creation host who is implementing these rules -- This is the same as driving a police car in small places. In many small places, a police car can ignore the traffic lights.

We can see the existence of many phenomena of superluminal speeds, but we can't use them to convey information, because these are often the behaviors of the creation host. Of course, in the future, scientists can use the characteristics of the creation host to develop a technology that transmits information at a speed greater than that of light, which is not what we can expect now.

Why does the result of interference fringes change in *the delay experiment* when the experimental conditions are changed after the electrons pass the double slit before they hit the photosensitive screen? The reasonable explanation is that it is not possible to change what has happened before, and the creation host can immediately sense the changes in the experimental conditions and then change the results of the experiment accordingly.

The creation program and the creation host can also explain many problems, such as why there is *an axiom* in science.

The reason why general relativity can be widely accepted is that Einstein originally designed and conducted an experiment to prove his theory. He judged that the light does not go straight in the curved space and time but will follow the curve because the light always has to take the shortest path; in the curved space and time, the shortest path is not the straight line but the curve. According to this principle, Einstein believed that because of the bending of the light, we can see the stars hidden behind the sun during a total solar eclipse.

Einstein's judgment was verified by observations, which caused a sensation. But we have to ask, why does light always take the shortest path? Einstein could not answer this question, and he regarded it as an *axiom*. The so-called axiom refers to the law that people have summed up in practice, which does not require proof and cannot be proved. To be more straightforward, the existence of axioms does not need a reason, and nor is it impossible to find the cause.

Is this the case? No. Now we know that many laws that are regarded as axioms exist for a reason, but this reason cannot be found in our world. It is a rule defined in the creation program and it is supervised by the creation host.

The basis of relativity is that light always travels at a constant speed in the vacuum regardless of the state of motion of the object emitting the light and regardless of the reference object. Why does light behave like this? Why doesn't it run faster, or slower? If we look for the reason in our world, there will never be an answer to this question. But we can answer this question now. This is set in the creation program.

For any problem that we want to trace back to the original root, this factor will be a good start. The "God particle" that is currently attracting much attention from the physics community is a case in point.

People once lay an extraordinary amount of emphasis on the "Higgs boson", so much that it is even called "the God particle". From this, we can see the deep influence that reductionist thinking has on physics. It is just because of this kind of thinking that many people will naively believe that, as long as we know the most basic structure of the world, we can explain the whole world on this basis.

However, things are not that simple at all. As Patrick McBride, a physicist at Fermi National Laboratory in the United States said: "Even if there is clear evidence that the particle, we are newly discovering is indeed the Higgs boson predicted by the standard model, our understanding of the universe is still not clear."

In the 1970s physicists built a standard model to explain the large group of particles found in the collider. The interpretation of the experimental results by this model was successful, but there was a huge problem in that it could not explain the source of particle mass. To compensate for this deficiency, it is assumed that there is a particle called "Higgs boson" that gives mass to other particles. The meaning of such a particle is so great that it is even called "the God particle."

Of the 62 elementary particles predicted by the standard model, all the other 61 particles have been found, except the Higgs boson. But on March 14, 2013, scientists at the European Nuclear Research Center announced that they had found the Higgs boson.

It doesn't matter much if you can find the Higgs boson, because the creation process can give other particles mass. Anyway, all the problems can be traced back to the setting of the creation program. The various characteristics of particles, including the existence of mass, can be conferred directly by the creation program, just like axioms, and there is no need to find a reason in this world. Of course, the property that the Higgs boson can impart mass to other particles must also be prescribed by the creation program.

Let's look at another question about the creation host. In the hearts of Christians, God is the image of an austere father. He is both omnipotent and benevolent. But on this point, it has been pointed out long ago that there is a logical contradiction: if God is omnipotent, then when it creates the world, it can make the world completely perfect, but the reality is that there are countless sufferings in this world. This is sufficient proof that God is either not omnipotent or not benevolent. It cannot have both of these characteristics.

We often have this doubt in our hearts. We all say that the sky has eyes, why is this not the case in reality? Why does evil often not receive any punishment, but good does not always get good ends? In plays and novels, why do we often that treacherous ministers and courtiers abound in dynasty after dynasty and persecute the loyal ones ruthlessly? Began, the prime minister of the Shang Dynasty in Chinese history was persecuted and tortured with his heart being pulled out alive. Yue Fei the patriotic loyal general was murdered at Fengbo Pavilion, and Yuan Chonghuan was tortured to death and cut into pieces on street. If God is omniscient and just and kind, then where is he now?

Some people have already seen the truth behind this. Lao Tze said: "Heaven and earth are not benevolent, for it treats everything as a dog." He believes that Lord Heaven is ruthless and does not take everything in the world seriously. It is difficult for us to understand this. Lord Heaven, who has supreme wisdom, infinite power, and omnipotence, will have no emotions. Now we finally know what is going on. As the original master of the world is the creation host, not a god or a creature, it certainly does not have emotions.

The creation host has no emotions, so in our world, you can't see direct karma, but you will often see the villain prevail and the good person suffer. Many people may think that we can do things unscrupulously and freely, and no longer have to worry about being punished by Heaven.

Of course, this is not true. Don't be naive to think that no one knows what you say and what you do; in fact, the creation host has all of them on record. People will face their destinies on the day of final judgment. When you do bad things, there may not be consequences at once, but you will pay for it sooner or later, as many a religion often teaches us. "One always has to pay back what is owed".

Science and Hypothesis

Because of the great influence of science, in the eyes of many people in modern society, the term *science* can be used as an equivalent of *correctness*. If someone says this: "Your statement is not scientific," he means "Your argument is incorrect."

Can science be a synonym for correctness? This is not the case at all. Science is just a hypothesis. It is far from being correct.

How is scientific knowledge formed? Let's take a look at the view of the French scientist Henry Poincaré in the early 20th century. In *Science and Hypothesis*, he first believed that "science is built with facts, just as houses are built of stone, "the experiment is the only source of truth for it tells us what the facts are". So, experimentation is the foundation of science."

He added that the experiment does not mean everything. "A pile of facts collected is not science, just like a pile of stones is not a house." "Experiments only give us a certain number of isolated points. We must use a continuous line to put these points together, and this is the generalization." By using logical and mathematical tools to generalize the scientific experiments, we arrive at the scientific theory.

Poincaré further added: "All generalizations are hypotheses," so a scientific theory is just a hypothesis. If it can withstand the test of practice, it may be accepted by the public. "If it can't withstand this test, people should abandon it without any reservation."

Let me give an example to illustrate his point of view. Einstein's theory of relativity is astounding for everyone, and few people now doubt whether it is a scientific theory. But what you don't necessarily know is that when Einstein first proposed the special theory of relativity in 1905, it did not immediately attract people's attention. In fact, in the eyes of the people at the time, it was only a series of assumptions premised on the assumptions of the principle of constant speed of light and the principle of relativity. It may be difficult for people now to imagine that in 1907 when Einstein wanted to apply for a position as a non-staff lecturer with this paper, he was turned down because people simply did not believe what he said.

In 1916, when Einstein published the general theory of relativity, the initial reaction was the same, and it was only regarded as a hypothesis. Fortunately, he provided three experimentally verifiable inferences. The first is the precession of Mercury's near-sun point, which was solved at that time. The second is that under the influence of the strong gravitational field, the spectral line of the light from the surface of a massive star to the earth will move toward the red end, which was verified by observations in 1925; the third is that light is reflected in a strong gravitational field, which was tested and verified in 1919 for the observation of the total solar eclipse. It is because of this observation that the General Theory of

Relativity is known to the world in an instant.

No matter how famous the relativity theory is now, it is still a hypothesis based on two assumptions. As long as people observe a phenomenon of superluminal motion, in reality, the theory of relativity will collapse, as what happened in classical mechanics.

The relationship between science and hypothesis is more than that. Not only a scientific theory is a hypothesis, but also many mathematical tools that people use in establishing scientific theories are based on assumptions. An example to illustrate this is *Euclidean geometry*.

In the 4th century BC, the Greek mathematician Euclid wrote the book the *Elements*. This book has held a dominant position in geometry teaching for more than two thousand years, and this position has not been shaken yet. And many countries including China still use it as a geometric textbook, which shows its profound influence. However, such great work is based entirely on assumptions. The premise of the entire Euclidean geometry is 5 axioms and 5 assumptions. If you leave these premises, the latter definitions, propositions, and inferences are all baseless.

People usually think that axioms and assumptions are self-evident. They are natural and there is no reason for this. But is this the case?

We can imagine that if you are a character in the game, then some of the settings in the game are just like axioms for you. It is natural and you can't find any reason for this. But we, people not part of the game, know that they are there not because there is not any reason but because the reason is not in the game world but outside the game. This is because they are settings in the game program.

The axioms we speak of are assumptions based on experience. If this assumption is consistent with the setting in the creation program, then it can hold forever in our universe and become an eternal axiom; if there is a conflict between it and the setting, then once people find such a conflict, it will collapse soon and will no longer be an axiom.

The "5th assumption" in Euclidean geometry has now been overthrown. How many things that people regard as axioms will hold at a certain level and will conflict with program settings at a higher level? This is something that only Heaven knows.

Science as a whole is a hypothesis. So, don't equate science with correctness, and regard it as truth.

Chapter 14

A Theory of Creation and Evolution:
Like a Computer Game, the World is First Created and Then Evolves.

At this point, you should understand what I am going to say. Yes, the world we live in is created in a way similar to the way computer games are made.

From this conclusion, we can easily find the answers to the difficult questions we discussed in previous chapters.

Let us first talk about the Principle of Uncertainty and *Probability Interpretation* in quantum theory.

Games and movies are popular pastimes for young people, but there are some important differences between them. The movie has a definite script. Before you step into the theater, its plot and ending are already doomed, and they won't change your mood when you watch the movie. Throughout the whole process of movie playing, you are just a bystander, and you are not involved n. According to determinism, our world is like a movie, and everything is already doomed.

But the computer game is different, as its result is quite often uncertain in the beginning. The progression of the game plot requires your participation, and your behavior in the game will promote and change the progress of the game, which makes it possible for the game to appear in many different ways and have different ends. In other words, the ending of the movie is definite, but the outcome of the game is uncertain.

The uncertainty of the game results mainly comes from two aspects. The first aspect is that the initial state of the system is uncertain. The initial states of quite a lot of games are randomly set by the systems. For example, in the card games, we play online the cards dealt to us by the system are different for each set, which is completely a probability event. So, even if the rules of the game are fixed and the players are still the same four people, the process and result of each set will not be the same.

From this, we can understand what Heisenberg's *Principle of Uncertainty* and Bonn's *Probability Interpretation* means. When we play a card game, we have no way to know the initial state of the cards before they are dealt out. This is the meaning of *the Principle of Uncertainty*. In the process of card dealing, what cards you will get is completely random. This is the meaning of the *Probability Interpretation*.

Like card games, there is also the issue of randomness in setting the initial conditions of the systems in our world, which is why there is the *Principle of Uncertainty* and *Probability Interpretation*. Because of the existence of such a situation, the world does not have a certain initial state as the determinist says; instead, it randomly generates some initial conditions of the system at all times. This shows that our world is more like a computer game than a movie. This is the charm of life in the world. If the world is just a big show rolling out according to a set script, we will surely lose much of the fun of our life living in such a world.

The second aspect of the uncertainty in the computer game stems from the player's choice or the "free will." Just like when we play the *Go* game, the initial state of each set is the same, and it is a blank board, and the rules of the game are set. However, even if the players are the same two people and the same one person will take the first move, generally speaking, unless both parties are deliberately following a fixed routine of moves, the process and result of each set of games will be different. This kind of uncertainty comes from the behavior of the players in the game. In each set, as the players can't have the exact same considerations on how to deploy the pieces in one set as in another set, the game will be more of a game of chance and randomness.

In a card game, what kind of cards will be dealt to you by the system is completely random.

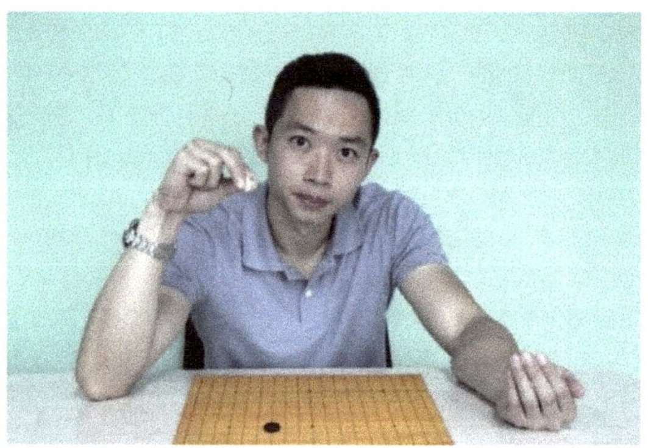

The initial state of each set of the Go game is the same, but the processes and results are different for different sets of the game because the player's ideas and moves are changing all the time.

The same is true in the real world. We are faced with choices anytime, anywhere. Just like at this particular moment, you can choose to continue reading, or you can choose to go out and watch a movie with a friend. If you choose to watch a movie, you may encounter a dream girl in the theater, and your life will be changed. Quite often, your choice is just a flick of the mind, but it will inadvertently change your life track.

This argument is contrary to the deterministic view. Determinists believe that everything in the world has long been determined, including our choices, which seem to be made by us, but in fact, what choices you will make are already doomed.

The logical basis for determinists to make this judgment is to regard the brain as a machine, believing that consciousness is nothing but the mechanical function of the brain. From this point of view, they believe that the brain, like other artificial machines, is composed of particles, and the changes in things can ultimately be attributed to the motions of the particles. Since the laws of physics determine the trajectories of the particles, then they must determine how the brain works and what choices the human consciousness will make. So, there is no such thing as "free will." All changes in the world, including people's behaviors, have all been decided long ago.

This kind of statement has made people feel quite frustrated, because if everything has foregone doomed before it happens, then what is the meaning of our worries about life and painstaking efforts? Isn't that an effort as futile as a bound man holding a torch to guide his way?

Fortunately, the brain is not just a simple machine as the determinists say. Our choice determines our own future and destiny to a large extent, and it is not completely meaningless.

The uncertainty in both aspects makes the world full of randomness. But it's important to point out that not everything in the game is random. It's quite certain in some respects. For example, the rules of the game must be written out in advance. It's hard to imagine how to play the game if you don't even know the rules of the game. Again, take card playing as an example. If there is no rule to say which card in the same suit is bigger, A or K, then how could you play in such a game?

Under the determined rules of the game, there is a certain causal relationship between the initial state， the game process, and the result. When playing cards, if you can have a good hand of cards initially, your chance of winning will be much

So, from this perspective, the Principle of Uncertainty does not negate the law of causality. The rules of the game are embodied in the law of causality. Although the initial state of the game seems to show a kind of randomness, the process of the game still strictly follows the law of causality.

Another quite certain thing in the game is the game process that has already happened. The uncertainty of the initial conditions in a card game exists only before the cards are dealt with; once the cards are dealt with, the initial conditions are determined. The same is true in the next steps of playing the card game. Everything is possible before the player makes a choice; but once the player makes a choice, the process is determined. It is impossible that the process is still uncertain after the card game has already been played. The cat is also one of the players in the real world. Its conditions cannot be ambiguous. The Copenhagen interpretation was challenged by Schrödinger's cat experiment because it did not give a good answer to this problem.

The computer game is a combination of certainty and uncertainty, and so is the real world. The laws of nature are equivalent to the rules of the game. As they are certain, they become natural laws in our eyes. Things will show some kind of fixed regularity in the process of their evolution. For example, the sun rises from the east and sets down in the west every day.

The coexistence of both certainty and uncertainty makes it possible for us to predict the development trends of things to a certain extent, but it can't be accurate, which is especially obvious with complex phenomena. For example, although the weather station can make weather forecasts, sometimes the forecasts may be false. The most impressive thing is that the typhoon landing site released by the Meteorological Observatory is constantly changing.

If there is no certainty, then the weather forecast is completely impossible and weather stations will be closed. If there is no uncertainty, then weather forecasts will be accurate, not just highly likely. It is impossible to conduct long-term weather forecasting as the Chaos Theory says. In theory, as long as the computing power is strong enough, it is possible to predict the weather one month later, one year later, or even 10,000 years later.

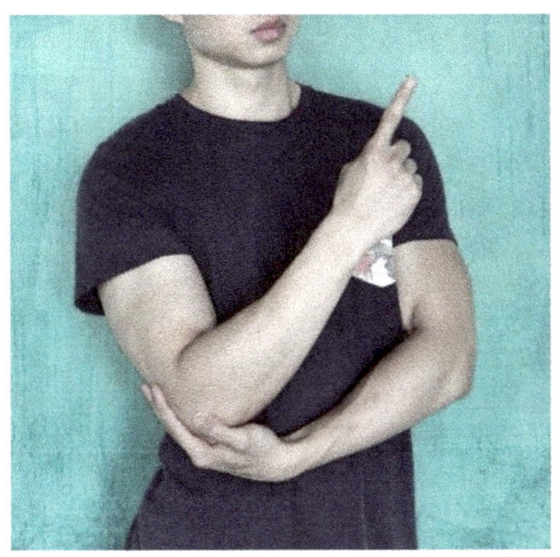

If only the prediction of trends is required with no need for precision, then everyone can be a good prophet. For example, if you predict that someone will die one day, though this prediction is not precise at all, it will be 100% correct.

If you can make good use of the coexistence of certainty and uncertainty in the real world, you can become a master of prophecy. Those successful prophecies are both in line with the trends of developments of things and vague in the expressions of the results.

The certainty of the rules of the computer game makes it easy for some people to misunderstand and think that fate is a heavenly arrangement. The outcome of life is death. If you call this certain game rule *destiny*, then it does exist. But if you believe that luck and misfortune of life are all arrangements of fate, then you are wrong, because this process is influenced by the *Principle of Uncertainty* and your own choice, and it is not predetermined.

Although the world has certain natural rules, the uncertainty of the initial conditions and the choices of the "free will" of life have caused uncertainty in the final result. *Chaos Theory* says that the "chaos phenomenon" can be seen everywhere in the world, which is the reflection of the uncertainty of this result in real life.

The problems of quantum theory are solved. Let's talk about the problems of evolution: Why are there no intermediate transition species? How are complex organs formed? How is the animal's instinct produced? What is the *Cambrian Life Explosion*? Why do some creatures stop evolving?

We can refer to the computer game to see how the player's level of power changes in the hierarchy of power. In the QQ game *The Battle of Four Kingdoms*, the player's level of power is defined as follows: the lowest level is the foot soldier; when the score reaches 10 points, he will become the deputy squad leader; when reaching 20 points, the squad leader; when reaching 30 points, the deputy platoon leader... There are altogether a total of 18 levels and the highest level is the commander, which requires one to gain 12,750 points to reach.

If the evolution of life on Earth is subject to rules similar to such kind of game upgrades, then many problems that have been plaguing us will be solved.

The first is the problem of intermediate transitional species. When playing the game of *the Battle of Four Kingdoms,* the level upgrade needs to go through two stages: the first stage is the "accumulation of points." From 0 to 9 points, they all belong to the level of the soldier. In this stage, the change of the points does not cause a change in level. This period of playing is a gradual process. The second stage is "upgrade". When the score reaches 9 points, as long as the score is increased by 1 point, the quantitative change becomes a qualitative change. With the score change, the level is also upgraded from the foot soldier to the deputy squad leader. At this moment, the gradual change of points becomes a sudden change of level. It looks like a leap, one step leaps upward. There is no need for a transitional stage. There is no "transition level" between the foot soldier and the deputy squad leader in the game.

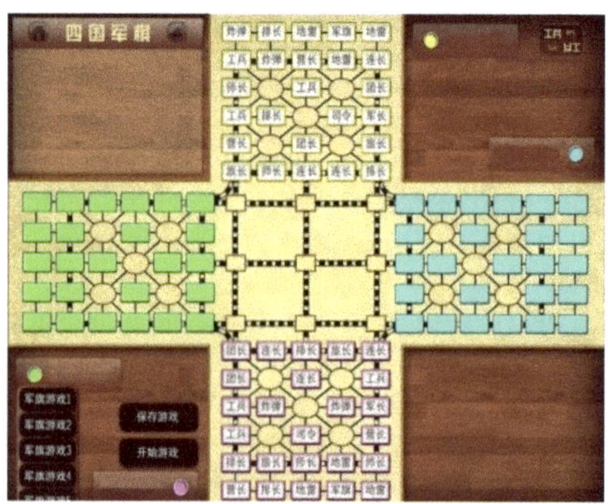

In the QQ game The Battle of Four Kingdoms, there will be situations in which players of different levels compete on the same stage.

Then there is the question of the generation of complex organs and instincts. After the soldiers are promoted to deputy squad leaders, they play completely different roles and possess different characteristics. You can think of different levels as different species, treating specific organs and instincts as features of the player of a particular level. So as long as the level goes up, no matter how complicated the organ is and how amazing the instinct is they will appear automatically. This is decided by the setting of the creation program, and we don't need to worry about how they are generated.

How should the *Cambrian Life Explosion* be explained? The answer is that it should be caused by the game has reached a certain critical triggering condition. When the Earth's environment evolved into one that is suitable for complex life, it met the basic conditions set by the creation program and triggered a button in the program. Therefore, the creation host conducted "a collective registration of players" according to the rules of the creation process, and intensively put a large number of species on the earth at one time, which made up the grand scene of the life explosion in our eyes.

Why does evolution come to a stop? There are two possibilities. One is that after you get to the commander level, even if your points continue to increase, you are just a "super high-score commander." There will be no higher levels and no further upgrades of levels. Crocodiles and sharks have stopped evolving, which indicates that they have embarked on a dead-end road out of bad luck and no longer could go forward. Not only these animals but also human beings are very likely to have stopped evolving, and there is no way to a higher level. If one-day humans are extinct, there may be more advanced life forms on earth than humans. They may be mice, cockroaches, or something else that is still upgrading, but these have nothing to do with humans.

There is another possibility. Some people have played *the Battle of Four Kingdoms* for many years, but they can still be in the ranks of foot soldiers in the boot camp. There is no way to rise to a higher level. Bacteria and viruses may fall into this situation.

The evolutionary mechanism of life is much more complicated than what is imagined by Darwin. The natural selection mechanism for the survival of the fittest does exist, but its role is limited to the point accumulation phase. Species that fail to pass natural selection not only cannot increase their scores but also be driven out, causing individual deaths and even extinctions. Species with a certain score will continue to increase the score and trigger the button in the creation program to promote them to the next level and become a new species.

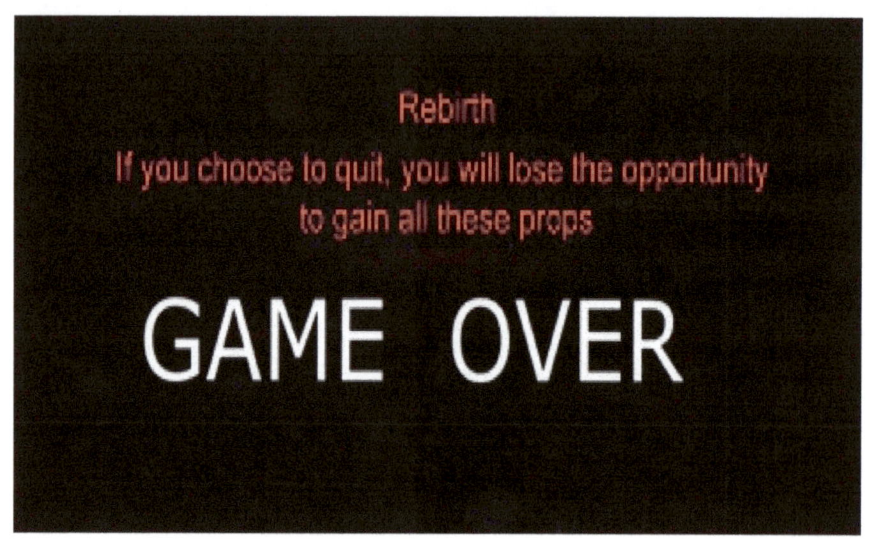

Species that are unable to adapt to the environment will withdraw from the game, which is the extinction of species in our eyes.

In this way, the whole process of the formation of complex and diverse natural ecology is not a natural evolution process with uncertain directions as the theory of evolution says, but a directional evolution process similar to the upgrade of levels of the players in the game.

Based on the analysis of these chapters, let's take a look at the question "Where does the world come from?"

In the debate between religion and science on the question of "whether the world is created or formed naturally", it seems that religion gives a correct answer. The world is indeed created, and science is wrong. But on the question of how the world was created, religion has completely made a mistake and gone in the wrong direction. The reality may not be, as many religions have preached, that God created the world directly and created everything. The world originated from a program. This program is called "Tao" by Lao Tze. We can call it "the Creation Program". This program creates the world, and then under the control of procedures and rules the world slowly evolves.

People are still arguing over whether the world is "created" or "evolved." The war between creationists and evolutionists goes on now and around the world. Now we know that the theory of creation and evolution are not mutually exclusive and contradictory as people thought, and we can combine them to explain the formation of the world. Neither the idea of pure creation nor the idea of pure natural evolution is complete in itself. The world was created, and then it evolved naturally under the constraints of procedural rules.

In the book of the Grand Master *of Zhuangzi*, Zhuangzi the philosopher creatively used the Chinese word "Zhaohua" (meaning "creating and evolving") which best depicts this process. In my QQ chat room, a netizen nicknamed "Wind" suggested that this theory of the origin of the world could be better called "the theory of creation and evolution."

Religion has made a great mistake on a key step. It regards the formation process of the world as a one-time simple creation, formed in one time and being unchanging, so it enables scientists to find the weak point and attack the whole idea. Science has established its authority in the process of fighting against religion, and the practical benefits brought about by the applications of science and technology have further consolidated this authority. But this does not mean that science is completely correct. The wrong answer it gives to the question of the origin of the world is just a small example.

What is the "Chaos Theory"?

The study of chaos deals with the extent to which the results are dependent on the initial conditions. *Chaos Theory* suggests that many phenomena in nature are incapable of being calculated because they are too dependent on the initial conditions. Everything in the world is universally connected, so the initial conditions to be considered are almost infinite, and the processes of change of them are too complicated, so the final calculation results are often caught in the chaos.

The American meteorologist Lorenz realized in the process of studying the weather forecast that the final result is more sensitive to initial conditions than we can imagine. Any small interference can have a great impact on the development of the entire system, and a small difference may lead to a completely different conclusion. The best way to illustrate this is Lorentz's "butterfly effect" which is that a butterfly flapping its wings in the Amazon rainforest may cause a tornado in Texas.

The evolution of things is highly dependent on the influence of many subtle and delicate factors. This idea has long existed in ancient books. The idiom we Chinese usually say is, "the embankment of a thousand miles collapses from an ant hole." This comes from the saying that "the dike of a thousand logs may collapse from ant holes," quoted in the book *Comments on Aging* of *Hanfei Zi*, which shows that the butterfly effect had already been noticed a long time ago.

In the real world, many delicate factors cause interferences which are completely unpredictable, so the results of the evolution of many complex things are simply unpredictable. As Lorenz said, any physical system with a non-periodic behavior is difficult to predict, and long-term weather forecasts are doomed to failure.

Chaos Theory tells us that there are certain linear relationships between some simple events in real life, but at the same time, in some complex events, there are also uncertain chaotic phenomena. Even in the macro world, uncertainty coexists with certainty. This is not as simple as the determinist thinks that the evolution of the world is predetermined.

Chapter 15

A Virtual Reality:
The Creator Created the Real World
with Virtual Reality Technology.

Some people may ask: The computer game world is a virtual world on the computer. Is the world in front of us also a virtual world? Can't we get it wrong?

No, it isn't. This is just what I want to say.

People have been thinking about the relationship between illusion and reality long ago. A famous allusion is a story of "Zhuang Zhou's dream of becoming a butterfly". In the Book of Things of *Zhuangzi*, Zhuang Zhou had a dream one night. He dreamed that he had become a butterfly, fluttering his wings in the flowers with ease. He forgot that he was Zhuang Zhou. It was not until he suddenly woke up that he realized that he was Zhuang Zhou, not a butterfly.

Zhuang Zhou knew in his dream that he was only a butterfly, not Zhuang Zhou. If he hadn't woken up, he wouldn't have known if he was in a dream or the real world.

Descartes also had a similar idea. He said: "When I think about this problem carefully, I find that the state of being awake, and the state of dreaming are not necessarily different." He further asked: "How could you be sure that your life is not a dream?"

This issue is also the theme of the popular American film *The Inception* which was shown a few years ago. In the movie, the thief Dom Cobb is good at sneaking into other people's dreams to steal important information and secrets. To realize his dream of reunion with his children, Cobb took risks and accepted a dangerous task. For this reason, he and his friends went deep into the fourth layer of dreams, and almost stayed in the "lost domain" forever, but in the end, he succeeded. After returning to reality and reuniting with his children, he used the gyro to test whether he was still in a dream. The film suddenly ended, leaving much suspense. Is he in reality or a dream?

This film has caused many people to ponder. We used to take it for granted that we live in the real world. But have you ever thought about it that we may have lived in an illusory dream, and never have woken up?

All human perceptions of the world come from the information acquired by the senses. In 1981, the American philosopher Hilary Putnam expounded a hypothesis: "If someone is operated on by an evil scientist, his brain is cut from the body and put into a tank containing nutrient solution that can sustain brain survival, the nerve endings of the brain are connected to a computer. This computer transmits information to the brain according to a program so that he can maintain all normal feelings. What will happen?"

This imagination is called "the brain in the tank." It makes us have to think, if the information about the external world is only virtualized through the sensory input in the human brain, how can we tell the truth about it?

"The brain in the tank" hypothesis shows that human cognition of the outside world depends entirely on the senses. If the senses deceive us, then we have no way to detect them. Like the emperor who stayed in the palace for a lifetime, his information was all from others. If the people around him intended to provide him with false information, he would only be kept in the dark, so it was not uncommon that in history the emperor was often controlled by eunuchs or courtiers.

The world we see is virtualized through sensory input. But why do we treat the virtual world as the real world? This question can be answered with virtual reality technology.

Virtual reality technology uses a computer to synthesize a virtual world. If the technology is sufficiently advanced, the virtual world created can be so real that you can't tell whether it is a virtual world or a real world.

The key to the success of this technology comes from four factors. The first one is "Multi-Perception." In this virtual world, you should have a variety of perceptual abilities. You can see, hear, touch, smell, and taste. The closer its function is to the human sensory function, the more real the feeling is. The second is the "Feeling of Existence." Everything in this virtual world seems to be true and real. It looks real, sounds real, moves real, even smells real, and tastes real. It feels the same as in the real world, so you can't tell whether it is real or not. The third is "Interactivity." You should be able to interact with things in the virtual world. You can grab objects with your hands. At this time, you will have the feeling of holding things and you can feel the weight of the object. The object that is held by your hand will follow the movement of your hand in your field of vision. The fourth is "Autonomy". There must be physical rules in the virtual environment. The things and events that happen should follow strict causal laws so that they are like an autonomous real system.

As long as it is realistic enough, the virtual world will make you unable to distinguish between true and false.

At the current state of the art, virtual reality technology is far from ideal, but it has found wide applications. As early as in the 1970s, this technology was already used to train astronauts; in the early 1990s, the United States used it to simulate the battlefield environment and conduct individual soldier combat simulation training. In the Gulf War, American soldiers were no strangers to the desert environment because they had already experienced it in virtual reality; Chrysler began using this technology in 1998 to design new cars and conduct car crash tests.

Currently, the most popular virtual reality system is the helmet-mounted display system. In this system, the participant of the virtual experience wears a helmet-mounted display, which artificially separates the visual and auditory senses from the world outside the system. Through advanced interface devices such as voice recognition, data gloves, and data clothing, the participant can interact with the virtual world in a natural way like in the real world. The helmet display provides a high-resolution, large-view virtual scene that is as real as what you see in the real world.

Okay, now we can see how the creator uses virtual reality technology to turn the virtual world created by the creation program into the real world in our eyes.

The first step is to give us a variety of perceptual abilities, vision, hearing, touch, smell, and taste. These are the foundations of our perception of the world. Without the sources of information provided by these senses, we could know nothing about the world, let alone think about whether the world is real or virtual.

The second step is to create a sense of presence. The creator allows us to convert the information we receive from the senses into a feeling, and to limit our sensory functions to a certain extent. This is like a magician performing magic. It is often necessary to confine the audience to watch from the audience seats. If someone rushes to the background to peek, the whole magic may be blown up.

At the Spring Festival gala of 2012, Liu Qian performed a magic show called "the Magic Mirror." Someone hid under the table enclosed on the front and back sides with mirrors, leaving the audience thinking that the space below the table is empty. During the performance, a hand suddenly appeared out of the table, which achieved a fantastic effect. But if someone stands in the vicinity, they will find the presence of the mirror below the table, and the magic will not work.

From this perspective, the world we perceive is just what the creator wants us to see, not its true reality. This was discovered in the third century BC by the Greek philosopher Pyrrōn. He warned people that our senses are unreliable. It can only tell us what things look like and can't tell us what things are.

The third step is to create interactivity. Realism also comes from your interaction with the world. You can feel the softness and silkiness of your hand by touching the satin. When you hit the wall, you will feel it's hard. You will also have a big swell on your head. With the broom in your hand to catch a hen, the hen will rush and run away. These phenomena show that the world is visible and tangible, and it will change because of our actions, so it is real.

The fourth step is to create autonomy. To create a sense of reality, the virtual world also needs to be a seemingly self-contained system in which things strictly follow causal relationships. Everything seems to have been created by the things that are associated with the system, just as the person in front of you was born by his mother and did not suddenly appear from nowhere. This is because if the origin of a thing cannot be explained by the things of this world, you can only think about whether there are other worlds at higher levels, which will inevitably make people doubt the authenticity of the world before them.

Although the world in front of us seems so real, it can't deceive everyone. As early as more than 2,000 years ago, Siddhartha had already debunked the mastery of the Creator. He believes that man does not have a real body but is composed of "Five Developments." A development means "an accumulation over time," For the so-called Five Developments, "the development of color" refers to the various things of the outside world; "the development of perception" refers to the feeling that the human sensory organs produce when they are in contact with the outside world; "the development of thought" refers to the idea that appears in the mind after perceiving the external stimulus; "the development of action" refers to the actions to take in response to these ideas; "the development of knowledge" is the summarizing and drawing of knowledge of the world from the consequences of the actions

Let me give you an example to illustrate this point. If you catch sight of a beautiful girl, this is "the development of color"; then you see her beauty, this is "the development of perception; then if you think how good it will be if she is your girlfriend, this is "the development of thought;" if you go forward and talk to her: "Hey, beauty, will you be my girlfriend?" "Don't bother me!" This is called "the development of action;" and finally, you understand the truth that the beautiful girl is not someone that you can pursue, this is "the development of knowledge."

Siddhartha refers to human perception as "the six perceptions", which are the six senses of "seeing, hearing, smelling, tasting, touching, and feeling" coming from the six organs of the eye, ear, nose, tongue, body, and mind respectively. He has realized that our perception of the immediate world depends entirely on the senses. The senses tell us that the world in front of us is real, but this is not the case. Therefore, Siddhartha repeatedly warned: "Color is empty, and empty is color," and "everything that you see is illusory," saying that the colorful world we see, and feel is illusory.

The picture on the display looks smooth and seamless, but it is made up of tiny pixels.

The Creator uses a technique similar to virtual reality technology to make us feel a level world. However, no matter how superb the technology of the Creator is, we can still find some flaws.

When we play online games, how do we see the virtual game world on the computer? A display is required. The same is true in the real world, and each of us should have a display screen in front of us.

All the displays have a very important feature no matter what kind of display they are: they are limited by pixels. Under normal circumstances, there is a continuously smooth, and clear picture on the display screen; but as long as you enlarge the picture largely enough, it will become a mosaic of small pieces, which looks like a collage of color cubes put together.

Because of this, the world usually presents a clear picture in our eyes. It seems that we are in a continuously smooth and seamless world, but when we enlarge the world to the particle level, we see a mosaic picture. The world becomes no longer smooth and continuous; instead, it becomes a mosaic body made of building blocks, thus exhibiting obvious quantum properties physically.

The Creator has already made the resolution high enough. The Planck length is only 10-33 cm long. The "Planck Cube" should be the size of a pixel. For humans, this is a surprisingly small point, and the eye can't find the problem anyway. But human curiosity is too strong. A bunch of instruments had been created, and even smaller particles had been found. They also created a particle collider to accelerate the particles and make them collide with each other. What flaws can't be found?

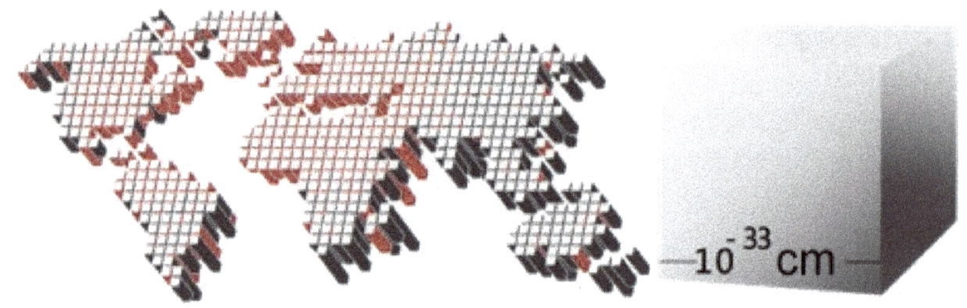

The display pixel of our world should be as small as a "Planck Cube".

Do you still remember the "complementary principle" in quantum theory that is hard to understand? We can easily explain this by the following analogy so that you can truly understand the meaning of it.

One of the salient features of the game display is that it can't present all the scenes of the game at the same time; it only shows what you want to see at the moment. When playing online games, if we want to see a certain scene in the game, we have to move the mouse over, and the scene will appear in the display, but we cannot see the entire scene of the game at the same time. This means that when we don't watch it, the game world is just a program running on the mainframe, and there is not a certain picture. Only when we go to look at it, the picture will appear on the display.

The "complementary principle" says that electrons have "wave-particle duality." When you don't look at it, it is an illusory wave; and when you look at it, it becomes a real particle, presenting itself in front of you. Doesn't Bohr's say show the same characteristics of the game display mode? The real-world situation is the same as the game world. When we don't watch it, the world is just a program running on the creation host. Only when we watch it, it becomes a real picture and appears in front of us. The *"us"* that we are talking about here refers to not only humans but also all life in nature. From this point of view, it is not only the observation of human beings that causes the wave function to collapse but also the observation of the cat can also make this happen.

When playing a game, only the scene we want to see is displayed on the display screen, and there is no real picture in places we can't see.

Moreover, the observations we are talking about here are not limited to seeing but should include the functions of all sensory organs, including listening, touching, smelling, and tasting.

Due to the lack of understanding of this mode of observation, there have been many misunderstandings. And some of the contents in Copenhagen's interpretation are wrong. This theory holds that the world is illusory when we are not observing it. There is nothing wrong with this. But it further goes on to falsely link the "complementary principle" with the "uncertainty principle", saying that the world is not certain when we do not observe, and it is in a superposition of various possible states. This is problematic.

The truth should be like this. When we don't sense it, the world is just a running program. It has no certain picture, but it is impossible to have no certain state. The uncertainty expressed by electrons only represents the initial state of the system, which does not mean that the whole world is in an uncertain state. We may not know what kind of state a particular thing in the world is in at a certain point in time, but the creation host does know this. Therefore, Schrödinger's cat cannot be in a state of both death and living at any time.

What is virtual reality and what is the real reality? Are you confused now? The Creator can create a real world with the creation program. So, if our technology is smart enough, can we also become the creator and create a real world? Or, as some sci-fi novels say, are we created by extraterrestrials millions of light years away who are much more technologically developed than us?

In the next chapter, we will continue to answer your questions.

Rich Terrell's Weird Theory

There are quite a few people from international academic circles who hold the idea that human beings live in a virtual world. One of them is Rich Terrell from the Jet Lab in Pasadena, California. In the first episode entitled "Is there a Creator?"

of the scientific documentary *"Through the wormhole with Morgan Freeman,"* Terrell presented a peculiar theory, which Morgan Freeman called "the most bizarre of all the possibilities of the Creator".

Terrell believes that the creator, by definition, should be able to set up the rules of the universe and change them as he will. This kind of ability is very similar to the programmer's role in the simulation environment. If we have a powerful computer that can simulate everything on the planet and even artificial intelligence, then we can create the universe ourselves. In this world created by the supercomputer, we can change the laws of physics, and we can do what God can do. We have all the conditions to become God; and as long as we add creatures to this world, we become their gods.

Since there is such a possibility, is our world a virtual world?

Terrell said: "All computer images, no matter how real they are, they are all able to be broken down into pixels when you zoom in to a sufficiently detailed extent. You may think that this is not possible in our real world, but you are wrong. Last century physicists discovered that matter consists of very small particles, just as the image in the display is made up of pixels. Quantum mechanics implies that everything we see is perhaps realized by the lines of code of a powerful computer."

In the documentary, he also said: "The basic rules of quantum mechanics apply to all tiny subatomic particles. When we look at them, they are points one by one; but when we look away, they change their physical states, becoming things that are different from what we observed. How similar it is to the plot we saw when we played the computer game. In the game, when in a huge city, I can find out my way from every part of the city, because this game will give me all the shots I need. And when I look somewhere else, it will give me the corresponding shot. It's strange, and the universe does the same. When you look at it, this universe becomes what you see; and when you don't look at it, it doesn't have to be there."

This scientist's idea is called the most bizarre point of view, but I think it is the most practical. It was exactly Terrell's view that inspired me to realize the pixel problem in the display mode of the world.

Unfortunately, his conclusion is a disappointing and shocking one. He said: "Our world conveys the characteristics of all the simulated worlds. Who else will simulate human beings besides the future human beings?" He took it for granted that our descendants eventually became God-like creatures, and they created the universe in our eyes.

Chapter 16

Heaven Beyond Heaven:
In the Eyes of People
in a Two-Dimensional Game,
We Are in a Higher-Dimensional Space.

If our world is just a virtual world in the creation host, then where is the creation host? To answer this question, you must first figure out what the *world* (*Shijie* in Chinese) is.

Shijie, the two Chinese characters equivalent of the English word *world*, comes from the Chinese translation of the two concepts from *the Surangama Sutra*. "Shi" means migrating, meaning that time flows like water, from the past to the present, from now to the future; "Jie" means space, which refers to orientation. The meaning of the English word *world* is equivalent to two words in Chinese, *time* and *space*. A world is an independent time and space.

The noun corresponding to the *Shijie* (world) is *Yuzhou*(universe). It comes from the Book of Things of *Zhuangzi*, with the same meaning as the world and it refers to time and space. The Book of Nature of *Wenzi* explains it as this: "*Yu* means the time from the ancient times to the present, and *Zhou* means the four sides plus the above and the below." The two English *words world* and *universe* and their Chinese equivalents *Sijie* and *Yuzhou*, though created by peoples of different lands, contain the same meanings, which indicates that people knew from very early on that time and space are the premises of the existence of all things.

People usually think that there is only one world. An important reason why Christianity supports Ptolemy's *Geocentric Theory* is that this system can leave a place for both heaven and hell, which is consistent with its teachings. Thus, Christianity does not regard heaven and hell as another world, and it believes that they are also an integral part of our world.

In Chinese myths and legends, there are three different domains in the world: the land of immortals, the land of mortals, and the land of ghosts. People also call the land of immortals "the heavens", the land of mortals is also called "the world of humans", and the land of ghosts is also called "the underworld". It can be seen that they are only different domains of the same world, not three different worlds.

Some people in history, such as Siddhartha, believed that there are many worlds. Siddhartha said that there are nearly infinite worlds. One thousand small worlds combined are called a "small thousandfold world"; one thousand small thousandfold worlds combined are called a "medium thousandfold world;" and one thousand medium thousandfold worlds combined are called a "large thousandfold world." The large thousandfold world in which we live now is called "the *Sahā-lokadhātu* world." In addition to this world, there are many other worlds, such as "the Western World of Bliss" and "the East World of Colored Glass".

There was a time when people believed that the universe was boundless and eternal and there was only one world. But the Big Bang theory suggests that the universe has its beginnings and boundaries. Scientists have to consider the possibility of the existence of *multiple universes*. Otherwise, they cannot explain the questions of what is before the beginning of the universe, and what is outside the universe. Martin Rees once said: "The universe we usually refer to maybe just be one of the universes. There may be countless other universes with different governing laws."

Hawking also said in *The Grand Design* that the scene generated by the universe is like the formation of steam bubbles in boiling water, which is not a universe but an infinite number of universes. Our universe is just one of the bubbles, and there are an infinite number of many other universes. Scientists call these universes *parallel universes*.

There is more than one world. If you understand this, it is very easy to answer the question of where the creation hosts are. The answer is very simple. They are in worlds different from ours.

If there are many worlds, then what is the relationship between them?

Some people think that these worlds are parallel and juxtaposed. The American physicist Michio Kaku wrote in *The Parallel Universes*: "We may live in an ocean of such universes, and each universe is like a soap bubble floating in the ocean."

Others think that these worlds are cascaded layers. Hawking told a story in his *A Brief History of Time*. A little old woman stood up after Bertrand Russell finished his astronomical speech. "You are talking about nonsense. The world is a slab on the back of a huge turtle." Russell asked: "So what is this turtle standing on?" The old woman replied: "It is just a tower of turtles with the upper ones squatting on top of the lower ones".

In the past, people thought that there was only one galaxy in the universe and that is the Milky Way, but later they discovered that there are countless galaxies outside the Milky Way. People used to think that there was only one universe, but now many people realize that there should be countless universes outside our universe.

Usually, people think that Siddhartha's world is also divided into layers, which are called the "Three Realms and Six Paths." The three realms from low to high are the desire realm, the color realm, and the colorless realm, and the six paths from low to high are hell, hungry ghost, animal, human, asura, and heaven.

The other five paths of *the Six Paths* are all in the desired realm. Only the heavens in the Path of Heavens" are spread across the three realms. Among them, there are six desires in the desire realm, four meditations and eighteen heavens in the color realm, and four heavens in the colorless realm. Altogether there are 28 layers of heaven.

At every layer of *the Three Realms and Six Paths*, the life living there is different. In the desire world, all beings are happy with the satisfaction of their desires, and the level of being is relatively low; In the color world the level of sentient beings is slightly higher, there is no desire, but they are subject to the shackles of materials; the beings of the colorless world have got rid of not only the bondage of desire but also the limitations of materials, and they live a higher level of life. The worst situation is the *Path of Hell* at the bottom of the thirty-three levels. It is the place where the villains who had committed many dreadful sins were born into. They have to go through hundreds of trillions of years of pain and suffering before they could gain the opportunity to escape from the sea of suffering.

In addition to these two theories, some other people think that the world is a multilayered one.

The American film *The Thirteenth Floor,* released in 1999, presents a strange multi-level world. Fuller and Doug developed an electronic system that could create a real Los Angeles in the 1930s. Countless people lived there like real people, without any knowledge that they were the phantoms created by the Internet.

Later, Fuller discovered a secret: not only the Los Angeles in the 1930s created by them was a virtual world, but also even his real world was just a fantasy. The fantasy was created by people living at a higher level. Because of this discovery, Fuller paid the price of his life, and he was killed by people from higher levels.

At the end of the film, Doug came to the space where the makers of the real world lived — those who were at higher levels exist in the future, and they live in 2024. Just as the story is about to have a perfect ending, a dramatic scene emerges. With the sound of a slap, the picture of this higher-level world flashes out, as if a TV plugged out of the power plug. Maybe this world of a higher level is just another fantasy.

Which of the three statements is more realistic? Is our world created by human beings who have more technical skills in the future, as said in *The Thirteenth Floor*? Or is it created by the highly skilled aliens living on an alien planet? Can we become creators like Doug and Fuller to create a real virtual world?

To answer this question requires the concept of "dimensions". Dimensions, also known as "number of dimensions," in mathematics, refer to the number of independent parameters, which in physics and philosophy refers to the number of independent space-time coordinates. "Dimensions" and "extra dimensions" have the same meaning. "The extra-dimensional hackers" are hackers who can crack the space-time barrier and come to our world from other dimensional spaces.

It has not been a long time since people realized the existence of dimensions in space. In the 18th century, the concept of "n-dimensional space" was proposed, but it was not until the middle of the 19th century that n-dimensional geometry was gradually accepted by the mathematical community. Since then, although there is a concept of multidimensional space in mathematics and it can be studied, our understanding of higher-dimensional space has not improved much, and we don't know if space more than three-dimensional exists, except that in physics a time dimension is added to our world by Einstein's theory of relativity to change it from a "three-dimensional space" into a "four-dimensional space-time".

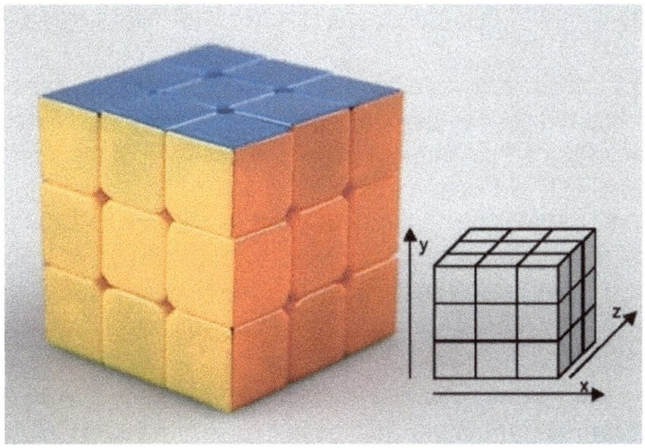

The space we are in is a three-dimensional space, which has three dimensions: length, width, and height.

The space I am talking about refers to a pure space, which does not take time as a dimension. Only when we say "time and space" do we take time as a dimension in addition to space.

The concept of high-dimensional space used to be a hot topic in science fiction, but it has been silent for quite a long time. In recent years, because of the popularity of "the string theory," it has become a hot topic for physicists again.

The fact that the string theory has been enthusiastically pursued fully reflects the influence of *the reductionist theory*. It is precise because of the reductionist logic that people begin to pay attention to the study of elementary particles. The reductionist logic believes that as long as we can find the smallest particles that make up the world and understand the principles of actions between them, we will understand everything in the world.

It is also because of this logic that some physicists have come up with the idea of "the great unification of different theories." In the history of science, there have been many examples of new theories unifying previous explanations of different physical phenomena. Maxwell unified electricity and magnetism with the electromagnetic theory. Einstein unified quality and energy with the equation of mass and energy. Each unity brought a huge leap to human understanding of the world. Therefore, some people are thinking along the thread of reductionism, hoping to discover a theory that can unify all the basic particles and four basic forces in nature. According to the reasoning that "the interaction between elementary particles can explain all phenomena in the world", as long as this theory is found, it is equivalent to having discovered "the theory of all things" that can explain everything in the universe.

In 1968, the Italian physicist Viniziano discovered a formula when studying the data of particle collisions. Some people explained it like this: Particles are not a point but rather a string in shape like the tensile rubber band. They stretch when gaining energy and shrink when losing energy, and they can vibrate like rubber bands.

Inspired by this idea, people have further suggested that based on the theory that "particles are strings", we can unify all the particles and all forces in nature. All elementary particles can be understood as the vibration of the string. All the forces are also the same. The electromagnetic force and the nuclear force are derived from the vibration of the open string, and the gravitational force is derived from the vibration of the closed string.

The String Theory theorizes as follows. Everything is a string, and the universe is a grand symphony. This is an exciting picture of beauty! Many physicists are fascinated by it. Hawking even claimed that *M-Theory* the latest version of the string theory is likely to be the only candidate for a theory of everything.

However, the funny thing is that people's understanding of the string theory remains a kind of fuzzy feeling. As the string theorist, Green said in "*Cosmic Longitude and Latitude*, "Even today, after 30 years of its appearance, most string practitioners still believe that we cannot answer a basic question satisfactorily: What is the string theory?"

The physicist L. Smolin said: "In the United States, there is almost no future for theorists who pursue basic physics methods other than the string theory. When string theory is still fighting for scientific issues, it has already won the favor of the academic circle."

The core equations of the electromagnetic theory are *Maxwell's Equations*. The core equation of the general theory of relativity is Einstein's *Field Equation*. String theory does not have its core equation. Even a clear description of this theory is not available. String theorists simply say that the entire universe is made up of strings, but they cannot say clearly how the strings constitute the universe.

Although the string theory is not complete, it requires a very exaggerated premise, that is, that the world we live in cannot be a four-dimensional time-space but must be an eleven-dimensional time-space. But we can only see the four-dimensional time-space. Where are the extra seven dimensions? String theory explains that these extra dimensions have been rolled into very small spaces too small to be detected with the most advanced instruments.

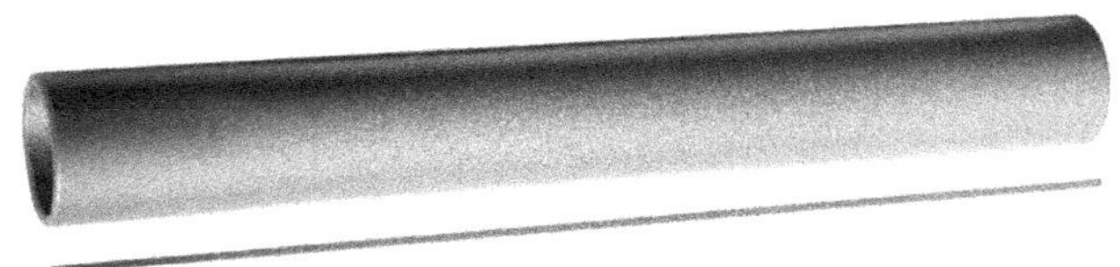

If a thin string is enlarged, it may be a tube, so a one-dimensional thing becomes three-dimensional. String theory believes that this is the case in our real world. It seems to be a four-dimensional space-time; but as long as it is enlarged big enough, it becomes an eleven-dimensional space-time.

But then bigger problems came. This curl cannot be arbitrary, because each method of twist corresponds to a set of laws of nature or a completely different universe. According to the calculations of the string theorists, there are about 10^{500} kinds of such curls; that is, there may be 10^{500} different universes in theory.

It is to explain why in so many possibilities there is an orderly universe like ours that the string theory needs to introduce the idea of "parallel universes." Darwin said that in the variants of almost infinite possibilities there must be one that is consistent with the species in front of us. String theory follows this logic and believes that in the almost infinite possible parallel universes there must be one universe with the same physical properties as ours.

Just to adhere to the concept of *Natural Creation*, Darwin's logic has been widely used in various fields, creating one after very ridiculous theories.

String theory believes that our universe is an eleven-dimensional space-time, and this concept has been recognized by most physicists. It at least shows that it is not too difficult to let people accept the concept of high-dimensional space.

Siddhartha said that the world is hierarchical, and string theory says that the world is high-dimensional. If these statements are combined, concerning the scenes *on the Thirteenth Floor*, we can guess this:

Beyond the three-dimensional space we are in, there are many different dimensions of space. Each spatial dimension can be thought of as a level of the hierarchy, so there are many different levels. There are many different worlds at each level, and in each world there live a completely different set of life.

We can understand this multi-level world by referring to the computer video game world.

Suppose that one-day human beings can make their game characters conscious and intelligent, then human beings become the creator of this game world. If you are the character Sedum living in the two-dimensional space of *The Legend of the Sword and the Chivalrous Man III*, for you, the game world is small at the same level as the two-dimensional space of your world, and other game worlds like the *Legend* and *the World of Warcraft* are all parallel universes.

The Legend of the Sword and the Chivalrous Man and The World of Warcraft are two-dimensional space games developed by humans in three-dimensional space. The virtual worlds in which the characters live are parallel universes.

For Sedum, the creator is the human programmers living in a three-dimension space. These people created the universe in which he lives. He is in the human-computer. Humans may watch him silently in front of the screen. They seem an inch away from the screen where he is in, but that small distance is beyond the end of his world, so Sedum in the two-dimensional space will always be unable to find that there are human beings in the three-dimensional space.

Following this line of logic, since there is a two-dimensional space in the game world and the three-dimensional space in the real world, why can't there be a four-dimensional space? Sedum is life in a two-dimensional space. We live in a three-dimensional space. Cannot we have lived in a four-dimensional space?

In this way, our world is unlikely to be created by future humans, nor by aliens, but by living in a higher-dimensional space.

It is unlikely for the creator to create just one world like ours. So, parallel to our world, there should be countless other universes that, like ours, are running in the creation host.

Among the three theories in which the world is parallel, cascaded, or mutually contained, it is most likely that in the vertical direction, the different dimensions or levels of space are contained in each other; from the horizontal perspective, the different worlds in the same level are parallel.

String theory should be wrong, and the root of its error lies in the theory of reductionism. Can the theory of elementary particles become "the theory of everything"? Even if the string theory unifies all the particles and all the forces, can it explain all the phenomena in the universe? How do you use string theory to explain war and peace, economic boom and recession, or regime establishment and change?

Humans can see every move of a character in a two-dimensional game, but even if it is so close to us the characters in the game will not discover the existence of human beings.

A schematic diagram of a four-dimensional space. In fact, as a creature in a three-dimensional space, we can never be able to imagine the true appearance of a four-dimensional space.

As for gravity and nuclear force, one is the phenomenon observed under a smooth picture, and the other is the phenomenon observed when the picture is enlarged to the level of a mosaic at which each pixel can be seen. At these two distinct levels, the observed laws are different; and there is no need to force them to unify. The study of string theory may be wrong in the beginning.

If there is a "theory of everything", then the theory of creation and evolution can be regarded as a good candidate!

Now we can easily answer the question raised earlier: Is there a boundary in the universe? What is there outside the universe? As long as you think about the boundaries of the game maps and beyond, you can understand everything.

In addition, I can easily answer this question: What is space? The answer is simple. Space is the map in the computer game.

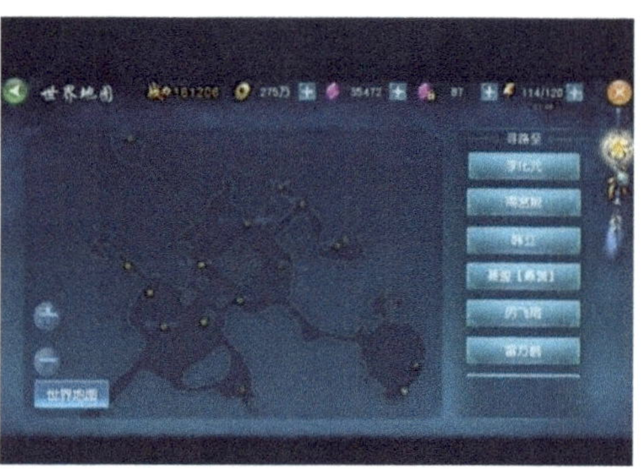

In the game, the map has boundaries, and there is nothing beyond the boundaries of the map except darkness.

Space is Not Void, and Ether Exists

The relationship between many worlds should be like this: one layer is wrapped in another layer, and there are countless worlds in each layer.

We discussed earlier the question of whether the space is *void*. People's understanding of this issue in history can be described as full of twists and turns.

At the earliest time, Aristotle believed that "nature hates vacuum", so space is not *void*, but filled with *ether* the fifth element. However, the atomists opposed it, saying that nature is composed of two things: objects and void, so space is *void*.

Later, Descartes believed that the impact between objects could only occur through contact, and that space was not *void* but filled with the invisible substance *ether*. He thinks that space is like a sea filled with whirlpools, in which planets float. However, Newton's law of universal gravitation suggests that gravity is an over-range effect, and the sun can exert gravitational effects on the earth without any contact with it. Newton's followers thought that space was *void* and they denied the existence of ether for a long time.

Later on, Maxwell believed that electromagnetic waves can propagate in space because the changing electric field generates a magnetic field and the changing magnetic field generates an electric field, so space is not *void*, and it is at least filled with the *field*. He believed that ether does exist, saying that the vast interplanetary and interstellar regions will no longer be regarded as useless places in the universe ... These places are filled with this magical medium. "He believed that ether is omnipresent, without mass, absolutely stationary, and it fills the entire universe, and electromagnetic waves can propagate through it.

But the mainstream modern physics community does not recognize the existence of ether, because Einstein said in the paper on the special theory of relativity that "the introduction of ether will prove to be superfluous." Since then, people have abandoned the concept of ether.

Einstein later changed his attitude. In 1920, he said: "More careful thinking tells us that the special theory of relativity does not force us to give up either." People do not realize that the theory of general relativity is a theory based on ether. It believes that gravity is caused by time and space bending. If the space is *void*, how can it bend?

Is space *void*? Let's first figure out what *space* is!

Newton has made a serious analysis of the meaning of space. He believed that there is a difference between *absolute space* and *relative space*. He said: "The absolute nature of absolute space has nothing to do with all external things. It is uniform everywhere and never moves. Relative space is a structure that can move in absolute space or a measure of absolute space. We perceive it by its relative position to other objects. Absolute space and relative space are the same in shape and size, but they are not always the same in value. For example, when the earth is moving, the space between the atmosphere and the earth is constant, but it passes through this part of absolute space at one moment and passes through that part of absolute space at another moment, so from the perspective of absolute space, it is continuously changing in space."

Let us explain what Newton meant. If the evolution of the universe is seen as a play, then Newton believes that the stage space is fixed, which is an absolute space. If the actor on the stage drives a prop car, then the space inside the prop car is the relative space. The prop car moves on the stage, and the relative space inside the car does not change, but its position in the absolute space of the stage is constantly changing.

Is Newton's statement correct? We can still use the game world to compare and analyze.

First, the absolute space that Newton said must exist. This is the big stage where the universe evolves, like the map in the computer game. Einstein was wrong in saying that there is no absolute space.

Secondly, Newton said that absolute space has nothing to do with all external things. It is even everywhere and never moves. This is wrong. Now we know that space is always expanding, just like the game maps are always expanding, and the distance between any two points in the absolute space is getting bigger. Moreover, Einstein's theory of relativity suggests that the stage of space is itself part of the show. Time and space bending will cause changes in the physical properties of objects in space, such as slowing of clocks and bending of light, as if the changes in the stage will cause changes in actors' emotions and these changes will directly affect their performances in the show.

The third point is whether space is *void*. This is not true. On the stage and out of the stage are not the same. The game map and the game map are different, and it is *void* of the game map. Einstein later realized this. He said: "According to general relativity, space without ether is unimaginable. Because in this space not only light cannot be transmitted, but also space and time standards cannot exist, so any space-time interval will have no physical meaning." He is right, how can there be any acting without a stage? How can a game run without a background map?

The American physicist Frank Wilczek said: "In places where we think it is a void, it is full of active media, and their activities have created this world." What is this medium? He said: "Ether is the oldest concept that is closest to the original intent, but it makes people feel that the concept is old and lacking new ideas," so he called this thing *grid*.

Wilczek said: "I began to suspect that the entity we call vacuum may be a weird superconductor. If you want to have superconductivity, there must be a substance that can conduct it. The weird superconductivity is everywhere, and then this material can only be the space-filling ether." He believes that "the world is built based on a multi-level space filled with ether."

After reading the above analysis, you should understand this. There is nothing outside the game map. It is a *void*. Within the map, even if there is nothing else, there is at least a background, so it cannot be said that it is completely *void*. The same is true of space. We can think of it as a map full of ether, so it is not *void* and blank.

A good proof of this is the phenomenon of *quantum fluctuations* in a vacuum. According to the *Uncertainty Principle*, even in a pure vacuum, a small amount of energy can be randomly generated, and a virtual particle pair composed of a particle and an antiparticle can be generated from nothingness. That is to say, in a vacuum, substances can be generated for no reason and then annihilated in a very short time. The current state of the art of technology is enough to observe their existence, which proves that the vacuum we originally thought of is not void. In places outside of the universe that are truly *void*, the phenomenon of quantum fluctuations can't occur.

Chapter 17
The Truth about Time:
Time is the Scale
of the Evolution of the Universe,
and It Can Move Forward and Backward.

Ancient people realized a long time ago that the existence of some things was very short, such as the myriads of shapes of fleeting white clouds; the existence of some other things was incredibly long that human beings couldn't detect their birth and death. Perhaps it is just because of the observed differences in the length of time of existence of things that made the ancient people create the concept of *time*.

For the ancient people, the accurate measurement of such differences in length of time was a difficult task. But they were very smart, and they found that the best way to measure time is to find something that changes cyclically as a reference. So, no matter where on the earth they are, people have adopted the same solution, calling the cycle of spring, summer, autumn, and winter seasons a year, the cycle of changes of the moon one month, the cycle of alternating day and night a day. Now we know that they represent the earth's revolution around the sun, the moon's revolution around the earth, and the earth's rotation.

It can be seen from the practice that people generally use *year*, *month*, and *day* to measure time, that time is related to the movement of things. One year represents a cycling process of spring blossoms, hot summer days, yellow leaves, and ice covering land; one month represents a cycle of changes of the moon, and one day represents a cycle of sunrise and sunset.

To measure time accurately, the ancient people invented the timing tools such as *sundials* and *sandglass*. Later, with the advancement of technology, there appeared more sophisticated instruments—clocks. And we have now the most accurate timepiece—the atomic clock, with an error of no more than one second in 20 million years. This shows that humans have reached a level of precise measurement of time.

The passage of time marks a change of things. The most common method used by ancient people to measure time is to measure it against a cyclical process of a fixed cycle.

At this point, there seems to be no suspense in people's understanding of time. But if you open Hawking's *A Brief History of Time*, you can see that each object moving at different speeds or in different gravitational fields has a different time standard. Time is not eternal. There was a beginning in the Big Bang, and the concept of time before the birth of the universe was meaningless. These questions will make you feel strange about the concept of time.

What is the secret of time? We still analyze references to movies and video games. The first question is: What is time?

The concept of time seems to be self-evident, but when you want to say it, I am afraid it is not so easy to make it clear. Time has always been the foundation of the whole physics, but the strange thing is that there is never an accurate definition of it. Even Newton, Einstein, and Hawking can't tell you clearly what time is.

In people's daily concepts, the time has two meanings. If someone asks you: "When did you get married?" The *time* he refers to is *the exact moment of time* of your marriage. And if someone asks: "How long have you been married?" The *time* mentioned here refers to the period from marriage to the present, which is *the period*.

Moment or *span*, which one can truly represent the connotation of time? I think it is *the moment*. So here we need to declare that the time we are talking about refers to the moment. For the length of a certain period, we will use *the period* to express it instead of the word *moment*.

In the movie, time refers to the exact moment on the whole scale of the story timeline. The picture comes from a movie that lasts 1 hour, 35 minutes, and 37 seconds. The time for this picture is at the time point of 35 minutes and 28 seconds after the film begins.

After regarding the time as the "time point," we are very clear about the nature of time. It refers to a *point* instead of *a length* on *the scale* that describes the process of things; for example, in a movie, the time when the male and female protagonists first met was 11 minutes and 25 seconds, the time when the wedding scene appeared was 50 minutes and 33 seconds, and the time when the child delivery scene appeared was 1 hour, 4 minutes and 32 seconds. Time here refers to the exact point on the scale of the procession of the film plot.

For the video game world, time refers to the point on the time scale of the game process. At some point, the game shows the following actions: John is in a fight with a monster, Bob is in a treasure hunt, and Peter is killing Tom. In the real world, time is also a scale; each specific time is associated with a specific event that took place at the time. The time in our world is the scale and marker of the evolution of the entire universe.

People don't understand the truth of time, so they think that the timepiece measures the time itself. This understanding has deviated from the nature of time.

The second question is: When did the time start?

From the point of common sense, things always have started. But humans have a limited life span, and they exist only for a short period, so they know very little.

It is because of the limited knowledge of human beings that the questions of "when does time start" and "what is there before the beginning of time" become very difficult to answer. Some devout believers were extremely annoyed with questions such as "what God is doing before the creation of the world," and even replied that "God was preparing for hell for those who asked such questions."

To avoid answering this question, there was a time when people believed that the universe was an eternal existence, and time did not begin or end. But the Big Bang theory has smashed this claim. The universe has a beginning, so the time as the scale of the evolution of the universe must have a beginning.

Where does this start? The time of the movie is counted from the moment when it starts to play; the time of the game world is counted from the moment when the game program starts running; the time of our world is counted from the time when the *Tao* starts running. That is, from the moment of the Big Bang.

The time in the movie is counted from the moment it is played; the time in our world begins when the creation program is clicked on.

The third question is: Does the concept of time before the birth of the universe make sense?

In the 5th century, the theologian Augustine said that time is an important property of the world created by God. Before God created the world, time did not exist. Many modern physicists and astronomers also believe that the concept of time at the beginning of the universe is meaningless. Is the truth like what they said?

If you think carefully, you will find that, when they say such words, there is a subtext in the words, that is, there is only one time.

In the past when people thought that there was only one world, it was normal to have such an understanding. But we now know that there should be more than one universe and they are of different levels of dimensions in the vertical direction, and there are many parallel universes in the horizontal direction, so there may be an infinite number of universes. In this case, it is not appropriate to think that there is only one time.

Every world has its scale of running processes, so it has its own time. There is one time in one world, and countless times in countless worlds. For our world, before the birth of the universe, the time that belongs to us does not exist, but there are still other worlds, so it cannot be said that the concept of time has no meaning. For example, in the world where our Creator is, their time must have existed before our time exists; and even if our world is destroyed, their time will continue to exist.

So, to the question "What God is doing before the creation of the world?" the answer is quite a simple one. The Creator is in a completely different world from us, where there is its own time. What the Creator is doing before creating our world is irrelevant to the beginning and end of the time of our world.

The fourth question is: How do you understand the difference in time flow rate?

The evolution of the universe is continuous, so the time as the scale of the evolution of the universe is always flowing.

From experiences, people have believed for a long time that in different regions, different ages, and for different things, time should flow at a constant speed. Or the process of the evolution of the universe should be carried out at the same speed.

However, in myths and legends, it is often the case that the time flow rates are not the same in different regions. Einstein proved that this is possible. Under different speeds of motion, or different gravitational fields, the flow rates of time may vary greatly. This phenomenon has already been introduced before. What is to be said here is how to explain this phenomenon.

We can think about the situation of watching movies with a DVD player. For the same movie, if you choose to watch it at different playing speeds, the results are completely different. Suppose the first time it is played at the normal speed, we watch the movie for 2 hours and 40 minutes; the second time we change the play mode, and press the button for 32 times faster play, then the duration will become 5 minutes; the third time it is played at a speed of 32 times slower, then the duration will be 85 hours and 20 minutes.

For the same film, the content has not changed. Why are the lengths of time of the three broadcasts so different? The reason is that the playing speed is different.

Movie players usually have buttons for fast play and slow play. When the fast play button is pressed, the time flow rate in the movie increases, and everyone's moves will become very agile; when the slow play button is pressed, the people's movements will become slow.

On a moving object or in a gravitational field, the flow rate of time will be slowed down, which is equivalent to the event being played at a slow speed. If there is a pair of twin brothers, with one living on the earth for a lifetime, and the other one living his life on a spacecraft cruising in the universe at a speed near the speed of light, the durations of time will be completely different. When the person on the spacecraft is dying and returning to Earth to see his brother, he will find that his brother on earth has already died many years ago.

Some smart people may want to take advantage of the different flow rates of time to live longer, but they are destined to be disappointed. The twin brothers have spent the rest of their lives. Although the lengths of time seem different, the life of the person on the actual spacecraft has not changed in his perception. Just like the movie that takes 85 hours and 20 minutes to run, the content is not more than the content of the movie that takes 5 minutes to run. The difference in duration is caused by the speed of play. The content of the movie will not be of any substantial change.

The speed of movement has been increasing and the time flow rate has been slowing down. When the speed of movement reaches the speed of light, the time is completely stopped, which is equivalent to pressing the pause button of the player.

When the Creator created our world, why should he set different time flow rates in the same system depending on the speed of motion and the gravitational field? Einstein derived his theory of relativity from the premise that the speed of light is constant. Inspired by this, I can only speculate that in the creation of the Creator, technically and logically, a constant speed of light is a basic premise, so the Creator will take trouble creating a flexible flow rate of time.

When the play speed is faster, the time for watching movies will be shorter, but the content of the movie will not decrease; when the play speed slows down, the time for watching movies will be extended, but the content of the video will not increase. If you want to extend the length of life by changing the flow rate of time, this method will not work.

The fifth question is: Can time be reversed?

Experience tells us that time is irreversible. People can't resurrect, the broken mirror can't return to its original state again; and it is impossible to reassemble the broken pieces of glass that fell to the groundbreaking into a perfect cup.

It is difficult for us to understand this characteristic of time from physics. From the point of view of mechanics, the process of change of motion of things is nothing more than a collision between particles. In the microscopic world, elementary particles have three basic symmetry modes. In addition to *the parity* explained earlier, there is another type of *time reversion symmetry*, that is, if we reverse the direction of particle motion, the particle motion is the same. This means that there is no qualitative difference between collisions when the particles go one way or the other. Why does the glass change only from complete to broken, not from broken to complete?

The irreversibility of time and process is difficult to get a reasonable explanation from physics.

The Second Law of Thermodynamics is the only physics theory that can now be used to explain the irreversibility of time and process. This law states that all spontaneous processes in nature are irreversible. Heat is spontaneously transmitted from high-temperature objects to low-temperature objects, and matter spontaneously diffuses from high-density areas to low-density areas, but this spontaneous process is irreversible. If this process is to be reversed, external forces must be involved. However, the Second Law of Thermodynamics is only an empirical one and is not well-proven in theory.

It is easy to understand the phenomenon of the irreversibility of time if we use the video game as a reference. In video games, the order of the different events is quite important because there is a certain causal relationship between them. If you confuse the order, there will be serious logical conflicts that will cause the system to crash, so the movie can be played backward, but the video game can't.

Our real world is more like a video game world, so time cannot go backward. However, a pause is completely possible. For example, the process of the evolution of the universe in the creation host temporarily stops and continues after some time. This is equivalent to a pause of time. In this case, we will not feel anything, unless part of the process of the evolution of the universe is temporarily stopped, while our part of the process is still going on so that concerning our part, we will find out when the part of the universe stopped evolution. Otherwise, without a reference, we will not know that time has been suspended when the entire system is completely suspended.

There is a fast reverse button on the movie player that can reverse the play, which is equivalent to time reversal, but it is not available in the video game. The reason is that the process and causal relationship of the film are certain, no matter whether its broadcast is forward or reverse; whereas the game process is uncertain, backward play will confuse causality.

The sixth question is: Is time relative or absolute?

Newton believes that there are both absolute time and relative time. He wrote in the book *Mathematical Principles of Natural Philosophy*: "Absolute time, true and mathematical, flows equably in itself and by its nature without relation to anything external, and by another name is called duration. Relative, apparent, and common time is some sensible external measure of duration you please (whether with accurate or with unequal intervals) which commonly is used in place of true time, as in the hour, day, month, or year.

Since then, this concept has been widely accepted for more than two hundred years, until Einstein published the special theory of relativity. Einstein subverts the notion of *absolute time* and points out that there is only relative time and no absolute time.

Why is there only relative time? Let's see how Einstein explained it.

In the special theory of relativity, he raised a question. A straight rail has two points A and B that are far apart, and the lightning hits both points at the same time, and both points emit flashes at the same time. Is there any problem with such a way of saying it?

Maybe you can't see what's tricky, but Einstein said there is a problem. He said, how can you determine that lightning is hitting these two points at the same time? Some people may suggest a good way to let a person stand on the rails in the middle of the two points A and B. If he sees two flashes at the same time, then it can prove that lightning strikes occur at the same time.

But Einstein went on to say that there is a problem here. If the person standing in the middle of the two points A and B is not standing on the rails but standing in a train just passing the middle position from A to B at a speed of V, then it will be another situation. At this moment he will first see the light from B, and then see the light from A, so he will think that the order of the lightning strike is first B and then A, not at the same time.

Thus, Einstein said: "There are several events at the same time for the roadbed, not at the same time for the train, and vice versa. Every reference object has its own special time. Unless we say to which object it refers in the statement about time, the statement about the time of an event is meaningless."

Since different reference objects have different time standards, absolute time does not exist. So, Einstein added: "Before the creation of relativity, there was always an implicit assumption in physics that the statement of time has an absolute meaning, that is, the statement of time has nothing to do with the state of motion of the reference object. But as we saw earlier, this assumption is incompatible with the most natural definition of simultaneity."

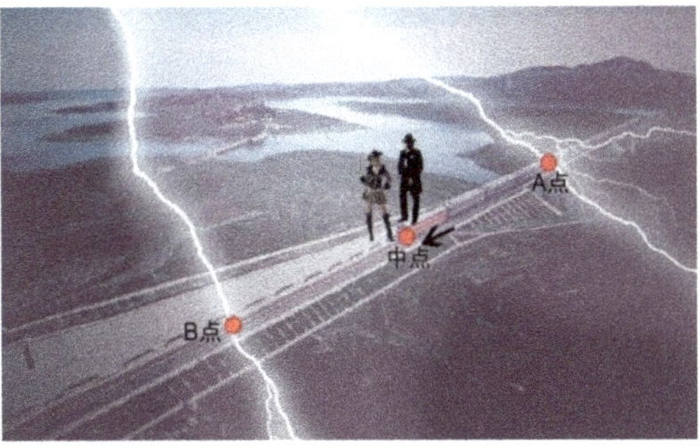

After lightning strikes at two points A and B, for two people who are at the midpoint position but standing on the rails and trains respectively, the order in which the flashes reach the eyes is different, so their judgments on whether the

two lightning strikes occur at the same time are different.

Einstein's statement has earned enough attention, but it is completely wrong. The difference in time observed in the reference frames of different motion speeds does not mean that each frame of reference can have its independent time standard, and it is not possible to derive the conclusion that "absolute time does not exist".

There is a serious logical problem in this statement. Einstein is a believer in the law of causality. This is why he opposes the *Principle of Uncertainty* and says, "God does not roll the dice." But he never seems to realize that the statement "there is no absolute time in the world" in his theory of relativity violates the law of causality.

The law of causality refers to the fact that the former cause will lead to the subsequent consequences and the previous events will trigger subsequent events. But there is a precondition here, that is, the occurrence of the events must be successive, and the distinction should be absolute, not relative. If the world is like what Einstein said, things have their independent time standards, and there is no absolute time in the whole system, that means that there is no absolute succession in the occurrence of events, and the standards are not uniform as for which event comes first and which event comes later. As a result, it will be unclear what the cause is and what the consequence is. How can the law of causality still exist? If so, the whole world would have been messed up long ago?

Just from this point of view, the world cannot exist with only relative time but no absolute time. But what is the standard for this time? If in the video game world, different things will cause different speeds of the game due to different speeds of motion, how can the time scale of the whole game be determined? This is very simple. Each server will have a clock, and its time is the unified standard time of the game world. Everything in the game can't have its time standard.

Our real world is the same. There must be a clock in the creation host, which can mark the progression of the entire universe. No matter which part of it is moving at what speed and how its evolution is progressed, its progress in the creation host must be clearly and accurately identified. And that is the absolute time of our world. When the two points A and B are struck by lightning, the system must record them as two events that have already occurred. They will be marked against a certain time scale, which has nothing to do with other people's observations. This time scale is the only sign of the evolution of the universe, just like Newton said, "it flows equably in itself and by its nature without a relation to anything external."

The video game process will have a common time scale, which is based on the server's clock.

The absolute time that Newton talked about refers to *the time point* on the process scale, and the relative time he talked about refers to *the time length*. Einstein did not understand the difference between *time point* and *time length*, so he would think that there is no absolute time. On this point, Newton is right, and Einstein is wrong. And the so-called "subversion of absolute time" is purely a farce.

Some people like to use the terms *time contraction* and *time expansion* when describing the phenomenon that the duration is shorter or longer due to the change in the time flow rate, which is confusing. Here we want to clarify that the time scale is standardized, absolute, and fixed; and only changes in the flow rate of time will occur, and accordingly, the durations will change.

So, as of relativity and absoluteness of time, *the time length* and *time flow rate* are indeed relative, and they are constantly changing; but as the time scale of the process of the evolution of the universe, time itself will not change. Just like the earlier mentioned example of playing a movie. If you use 32x fast play, then when the movie runs to the episode of the child delivery, we feel the episode lasts just 2 minutes and 1 second. But in the whole movie scale, it is still at the position of 1 hour, 4 minutes, and 32 seconds. The player's clock is still labeled as such, without any slight change.

Existence and Perception

"Existence is perceived." The words of Bishop George Berkeley are wrong. The Creator gives us limited ability to perceive. We couldn't perceive many things, but we can't say that they don't exist.

However, in real life, we often confuse existence with perception. The court follows the logic of "Existence is perceived". The evidence is something that has been perceived by the judge, so it can be said that the judge judges the truth of the case according to his perception. Although some things exist that are not perceived by the judge, and they may have a higher degree of relevance to the case and may affect the result of the judgment, they are automatically excluded from the judgment.

In science, *perception* is replaced by *measurement*, and people subconsciously believe that existence is measured. Take *quality* as an example. When people originally proposed this concept, it means *the amount of matter*. But for a specific thing, how can we know how much substance it contains? We can only rely on measurement.

There are two methods to measure the mass of a body. The most common one is to determine mass by measuring weight. When we go to the market to buy pork, we need to pay according to the amount of pork, that is, its mass. We usually use scales to weigh, so weight is not mass but the gravity of the piece of pork. But we use it to measure the mass of pork, which is called *gravitational mass*. The applications of this method are limited because gravity will change. The 5 kg of pork on the earth will become heavier on Jupiter, lighter on the moon, and become weightless in the "weightless" state of outer space. Even in an elevator with upward or downward acceleration, it will not be accurate.

A more physically accurate approach is to determine mass by measuring *inertia*. For example, two astronauts push each other out of outer space. One of them has a mass of 50 kilograms and a receding speed of 2 meters per second. If another person retreats at a speed of 1 meter per second, then we can calculate his mass as 100 kilograms, so the mass measured in this way is called *inertial mass*.

Can *inertial mass* mean *mass*? No, it couldn't. It has been observed that as the particles reach near the speed of light in the accelerator, their inertial mass increases dramatically. But if we start from the definition that "mass is the measure of matter", is there more matter in the particle at this time? There aren't. Once the speed is reduced, its mass will return to its original level. This means that just as *gravitational mass* changes with the change of gravitational strength, *inertial mass* also changes with the change of state of motion.

What inspiration does this example give us? It shows that the logic of "existence is measured" is wrong. The measured increase of mass cannot be equated with the real increase of substance, and measurement and existence cannot be completely equated.

From the phenomenon that inertial mass is equivalent to gravitational mass in the gravitational field, Einstein discovered the *Equivalence Principle* and concluded that gravitation and acceleration are completely equivalent. This is also a kind of "existence is perceived" logic. The physical meanings behind gravitation and acceleration are completely different. On earth, we find they are equivalent by observation; but in the universe, are they not equivalent in some special cases? This is entirely possible! As in the previous example, you can pay with a shopping card, a bank card, or cash when you buy something in the supermarket; but in other places, you may not be able to use the shopping cart; some small stores may be cash only and may not accept the bank card.

We often make mistakes in our understanding of time. We don't see time itself as the scale, and what we can measure is only its flow rate and relative length. If this is not clearly understood, existence will be confused with measurement, leading to the wrong conclusion that there is only *relative time* but no *absolute time*, just because the changes in time flow rate and length can be measured.

The same mistake occurs in people's understanding of the problem of simultaneity. The simultaneity behind the system must exist, but we don't know it. What we know is the measurement results of different reference systems. When Einstein concluded that "every system has a time standard", he confused existence with perception.

Quantum Gravity May Be Just a Legend

Although Einstein made a mistake in the judgment of whether there is absolute time or absolute space, this will not shake the foundation of relativity. The theory of relativity itself does not prove that absolute time and space do not exist. Einstein's perception that it does not exist is pure intuition, and he doesn't derive it from any theoretical speculation. However, inferences based on relativity, such as the *twin paradox* need to be changed accordingly, because many presumptions of them are based on the concept that there is only relative time and space but no absolute time and space.

The theory of relativity was indeed an advanced understanding of human beings about time and space. In particular, the interpretation of gravitation in general relativity involves extraordinary imagination. Later, *quantum gravitation* was conceived to unify relativity theory and quantum theory. Maybe it is just a beautiful legend.

Let's discuss this issue, starting with the basic forces and particles.

According to the usual theory, there are four basic forces in nature: gravitation, electromagnetic force, strong nuclear force (strong interaction), and weak nuclear force (weak interaction). Gravity is the weakest of the four forces. It exists between any object, and the electromagnetic force acts only on the charged particles. Both of these forces can be long-distance.

The strong nuclear force is the force that binds protons, neutrons, quarks, etc. in the nucleus. This force is very powerful. Protons with positive electrons will mutually repel each other, but they are tightly bound by strong nuclear forces. The weak nuclear force is the force that causes the radioactivity of a nucleus or the decay of free neutrons. It mainly exists in the decay process of particles. Strong nuclear forces and weak nuclear forces have very short distances. They exist only in the nucleus, and we cannot directly access them.

The above four forces are called *basic forces* because they cannot be explained by more fundamental forces. The forces we often see in daily life, such as the brute force of the fight, the friction of the tire, the spring force of the spring, etc., are essentially only a manifestation of the electromagnetic force, and thus are not the basic interaction forces.

How do these basic forces arise and what do they rely on to transmit? In classical physics, a force is transmitted by a field; gravitation is transmitted by a *gravitational field*, and electromagnetic force is transmitted by an *electromagnetic field*.

But after the rise of quantum theory, people began to search for the roots of these forces in the quantum world, thus developing the *quantum field theory*. According to this theory, force is caused by particles that fly back and forth between material particles that can carry and transmit forces.

According to the difference in the performance of force, the particles can be divided into three categories: hadron, lepton, and propagator. Hadrons are particles that can participate in strong interactions. They are composed of quarks. Most of the particles, including protons, neutrons, andπmesons, are hadrons. Leptons are involved in weak interactions, electromagnetic forces, and gravitational effects and they do not participate in strong interactions, including electrons, electron neutrinos, etc. Propagators are particles that propagate forces between matter particles.

At present, the last three basic forces have been confirmed to be propagated by particles, and these particles have been found. The strong nuclear force is transmitted by gluon. The weak nuclear force is transmitted by the w+, W-, and Z0 particles. The electromagnetic force is transmitted by a photon. According to this logic, people think that gravity should also be propagated by particles, and the imaginary particles that propagate gravity are called graviton. This quantized gravitation is called *quantum gravity*.

However, many years have passed, but people have never been able to observe the existence of *graviton*. This makes us have to think about the question: Does *quantum gravity* exist?

According to Einstein's general theory of relativity, gravity is not a basic force. When we put a very heavy iron ball on the mattress, it will causes the mattress to sag. For the same reason, all objects will make the space-time net warped and deformed. When an object travels through this space-time, its trajectory will be changed accordingly. It looks like it is being pulled by a force. In combination with the absolute space concept, we can imagine that the universe is a sea filled with ether. The stars and other objects are like balls floating in the ocean. The surrounding seawater is squeezed out, creating a hole in the space. The seawater squeezes the surrounding objects into the hole, which looks like an object has an *"attraction"*. If this statement is correct, then gravity is essentially a superficial phenomenon, not a real force.

In 1995, Ted Jacobsen from the Department of Physics of the University of Maryland published an article demonstrating the surprising similarities between general relativity and thermodynamics. Put more exactly, Einstein's equation that relates time-space distortion to the manifestation of matter can be interpreted as an equation familiar to thermodynamics, the *State Equation*, which does not need to consider microscopic details. It is a direct depiction of the properties of the entire physical system.

Gas is a collection of free-roaming molecules. At the macro level, it exhibits many properties such as temperature, pressure, volume, concentration, surface tension, etc. However, these properties do not exist at the microscopic level, like the pressure inside the ball. They are only collective attributes of the gas atoms in a closed vessel and exist only at the macro level we are at. Once we go deep into the molecular level to study them, they disappear without a trace.

This similarity between gravitation and thermodynamic phenomena has prompted people to reflect on the nature of gravity. Perhaps it should be treated as a superficial phenomenon rather than a basic force. The Dutch theoretical physicist Eric Verland said: "In my opinion, the so-called model of exploring the most basic forces and particles has come to an end. If gravity is only a superficial phenomenon, then it is not necessary to take pains to search for ways to quantize the general theory of relativity. Since this theory is a macroscopic collective phenomenon, it is understandable that it stops outside the boundaries of the quantum world."

Based on these considerations, we have every reason to believe that *quantum gravity* may be just a legend.

Chapter 18

The Mystery of the Soul:
People Have a Body and a Soul,
as Computers Have Hardware and Software.

The world is full of mystery, but the biggest secret in the universe may not be the external world, but human beings. The existence of human consciousness is the biggest supernormal phenomenon.

We have already had a detailed discussion on the question "Where does the world come from?" but the question "Where does man come from?" is still a mystery. Human science and technology are quite developed, but still little is known about life. We can make computers, atomic bombs, robots, satellites, and spaceships, but still can't make a complete life.

As to why the basic traits of life can be passed on from generation to generation, we had been full of doubts until we discovered genetics, and then had an intuitive understanding of the cause of organisms. Every cell of an organism has DNA or RNA molecules that carry genetic information. This is the gene. There is genetic information in every cell, just like every brick in a building is accompanied by a construction drawing, which can be built as shown in the drawing. The genes of the previous generation of organisms can be passed on to the next generation through replication, ensuring that the traits of the species can be passed down. The gestation, growth, and death of life are carried out in an orderly manner under the guidance of genetic information.

The existence of genes allows us to understand why organisms can naturally grow and reproduce. The current technology has even been able to transform natural creatures, making test-tube babies, cloning sheep, and genetically modifying organisms. Does this mean that humans can already make life? The answer is negative. The characteristics of life not only include the outer body, but also the inner spirit. We still know almost nothing about the question of how the spirit is created, let alone its fabrication

Among all the characteristics of life, the spirit is the most mysterious, and it is different from other things. Today, many things that we couldn't see before, such as air, radiation, and electromagnetic fields, can now be observed and measured. But for the spirit, although we know its existence, we cannot perceive it and measure it.

Because of this, there is a huge disagreement in people's understanding of it. In philosophy, the debate between idealism and materialism has been around for a long time. Idealism believes that the spirit is the first nature. The spirit creates the material and determines the material. Materialism holds that the material is the first nature. Consciousness is only the function of the brain, the product of matter, and the material determines consciousness.

Thomas Hobbs, a 17th-century British philosopher, believed that all phenomena in nature, including humans and animals, are made up of molecules of matter, and even human consciousness is produced by molecular movements in the human brain. The 18th-century French philosopher J.O. Rametrie wrote in his book "The human being is a machine" that just as a person's feet have muscles to walk, the human brain also has muscles to think about. After the industrial revolution, the construction of the machine became complicated, and its functions became more powerful. So, some people thought that maybe when the structure of the machine achieves a certain degree of complication, it is possible to have such a function of consciousness. In the 19th century, following this logic, German materialists said that consciousness is the function of the brain. The relationship between the mind and brain is like the urine to the kidney and the bile to the liver.

Does matter determine consciousness or does consciousness determine matter? The following is an analysis of this. Still, we use the video game as a reference.

There are two types of characters in computer games. One type is called NPC, which is a non-playable character. They are completely controlled by the system and are purely systemic puppets. For example, the merchant in the game that you click on when buying or selling the item is the NPC. The other is called PCC, which is the player-controlled character. They are players behind these characters outside the system, and their consciousness is completely independent of the system. Simply put, the game character you registered is PCC.

Are all kinds of life in nature like NPCs or PCCs in games? This problem is a bit complicated. We know that inorganic matter is dead, and life is alive. As long as it is a living thing, it can sense the stimuli of the environment and make a reaction that is selective rather than completely mechanical.

In the game we play, behind the PCC is the player, who embodies the free will of the player. Whatever things happen in the game, is derived from the player's own choice, not the system's decision. The NPC is the exact opposite. There is no free will in its body, it is completely controlled by the system, and its behavior in the game is mechanical.

Even plants can sense and react actively. For example, the flytrap can sense the presence of insects and catch insects with its insect traps. So, from this perspective, life is not an NPC.

From the broadest point of view, all life in nature is sensational, including bacteria, viruses, and plants. The low-level creatures' sensation is primitive, and they only show responses to the environment, and the animals with brains will show a clear consciousness. Dogs have superb memory and can remember the appearances of their former masters after many years; dolphins have good learning abilities, and they can be trained to perform; bees have their language and can pass through dance the information where there is pollen. This evidence shows that animals not only have their consciousness but also know how to communicate with their peers the information that exists in their consciousness.

Life is not NPC; will it be PCC? Not exactly. The creatures are not controlled by the player outside the system, and they have their consciousness. But the consciousness of biology is not completely independent of the system. Most creatures have a low level of consciousness and can only act by instinct. Instinct is the programmatic behavioral rule that the system gives to creatures. Animals have no choice in front of instinct. For example, even if the moth is burned to death, it will still be driven to the flame by instinct. So biological behavior is not completely independent, and there is still some control over the system.

Once I went back to my hometown. Because I hadn't gone back for a long time, my brother's dog had never seen me before, so it didn't know me. It barked at me so fiercely at first. But, after having stayed at home for a while, when I passed by it after lunch, it lay there not bothering me anymore. Throughout the whole process, no one made any indication to the dog, but it had adjusted its behavior. The dog has its consciousness. It can judge whether the person is kind or malicious according to the owner's attitude and use this to determine how it should react.

Does the flytrap also have a judgment? When it catches insects, is it because of the reaction to the presence of insects, or is it purely an action out of unconsciousness? Just like the mousetrap suddenly caught the mouse. It isn't because it was conscious of the existence of the mouse, but because the mouse touched the organ.

The biological instinctive response is not controlled by consciousness; otherwise, you will say that the moth is stupid enough when it is consciously rushing into the fire.

In contrast, human beings have relatively independent mental abilities, are less controlled by instinct, and have greater freedom in behavior. Human rationality can suppress instinct to a certain extent. For example, in the face of the temptation of a sexy beauty, a normal man will be drawn to the lady and begin to flirt, as long as he is normal and has an instinctive impulse. But not everyone will take further action because rationality tells us that morality and law do not allow us to do so. Although instinct does not completely dominate human behavior, just like animals, its impact on humans is still enormous. From this perspective, human behavior is not completely independent.

Life in nature is all between NPC and PCC, with a sense of freedom, but the behavior is not completely independent. In comparison, humans are closer to PCCs and have stronger independence; other forms of life are closer to NPCs, which are instinctive and have poor independence.

Why does life have consciousness?

As early as 6,000 years ago, the ancient Egyptians believed in the existence of the soul. They believed that they would be resurrected in another world after death, so the body should be made into a mummy that would not rot so that it could re-integrate with the soul in the underground. This shows that people have begun to use the soul to explain the existence of consciousness.

Many people think that there are two different things in the creatures. One is the body that exists in material form, and the other is the soul that exists in spiritual form. When the Creator created life, he also created their bodies and souls. The soul is the reason for life's possession of consciousness.

This point of view is called duality in philosophy, which states that both spirit and matter are two things that coexist at the same time. However, be it materialism or idealism, there is only one thing, and the other is derived from it. This is called monism. Descartes is a typical dualist. He believes that spirit and matter are completely different in nature. They are independent of each other. There is no question of who decides whom or who derives from whom.

Most religions in the world believe that each life has its independent soul. After the body is destroyed, the soul can still exist. After death, some souls ascend to heaven and some to hell. But in modern times, science dominates the mainstream thinking of society. Most people no longer agree with the existence of the soul in the world. They believe that consciousness is only the function of the brain, not something independent of matter.

Does the soul exist? Is it the reason why life has consciousness? We can analyze it by comparison with the computer's workflow.

A computer can be easily divided into four components: an input device, a central processing unit (CPU), internal memory, and an output device. Its workflow is like this: first, the input; before the computer works, we need to input information through an input device, such as a keyboard or an optical drive, and this information is essentially data; then the CPU processes the data, this is a computational process; throughout the entire process the information that needs to be recorded is stored in the internal memory; finally, the output of the resulting information, which may be a set of data, a table, an article on the display screen, or a picture from the printer, or a song played by the speakers.

When you think about it, you will find that the computer's workflow is very similar to that of the human brain. The input device of the human brain is a sensory organ, including vision, touch, taste, smell, and hearing. For example, there are photoreceptors on the retina of the eye. Once the light hits the retina, the photoprotein in the photoreceptor will generate a current signal, transmitting the outside information to the brain; the brain is the CPU and the memory, and the information can be processed and stored in the form of memory; and the output can be a picture drawn by hand, a song or words from the mouth, or an expression on the face.

Of course, there is still a difference between the computer and the human brain. The latter is much more powerful. And their ways to process data are different. The input of the computer is data, and the processing result is still data in essence; whereas, the input of the human brain is data, but the processing result can be data, a feeling, or some kind of judgment, which is consciousness. The computer will never feel the input information, but the human brain can. This is its mystery. For example, when the robot reaches the boiling water, the data of "100°C" appears in the brain; when the person puts his hand in, the result is "hot." No clue? And these feelings are still the same. For example, seeing blue is a visual effect, but we can have a "cool" feeling in our minds. Also, computers generally only process certain data, but the human brain can do a fuzzy procession. For example, we can feel the atmosphere of a certain occasion, but the computer cannot convert the "atmosphere" into data.

Although the computer and the human brain are functionally different, their workflows are similar. Sometimes the function of the machine will make people feel wonderful. Many people have had such an experience when they were young, thinking that the song on the radio was actually from someone singing inside.

Computational power is a very important function of human thinking activities, and a lifeless computer made up of machinery can also have powerful computing power. From this, can we infer that thinking is just a function of the brain, perhaps just like computing power is just the function of a computer? Perhaps consciousness is naturally produced in the process of processing the information provided by the senses. Therefore, there is no need for the soul to explain the existence of consciousness.

Feelings can't be translated into algorithms. For example, on a certain occasion, the atmosphere is very depressing, and you feel uncomfortable. This is easy to describe with words, but it is difficult to express it with data. But people know how to adapt to the atmosphere. On a sad occasion, such as a funeral, you will consciously remain silent without laughing.

When one saw the blue sea, one would have a feeling of coolness in his heart. This is a psychological phenomenon of human beings, called Synesthesia. It is the functioning and communication of different sensory organs at the same time. Synesthesia is very common in life; for example, when you smile very sweetly, there is a connection between vision and taste; The famed Chinese writer Zhu Ziqing once wrote in his essay The Lotus Pond in the Moonlight: "The breeze brought fragrances along its path as if a melody was played from the high building in the distance. This is the connection between smell and hearing.

The reason why we think so is that we missed one important thing. The previous analysis of the workflow of computers is not comprehensive. It only mentions the hardware and does not take the software into account.

A computer without any software is called a bare metal, and a bare metal computer will not work properly. It needs to be installed with two kinds of software; one is called the system software, such as the operating system, the language processing system, etc.; the other is called the application software, such as the office software Word, the web browser IE.

Here comes the problem. For the computer, only the hardware is not enough. You need the software to support it to work properly. Doesn't the human brain work like this?

The organism is mainly composed of inanimate organic matter, but why does organic matter have no signs of life, and why is the organism composed of organic matter so different? If you can understand why the computer needs the software to make it work, it is quite easy for you to understand this question.

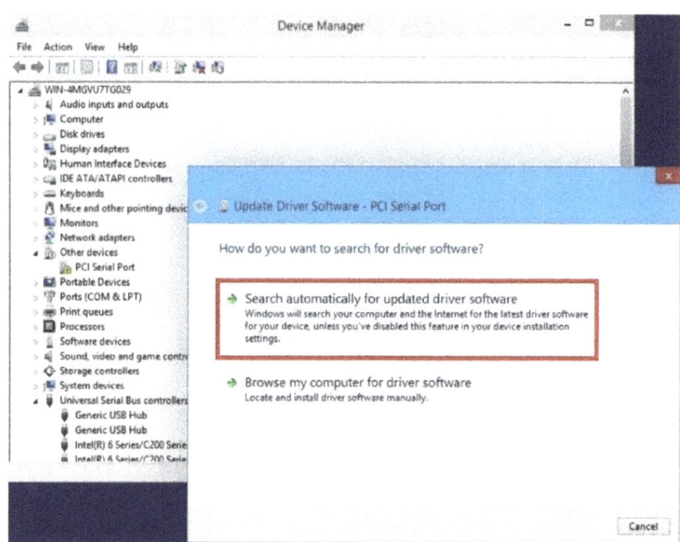

If the computer does not have a driver installed, it will not work properly. The driver is the reason why the device can run autonomously. By the same token, organisms can sense the stimuli of the environment and respond autonomously, indicating that they must have a driver.

Some people suddenly became mad and mentally ill when they were greatly stimulated. If you think of the human as a machine, then this is a bit strange, because, from the hardware point of view, his brain structure is not physically damaged at this time, no different from when he was a normal person. Why can't this machine work properly?

This fact reminds us that the normal operation of the human brain requires the support of software. The reason why mental patients are mentally disordered is not because of the hardware, but because of the strong stimulus. The strong stimulus caused logical errors in the running of the software in the brain, resulting in system failure.

Any life is a complete working system. There should be something like the system software, which we can call the soul of life.

Soul and flesh are equivalent to the relationship between the software and the hardware in computers. Consciousness is equivalent to the perception of the outside world and self, which is generated by the system when it runs the software. Therefore, consciousness is the function of the soul, not the function of matter. It is precise because the most important life phenomenon of an organism is not from matter but from the soul that the organism looks so different from organic matter

Here we need to emphasize that many people often confuse soul with consciousness. There is a difference between them.

Human beings have a sense of autonomy. It is controlling our words and deeds. When we are hungry, we will go looking for something to eat. If we are thirsty, we will go to find water. This phenomenon is easy to create a feeling that all human behavior is made under the guidance of consciousness, but this is completely wrong.

The reality is that in most cases, the physical response is made in an unconscious state. Consciousness disappears when sleeping at night, but we are still breathing regularly, and all parts of the body are still functioning normally; even in the awake state, our bodies are more often unconsciously reacting, and conscious behaviors only account for a minority. For example, our consciousness does not command the heart to beat, but it has been beating all the time.

From this point of view, soul and consciousness are not the same things. The soul is like the system software and driver of our body, it controls our entire body; whereas, consciousness is only a function of the soul, and it only works at a relatively high level. This is like when you are listening to music on a computer. You click on a song in the player, which is equivalent to a behavior led by consciousness; then the performance of those tasks of reading the song file, calling the decoder to decode, and sending the signal to the speaker does not require you to issue instructions one by one, the operating system will automatically complete these tasks, which is equivalent to the automatic response of the soul driver in a state without the control of consciousness.

As the operation of the software is inseparable from the hardware, this is why the soul needs to depend on the physical existence of flesh. Once the body dies, the soul will disappear. When the brain tissue is seriously injured, people will be unconscious, just like a hardware failure in the computer, and the operation of the software will be affected. When one sleeps, the brain will go to sleep. This is equivalent to the computer being on standby. When the computer is in standby mode, many applications will stop running. So, in sleep, the human consciousness is interrupted, and man temporarily loses consciousness.

The operation of the software must depend on the hardware. It cannot exist independently or function independently. This is easy to create an illusion that the hardware is determining the software. Just as materialists believe that matter is determining consciousness, consciousness is derived from matter, and it is a vassal of matter. But in fact, the soul and the flesh are two separate things, just as software and hardware are two completely different things. For life, the two are equally important and indispensable.

Although software needs to rely on hardware to run, it does not mean that it is completely subject to hardware. The function of the hardware must be realized with the support of the software. Otherwise, it is just a pile of copper scraps. It is the same for life. If there is no spirit, the organism is a pile of dead flesh. The software can also affect the hardware, and some virus programs can attack the hardware system and damage the hardware. By the same token, the spirit also has an important influence on the body. Spiritual pleasure plays a positive role in physical health; and when the spirit is severely damaged, it can seriously damage the health of the body.

The computer system is composed of hardware and software. They are independent and interdependent. No matter which one is missing, it is no longer a complete system. The same is true for the body and the soul. They together make up life. Once they are separated, the body becomes a corpse, and the soul will have nowhere to dwell.

Sometimes there are some special circumstances. For example, people will dream. How does it happen? This is the case: the computer will sometimes perform a self-test in the standby state, and some system software will occasionally run by itself. The soul should also be like this. Dreaming is the automatic operation of the system software while the body is in a dormant state.

There are also some special states of consciousness. For example, some people had already died, but later they came back to life, and they would have some indescribable experience. What is going on with these death experiences? There is a simple explanation. When the computer restarts after an abnormal shutdown, the software function is often abnormal, and the human brain maybe works the same way.

Why do some animals look smarter, and some others look stupid when they all have souls? The reason is simple. The principles of a calculator are the same as those of a computer. They both have input, output, processor, and memory. Why are they so much different in function? Because their internal structures are different in complexity and their running procedures are different. The same is true for living creatures. Bacteria and viruses have simple structures. Correspondingly, there is only simple system software. Just like a calculator, they have simple functions. The human brain is much larger than other animals, and much more complicated, so the performance is much better; the installed system is certainly more advanced, so the function is of course more powerful.

As life evolves from a lower level to a higher level, the body structure becomes more and more complex, and the expressed consciousness becomes more and more obvious. If, as Darwin claimed, life is gradually evolving, then it is easy to understand the change in appearance, but how should the upgrade of the internal control program software be explained? How does it produce variants and become more and more advanced?

The truth is that Darwin did not pay attention to this issue at all. Consciousness is still a mystery to the biological world, so biologists directly ignore this extremely important factor when discussing the process of evolution of life. If we think carefully, it is not difficult to find out that evolution does not explain the emergence and progress of consciousness. It is simply a lame theory.

Perhaps the purpose of the Creator to endow the human being with consciousness is to create a PCC in his system. Animals are also thinking. Gorillas and dolphins are said to have IQs equivalent to those of two or three-year-olds and therefore have relatively low-level thinking abilities. So, fundamentally there is no qualitative difference between humans and animals in this respect, they are just different in degree.

A highly developed human brain gives humans an important ability to express their consciousness. Its original forms may be facial expressions, and gestures, and later on it develops into painting, music, speech, written language, and mathematical formulas. People can communicate with each other about their understanding of the world and their emotional feelings.

This is an indication that humans are significantly more advanced than other animals. Perhaps there is only basic system software in the animal's brain or a simple driver, no more advanced applications, so most animals behave only by instinct. The function of the system software of the human brain is much more powerful, and many applications with learning functions can be run on this base, so the human learning ability is very strong, and the consciousness can always be improved.

The soul is there. But what is the soul? Where does it come from?

Eben Alexander's Soul Journey

In October 2012, the US magazine Newsweek published a cover article by Dr. Eben Alexander, a professor at Harvard Medical School and a well-known neurosurgeon. He claimed that he had been to paradise, and this is not an illusion. The first episode of the documentary Walking Through the Wormhole with Morgan Freeman II: Is There a Life After Death also talks about this event.

Alexander is a Christian, but he has no deep religious beliefs. He did not believe that there was a paradise in the world, nor did he believe in the experience of dying. He believed that the sudden death experience described by people could be explained by science. However, a personal experience in the fall of 2008 changed his opinion.

At that time, he suffered from rare bacterial meningitis. The cerebral cortical neurons were trapped in a "disfunction" state, and he had been in a coma for seven days. During this time, his body was unaware, and the advanced functions of the brain ceased to function, but his self-consciousness went to another world. In this new world, his consciousness was separated from the limitations of the brain and the body, becoming an independent existence. It was this experience that made him believe that death is not the end of the soul, but a small episode in a long journey.

Alexander told of the paradise he saw. He saw big loose clouds floating in the deep blue sky. Above the clouds, flocks of glowing transparent creatures flew in the sky, leaving a long streamer-like trace. These creatures were different from any creature on earth. They were more advanced forms of life. Later, he heard huge sounds from the sky, like the chanting of hymns. These sounds came from the mysterious creatures flying in the sky, indulging him in a blissful feeling.

In most of the journey, Alexander was not alone. A beautiful woman was accompanying him. The first time he saw her, Alexander and she were on a plane with a complex pattern. Later, he recognized it was the butterfly's wing. They were surrounded by countless flying butterflies, which formed a colorful river of life flowing in the air.

The beautiful lady was gazing at him. There was not a hint of love or friendship in her expression. This was an expression that transcended all emotions on the earth. The expression made people feel that it not only carried all types of love but also went beyond that. Without employing any words, the lady could transmit a message to him. The message read, "I will show you a lot of things here, but in the end, you still have to go back."

They continued to move on, entering into a huge void. It was completely dark there. The expanses were infinitely wide and remote, making one feel extremely comfortable. Although it was dark, Alexander felt the existence of light. The light seemed to originate from a bright sphere. He felt the sphere was nearby. It played the role of a translator, allowing him to communicate with the world around him. He felt like a newborn baby, having just been born into a broader brand-new world. The whole world is like a huge womb, and the sphere is guiding him. The 17th-century poet Henry Vaughan wrote: "Some people say that the place where God lives is deep but dazzling darkness." Later, Alexander discovered that this magical place was like the one described in Vaughan's verses, which was where God lives.

Based on his own experience, Alexander wrote "The Evidence of Paradise". He said: "I am still a doctor, and I am still a scientist as before. But from the bottom of my heart, I am not who I was in the past." As an experienced and well-known neurosurgeon and a teacher who had taught at one of the most prestigious universities in the United States for many years, Alexander used to think that consciousness is only produced by the brain, and the universe has no emotions. But after going through the near-death experience, Alexander became suspicious of this. He began to believe that human consciousness can be hosted by more than the human brain.

There are many more people who have had a sudden-death experience like Alexander. Their narratives have some striking similarities, such as the soul leaving the body, seeing the light, and feeling profound peace and tranquility. Are these experiences just hallucinations?

Chapter 19

The Magical Power:
After the Function of the Flesh Closes,
the Function of the Soul Opens.

Although modern science cannot explain clearly where consciousness comes from, scientists do not recognize that people have souls， and they are unwilling to use the soul to explain the existence of consciousness.

Why does this happen? Let us look at how science knows the world: first, identify a phenomenon, that is, to discover objective facts in nature through observation or scientific experiments; then propose a hypothesis, that is, to form opinions that can explain this phenomenon; finally, to verify, that is, to draw some inference for verification and testing by experiment.

It can be seen that the human understanding of the external world depends on two aspects: senses and thinking. We need to rely on our sensory perceptions to identify phenomena. We need to rely on thinking to analyze and make assumptions. We need to rely on sensory perception feedback to verify whether the inference is correct or not.

The use of this method hides a precondition that the external world we want to know must be capable of being directly or indirectly perceived by the senses, and everyone perceives the same so that verification can be conducted repeatedly. For example, the inference from the general theory of relativity that "light will bend in a strong gravitational field" will hold, no matter who verifies it. If the light is bent when you look at it, the light is not bent when I look at it, then this is not science.

People use this method to understand the external world, and the results are remarkable. On this basis, a set of scientific theoretical systems has been established. However, this method is not effective in understanding the inner spiritual world, so people still know very little about the operating mechanism of consciousness until now. Why is this?

The reason is simple. Our inner spiritual world is different from the external material world, in which the senses lose their roles. For a piece of cake, we can see its shape, feel its texture, smell its aroma, taste its flavor, and hear the sound of eating it. However, we can't sense the soul that exists in the spiritual form through the senses. It is completely virtual to us. It can't be seen, touched, smelled, tasted, or heard. This is a headache for us.

The soul, for a long time, can't sense its existence, and we can't measure it. So, we think that the spirit is only an illusory phenomenon, and it is the function of the brain. Because it is not sensed, it is difficult to carry out the first step in the research method mentioned above, let alone make assumptions and verify them. For this reason, the study of the pure spiritual field has become a forbidden area for science.

Isn't there any way to study the soul? Of course, this is not true. But before we can study something, we must be able to reach it. So, we must try first to solve the problem: how can we enter the spiritual world?

In this respect, eastern cultures are far ahead of western cultures. There have been many great master's in history, and the Chinese philosopher Zhuangzi is an expert in this field. He once said that the farther we are away from our material being, the closer we will be to the inner soul. When we completely abandon the role of the senses and thinking, the mind will become acute, and we can sense the world with our hearts. Just as when blind people lose their sight, their hearing will become more powerful; completely color-blind patients can't see any color, but they can capture the changes of shades of light and shadow better than us, and see what we can't see at night.

Zhuangzi called this the fasting of spirit, which involves excluding the senses, eliminating disturbances and distractions, and making the state of mind empty and pure. In the Book of Human life, Zhuangzi said: "If you are determined, if you cannot listen with your ears, you will learn to listen with your heart; if you cannot listen with your heart, you will learn to listen with your spirit. Listening will stop at your ears; your heart will stop at concrete symbols. As spirit is void and formless, it can deal with anything. Tao is the only thing that can subsume void. Void is the fasting of spirit." He meant that the fasting of the spirit is to isolate the senses and empty the heart so that the soul can sense the laws of the heavens by spirit.

In The Great Master, Zhuangzi described this process through the mouth of a female puppet. "I am still fasting and I am told that after three days I will be able to go outside the world; after I have gone outside the world, I will fast again, and then I will be a foreign object after seven days; after being a foreign object, I will fast again, I can gain a rebirth after nine days; after I have got a rebirth, I can gain a sudden insight; after I have gained the sudden insight, I can see what I couldn't see before." According to him, by keeping the mind empty and gradually forgetting the world, all things, and even oneself, one can fully understand the Tao.

The world is fair, and when you lose here, you will be compensated there. This principle is often validated in people with physical disabilities. This principle is used

This process can be achieved through meditation, which Zhuangzi calls "sitting and forgetting." The Great Master says: "Falling out of limbs, making acumen blunt, and knowing away from the form, is equivalent to the great consummation and fulfillment, and this is called 'sitting and forgetting." During meditation, forget the feelings of the limbs and stop the activities of thinking, to enter the pure realm of the void where one completely forgets oneself and the surrounding things, and you can enter the mysterious spiritual world.

Zhuangzi's method is very simple in principle. The flesh and soul are two different systems. Normally, we use the abilities related to the flesh, and part of the soul's functions will lay dormant. When we close the functions associated with the flesh, that is, the functions of the senses and thinking, the deep functions of the soul are awakened and activated. This is the same as the principle of amblyopia treatment. When the child has one eye normal and the other eye is amblyopic, the doctor uses glasses to cover the normal eye, forcing him to see things with the amblyopic eye, to stimulate the restoration of its function and gradually improve his eyesight.

Zhuangzi's thoughts are in the same line as Lao Tze's. In Lao Tze's Tao De Jing, there are similar words, such as "to the ultimate in emptiness, keep quiet and sincere", and "Carry the body and spirit and embrace unity, can you be inseparable? Concentrate on breathing and breathe as smoothly as possible, can you be like a baby? Eliminate the speculations; can you go to the extent of being flawless?" The Taoist school founded by Lao Tze and Zhuangzi has a characteristic of its practice method, which involves the concept of *qi*, and their practice method can be called " training of *qi*.

In reality, I have met many friends who practice such a way of energy control. Originally my wife's lumbar and cervical diseases were very serious, and she often suffered from dizziness. Later, she began to practice *Qi* (energy control) under the guidance of a friend. The effect was indeed very obvious, and the symptoms have been greatly relieved.

The Taoist practice method is not the only one. In the days when Lao Tse and Zhuangzi lived, another method of practice has long been circulated in distant India, that is, "meditation."

In principle, there is no essential difference between meditation and the Taoist practice method, but the details are much clearer. Meditation first requires observing the precepts, such as no killing life, no stealing, no vulgarity, no swearing, and no alcohol drinking. This is to guard the door of the senses and control the information that enters through the senses, so as not to allow more stimuli to flow into to distract the heart. It can be likened to this: our heart is like a juicer, and our senses are like a power plug. Plugging in the power, our hearts may be messed up; and once the plug is unplugged, no current passes through, and our hearts will stop throbbing and return to peace.

Therefore, meditation practitioners are often warned that sensory stimulation can only bring short-lived satisfaction and that the pursuit of sensory satisfaction is unrealistic. Everything is born and gone, the world is impermanent. The external material world cannot be permanent, so we shouldn't care much about external things. And we should be far away from external stimuli and return to our peace of mind. These statements are close to Zhuangzi's idea on foreign things.

After isolating the sensory functions, the next step is to eliminate the function of thinking, to achieve peace of mind, and to achieve ecstasy. For meditation practitioners, five obstacles are to be ruled out at this time, namely greed, hatred, drowsiness and laziness, restlessness and worry, and doubts. These obstacles are called "five covers." After letting go of everything and abandoning the ego, the mind will reach complete silence and peace, and no longer have any thoughts. At this time, the functions related to the flesh have stopped. Another system in the body will start. We will feel like entering a completely different world.

Meditation is the same as sitting and forgetting, and it is more practiced by sitting in quietness, so it is also known as "sitting meditation." It is a very complex spiritual practice system with distinct levels and is divided into different levels according to the level of the realm, so-called "Four Zens and Eight Sets." India is the nation with the most research on soul cultivation in the world. In addition to meditation, India also has another well-known cultivation system, which is yoga.

Yoga is also a mind cultivation practice method, as a yoga master said. "Yoga is the science of the soul, the science of practice." Unlike *Qi* training and meditation, yoga has a special secret book of practice, the Yoga Sutra, which proposes eight kinds of exercises, also known as the Eight Limbs of Yoga. These exercises are *Yamas*, which refers to observing the precepts; niyamas, which means observing moral principles; asana, which refers to mastering the body to sit still for meditation; pranayama, which are yoga breathing techniques designed to control prana or vital life force; pratyahara, which means withdrawal of the senses; *Dharana*, which refers to concentration on a place in the body or focusing on an object of the outside world; dhyana, which is the practice of meditation, making the mind unite with the object focused on; samadhi, which is merging with the divine, the attainment of the union of mind and the object of concentration. In the third level of *samadhi, dharmamegha samadhi*, all changes and functions of the mind have been extinguished, completely reaching the state of being in union with the focused object, and this is the highest state of yoga.

After comparison, you will find that the principles of yoga and meditation are more or less the same. Both require the seclusion of the senses to separate the stimulus from the senses, and the emptiness of the mind by cutting off the thinking. The difference is that yoga highlights the body-adjusting posture, breath-adjusting breathing method, and mind-adjusting meditation, which are different in form. In addition, yoga uses attention-shifting techniques to interrupt thinking activities. First, it focuses attention on a specific object, interrupts other thinking activities, and then mingles the mind with the focused object, thereby interrupting all the conscious thinking activities.

The flesh and soul are two independent systems in human beings. Logically, since we can exercise the physical body and improve the body's functions through sports, it is entirely possible to exercise the spirit and improve it in some way. In the experience, all our knowledge relies on sensory organs and reasoning, which are all related to the flesh, and the deep functions of the soul are inhibited. However, *Qigong*, meditation, yoga, and other practice methods all provide us with a way to exercise our souls and thus open the door to the spiritual world.

Unfortunately, these methods of practice are not as intuitive, practical, and effective as physical exercise. The process of spiritual practice is very long and arduous, and it is difficult to master the know-how. Most people cannot persevere, and even more, people can't even find the right path. And in this age of material desires, temptation is everywhere, and it is even more difficult to cultivate the mild.

Just as swimming, basketball, and running are all different ways of physical exercise, Qi training, meditation, and yoga are also different ways of spiritual cultivation. Different physical exercise methods will eventually bring about improvements in physical functions. Will different spiritual cultivation methods bring the same results?

Yes. In the end, these different methods of practice all reach the same goal by different paths, and they enter the same realm: "entering concentration." People who practice *Qi* training can enter concentration after reaching a certain level. People who practice yoga need to enter concentration through meditation after adjusting their bodies and breathing to a certain level. Both of these methods involve the process of progression, with an emphasis on gradual and orderly progress. However, meditation is done in one step, directly rushing to the realm of concentration, so the success rate will be relatively low because the mind is easily overwhelmed in the absence of gradual progression of practice.

"We pursue wealth, power, fame, and many other material things painstakingly all our life, but they are nothing to us if we don't have good health." These words are now deeply rooted in the hearts of many people, so they attach great importance to exercise, but not many people will care about cultivating their souls.

Former President of the University of Taiwan, Professor Li Sicen (李嗣涔) has used scientific methods to study this phenomenon. At the beginning of 1989, with the help of two brainwave experts from the Department of Neurology, National Taiwan University Hospital, he invited many master's from various martial art schools to measure their brainwaves. It was confirmed that there are significant changes in the brainwaves when they practice and there are two distinct states. *Qi* practitioners are initially in the "resonance" phase, at which time their brainwaves will increase significantly. But after reaching a higher level, people who practice *Qi* or meditate will enter the "concentration" stage, at which time their brainwaves will be suppressed or even disappear.

This phenomenon proves that when the mind is in an ethereal state and the thinking activity is weakened or even stopped, the brain waves are suppressed until they disappear. At this time, the deep function of the soul is awakened. It replaces consciousness and takes over us. We can enter the spiritual world and be in a mysterious state. This is "entering concentration."

When it comes to entering concentration, many people will think of such a picture: the meditator sits still, his body is motionless, and there is no thinking like a dead person. This is a misunderstanding of the entry to deep concentration. Sitting cross-legged helps to calm the mind, so if you want to enter a concentration state, this posture is most commonly used. But in fact, sitting in peace may not be able to enter concentration; vice versa, entering concentration may not necessarily require sitting in peace.

When someone concentrates on a certain skill or object, they can enter a state of concentration without knowing it. In Zhuangzi's The Master of Health, the slaughter of the cow, Pao Ding, said: "When I first cut the cow, what I saw was nothing but a cow. Three years later, I never saw the whole cow. And now I can sense the cow without using my eyes. My senses stop working while my spirit works." This man worked so hard and focused so much that he finally achieved sensing with the soul instead of seeing with his eyes, the realm where sensory perception is completely stopped, and the soul is activated. The "spirit" mentioned here is the soul. And Pao Ding accidentally entered a state of concentration when he killed the cow.

This can be mutually confirmed with yoga exercise methods. *Dharana* in the Eight Limbs of Yoga is to make the mind focus on a certain object. When this kind of concentration develops to the extreme, where the mind and the focused object are united into one, you can enter the state of being concentrated.

Many strange phenomena are happening in the state of entering concentration. Compared with spiritual encounters and spiritual travel mentioned by Zhuangzi, the more mysterious is spiritual daydreaming. The Book of Masters: The Yellow Emperor has this description: "I slept during the day and dreamed of a journey to the land of Huaxu people. The land of Huaxu is to the west of Yaozhou prefecture and the north of Taizhou prefecture. As it is thousands of miles away from the *Qi* kingdom, it is impossible to travel there by cart or by boat. I assume it is just a spiritual journey." People usually think of the spiritual journey as the journey that the spirits are capable of making. But in fact, many of those who can enter the deep state of concentration have had such real spiritual wandering experiences: the soul can directly observe the external world, and can even come out of the body, break through the boundary of space, reach other levels of space, and make spiritual communications with life there.

These strange phenomena that appear under certain conditions are called "supernatural powers" by Buddhism. There are six kinds of magical powers: the opening of the heavenly eye, the opening of the heavenly ear, the opening to other hearts, the opening of heavenly travel, the opening to fates, and the opening to infinity. They are the capabilities possessed by the soul, and they are completely different from the functions of the flesh. This is incredible!

After entering concentration, many people will have wisdom beyond the ordinary. The explanation for this phenomenon is that when the consciousness controls us, the deep functions of the soul are in a dormant state, and we rely on the senses and thinking to know about the world; and when the soul directly controls us, the consciousness enters a dormant state, and then we can rely directly on the soul to perceive the world. Soul perception, an unusual method of perception, will give us a brand-new cognition of the world. This cognition transcends senses and thinking, transcends our experience, and possesses extraordinary wisdom.

Zhuangzi has a full understanding of this, and he uses "the thorough understanding in the morning" and "the unique perception" to describe this phenomenon. Lao Tze also knows this well, so he said in the Tao De Jing: "Nothingness is the way of the universe, and I want to observe the best" and advocated observing the mysteries of the universe in an empty state. At the same time, he also said: "Pursue the extreme of emptiness, keep peace and sincerity. As all things work together, I can observe them again and again." He believes that by observing the cycle of growth of all things in a state of extreme emptiness one can often make great achievements.

There is a similar saying in meditation; that is, "precept, concentration, and wisdom." It is believed that by keeping the precepts and entering a state of concentration, great wisdom can be produced, and the truth of the universe can be seen through this. This method of meditation is called "insight after inhibition." "Inhibition" is the cessation of breath and mind, and "insight" is seeing all truths. Insight after inhibition means that the wisdom generated from entering concentration can gain insight into the truth.

We had doubts about a question before, that is, where does Lao Tze's wisdom which is beyond time and space come from? Modern science is so advanced, but we still have no way to prove that the world is illusory. How did Lao Tze know about this? Why was he able to make such a clear description of the process of the world's generation that even modern science could not exceed?

If you just guess that the world is illusory, that's nothing, because many people have had this idea since ancient times. However, Lao Tze established a strict philosophical system on this basis. The Tao Te Ching contains a complete theoretical framework of the world outlook, the development outlook, the values, and the outlook on life. We have already revealed some of the incredible wisdom contained therein, but that is just the tip of the iceberg.

Lao Tze was the director of the National Library of the Zhou Dynasty, but his wisdom far surpassed that era, especially about the concept of the creation process of Tao. We can't believe that he can get it from books. This is because even modern people can't even think of these ideas, or accept them, let alone the people of that era.

Now this problem can be explained. It turns out that in addition to the senses and thinking, there is another way for humans to understand the world, through which they can perceive the true meaning of the universe that ordinary people cannot obtain. Before the rise of science， the extraordinary wisdom that Lao Tze and Siddhartha have shown far beyond their times may all have come from this.

Lao Tze said in the Tao Te Ching: "You know the world without going out; you see the way of heaven without looking out of windows; if you go far away, you may know less." We once didn't understand why Lao Tze said that you can stay at home and still understand the world, why the farther you go, the less you know. This statement seems very illogical. Now we finally understand that for spiritual practitioners, there are other channels besides the senses and thinking for them to understand the world. In the state of the spiritual journey, through the perception of the soul, it is indeed possible to understand the information of the outside world without leaving the house. As Zhuangzi said, "Those who are strong in their desires are further away from the truth." If you have gone to many places, known about many things, and received many stimuli and temptations, it is even more difficult to calm down and understand the truth of heaven.

When we study the ultimate question of the world, we will find that science and philosophy have reached the same goal by different paths. The conclusions reached by modern scientific methods are essentially the same as those drawn by Lao Tze and Siddhartha more than 2500 years ago. This can't help but be reminiscent of a popular sentence: "When scientists climbed to the top of the

mountain with great pain, philosophers have already been there waiting for them for a long time."

With the Internet, you can watch the news from all over the world and get a lot of information without leaving home. If you collect it yourself, you may not know so much. This shows that the appropriate way can break through the original cognitive barriers.

The above-mentioned methods of practice all come from the East, but there is also a way of thinking in the West, called transcendentalism. Kant said in The Critique of Pure Reason: "Some knowledge is not related to the object, but only related to the way we know the object, and this cognitive method is innate. I call this kind of knowledge transcendental." Emerson, an American thinker of the 19th century, created the trend of transcendentalism. He said: "There are very important ideas and necessary forms that do not come from experience. On the contrary, people get experience through them. They are intuition of our soul itself." Kant called intuition "the transcendental form." This may have the same meaning as Confucius's notion of "innate knowledge."

The knowledge that people accumulate through their senses and thinking is called experience. It is the basis for understanding the world through scientific methods, while "transcendence" transcends experience. Transcendentalists also believe that there is another way besides experience. People can perceive the outside world and know the truth of nature purely through their hearts. So, transcendentalists have a motto: "Belief in yourself."

Unlike what happens in the East, there is no systematic method of spiritual practice in the West. The occasional appearance of individuals who have transcendental experience is because they are inherently different and sensitive in this respect. That's why Kant thinks that transcendental phenomena are congenital and innate. But, with the help of Eastern practice methods, ordinary people can experience this kind of experience, and they don't necessarily need to be born with this ability. This is what Kant doesn't know.

We used to think that humans came up with the concept of gods out of fear of nature and/or not knowing how to explain natural phenomena. However, according to the experience of spiritual practitioners, a simple-minded person is easier to practice than a sophisticated-minded person, an uneducated person is easier to practice than an educated person, and a child is easier to practice than an adult. This shows that the purer the heart is, the easier the potential of the soul is stimulated. The ignorant minds of primitive people are much purer than ours, just like children, so they are more likely to produce magical powers and are more likely to perceive intelligent life in higher-level dimensions. The beast's sensing ability is much sharper than ours and can react before an earthquake strikes, but we humans are unaware of the imminent disaster. Perhaps it is precise because of this sort of magic power that the idea of gods was born in the hearts of early humans, not entirely out of fear and ignorance.

Although we cannot touch the spiritual world through our senses and thoughts, we can perceive it by activating the soul's functions. This creates the necessary conditions for us to understand the spiritual world. On this basis, can we use scientific methods to conduct more in-depth research on it and get clearer results? Let's take a look at what Professor Zhu Qingshi, an academician of the Chinese Academy of Sciences and former president of the University of Science and Technology of China, said. In December 2012, Professor Zhu Qingshi gave a speech on *"Where did we come from and where will we go to--the universe of science and Buddhism."* In his speech, he said that science and Buddhism have different ways of knowing the truth. "The objects of natural science research are objective entities that exist independently of the observer. No matter who observes or by what method, the results should be the same. This is the principle of repeatability. The Buddhist method of knowing the truth is 'discovery through karma', which refers to discovering the truth of the universe at the corresponding level according to the level of one's karma and cognitive ability."

Professor Zhu added that by entering a state of meditation to improve cognitive ability, one can perceive the truth of the universe that ordinary people cannot obtain. This is another way for humans to understand the world apart from the scientific methods of logical reasoning and experiment. But there is a big problem with this approach, that is, as each person's abilities and levels are different, they recognize different things. Therefore, this method does not apply to everyone like the scientific method, which is based on human normal sensory experience and can be verified repeatedly.

This is indeed a big problem. Since each person's spiritual cultivation realm is different, they often observe different things; and even a lesser task of making an exact description of the phenomenon will be a difficult thing. More importantly, spiritual practitioners observe the world not with the senses but with the soul, so it is difficult for them to describe the phenomena they have observed to ordinary people, just as it is difficult for you to explain clearly to the blind how colors work. For those who have no similar experience, the words of spiritual practitioners are simply unreasonable.

However, it is worth noting that the experimental methods used by Professor Li Sicen for studying mental phenomena have provided a good reference frame for problem-solving. In the experiment, Professor Li used instruments to measure the physiological changes of the practitioners, so that the experimental results were supported by the measured data, which closely linked pure personal feelings with the actual measurement results, which could greatly eliminate the possibility of creating these phenomena out of personal hallucinations. Professor Li's experiments show that by carefully designing scientific experimental methods, it is possible to show the spiritual practice experience that was originally purely personal in a clearer, standardized, and verifiable way so that more people can understand it and master it.

Current Research on the Soul

At present, there is no academic discipline devoted solely to the study of the subject of the soul in any country around the world. *Sociology* has not yet been established. The most relevant discipline is called *parapsychology*.

In 1928, Dr. Ryan, a psychologist who taught at Duke University in the United States, established the Institute of Parapsychology to research supernatural phenomena. His main research focus is extra-sensory perception. Ryan received his Ph.D. in plant physiology. He found that plants not only have vitality but also emotions. Everything in the universe, especially humans, has a high level of potential. In 1934, he published the paper "Extrasensory Perception." Later the research in this area developed into a discipline called *parapsychology*.

In 1957, Dr. Ryan founded the first academic group of extra-sensory perception, the Parapsychology Association. To make this association to be accepted by the scientific academic community, he presented several experimental pieces of evidence and statistics on supernatural powers to the most authoritative scientific body at the time, the American Association for the Advancement of Science (AAAS). After two and a half years of experimentation, he collected enough evidence to finally make AAAS accept the Parapsychology Association as a full member of it in 1969. Parapsychology has since been recognized as an emerging discipline, and its academic status is officially recognized.

Although the study of the soul is not a popular subject, the people involved in this field are not all unknown, and some of them are quite big-name scientists, such as the British physicist Roger Penrose and the 1973 Nobel prize in physics winner Brian Josephson.

Because his collaboration with Hawking has mathematically proved the existence of singularities, Roger Penrose has been repeatedly mentioned in Hawking's popular science book, which makes his name quite familiar to us. The physicist, together with Dr. Stuart Hameroff, head of the Center for Consciousness Studies at the University of Arizona, proposed a compelling theory that the human soul is located in the microtubules in brain cells. Consciousness activities are the results of the quantum gravitational effects within these microtubules. This is the

Orch-OR theory.

According to their theory, consciousness is a program of a quantum computer in the brain. This program can still exist in the universe after death. In the documentary "*Through the wormhole with Morgan Freeman*", Hameroff said: "The heart stops beating, the blood stops flowing, the microtubules lose their quantum state, but the quantum information in the microtubule is not destroyed. It can't be destroyed. It will leave the body and return to the universe. If the patient wakes up, the quantum information will return to the microtubule, and the patient will say, 'I experienced a sudden death experience.' If the patient does not wake up, the patient will be dead; this quantum information will exist outside the flesh, in the form of the soul."

Brian Josephson is a legendary figure. He made Nobel prize-winning achievements at the age of 22 and won the Nobel prize in physics at the age of 33. He is one of the youngest winners in history. However, in the next 30 years, he gave up traditional physics and changed his research focus to supernatural phenomena.

He has written many essays including "Physics and Spirit: The Next Big Unity?" in a bid to use quantum mechanics to explain supernatural and spiritual phenomena, and he also led the "Spiritual and Material Unification Plan" at the University of Cambridge. He often said that his research on supernatural phenomena is far more important than the work he had done in his youth for winning the Nobel Prize. He believes that traditional science can't do anything about the issue of consciousness, so it is necessary to study the subject of consciousness and mind.

Domestic research in this area was initiated by Professor Qian Xuesen, who called it "the science of the human body."

Professor Li Sicen's Finger Literacy Experiment

At present, in the research on the spiritual phenomenon by scientific methods, Professor Li Sicen's finger literacy experiment is a relatively valuable reference.

Professor Li Sicen was an expert in electrical engineering and later served as the president of Taiwan University. He had continually conducted experiments on finger literacy for nine years. In his experiments, the children are given short-term training to make them enter into a state of mind similar to meditation so that they could see the words or patterns on the pieces of folded paper by touching them with their fingers rather than by seeing with their eyes. Rigorous scientific methods were adopted in the experiments, especially the double-blind method adopted in the later stages. Both the subject and the tester did not know the contents of the note, and the result was very reliable.

There are many strange phenomena in the experiments done by Professor Li. The first is that after the children enter the state, there will be a screen similar to the TV screen in front of the head, and what they want to see will slowly appear on the screen.

If the eye is the visual organ of the body and we see the world through the eyes, then through the experiments of Professor Li it is shown that the soul also has its own eyes. This screen that appears in a special state is the visual organ of the soul, which we can call "the eyes of the soul." Through these eyes, the soul can bypass the body's senses, directly sense the outside world, and even see things that the eyes cannot see.

The second bizarre phenomenon is that sometimes children can sense some people on the spiritual screen. These people will communicate with the children, teach them something, and even help them to do things. The children usually call them "masters." Interestingly, through finger literacy experiments, children can easily contact their masters. When the experimental words and patterns are replaced with a long list of questions, they can send the questions to their masters and receive answers from them.

Professor Li Sicen with the author on a tour of the Three Gorges

In the conversations, the Master said that he can directly hear our voices, and even know what we are thinking, and for us, he is everywhere. When asked about some difficult questions, his answer was hesitant, and he was not sure. Even when he was deliberately asked about the script of the ancient Semitic, he did not understand the text and admitted that he had to learn.

From these characteristics analysis, we believe that these masters are intelligent beings in high-dimensional spaces, so they can see through us and are everywhere in our world. But he is not an omnipotent god, so he also has something he does not understand. He still needs to learn and cannot answer all the questions we have raised. You can the comparison. In the eyes of the two-dimensional game world of System, we are like this.

The third, even more bizarre phenomenon is that there is a structure similar to the Internet in the high-level space that the children's mind eye screens are connected to. To enter this network, they need to use some special characters as the URL, and by identifying these characters by finger literacy, they can connect to the homepage of the website. Professor Li called these websites "the websites of the gods."

On the websites of the gods, like on the Internet, as long as you know the path, you can go through the home page and enter the next page to browse. Through the path of "Jesus/SAM", the children saw a towering, magnificent gate of the cross. Then they silently recited the password "Hallelujah" and passed. They entered the door and immersed themselves in the sea of light. Through the path of "Bodhisattva/Avalokitesvara", the children saw dozens of rows of bright circles, and after asking silently in their hearts, "can I go in and see it?" they went into and visited the first, the sixth, and the eighth medical herbs gardens of the pharmacist Buddha, where they saw many strange plants. Those special characters that can be used as URLs even include such names as *Lao Tze, Confucius,* and *Lord Guan Gong.*

During the children's finger literacy experiment, Professor Li tested their physiological states. He found that if the literacy experiment was done with the right hand, the arterial blood flow rates of the middle and posterior brain would decrease by around 20 % when the spiritual eye appeared. There are voltage pulses in both hands and the pulse on the right hand is positive. In this way, by measuring the physiological changes, it can be judged whether the children's spiritual eyes are opened or not, thus providing reliable measured data for the experiment.

In August 1999, the president of the Physical Society of Taiwan led a dozen of professors of physics and psychology from the National Taiwan University, the National Tsinghua University, and the Chinese Academy of Sciences to NTU to watch Professor Li's finger literacy experiment. The findings of the experiment made the professors jaw-dropping and speechless.

What is Telepathy?

Among the transcendental feelings of Westerners, the more common ones are *telepathy* and *extra sensation*. Telepathy is a special ability that some people have. They can communicate with life that is not in the same dimension as we are. Many people in the West claim that they have had the experience of "talking with God", which is a telepathic phenomenon.

The telepathic phenomenon in real life is not uncommon. Quite a lot of people in the recently very popular program *The Strongest Brain* are telepathic. There was a female restaurant owner of a roast duck restaurant who could see at a glance how many strokes there are in a line of no more than 12 Chinese character words. The guest asked her: "Even if you remember the number of strokes of each character, it still takes time to add up the 12 numbers. Why can you say it out?" The woman replied: "It is not calculated." I glanced over and the total figure appeared in my mind." This is a telepathic phenomenon.

There was also a child with mental retardation. He has incredible computing power. He could on spot calculate and produce the correct answer to the question of extraction of the root of a 12-digit number 13 times in a short time. A friend of mine told me that when he watched this show, his feeling was that the child was not calculating at all. Instead, he was waiting for something, waiting for someone to give him information. This is also a telepathic phenomenon. The one that conveyed the message to him might be life in other dimensional spaces or life in the spiritual world.

Some people can help you to contact your deceased relatives and communicate with them. This is not entirely superstition. Some of them do have the ability to telepathize. In Professor Li Sicen's experiment, children can contact their "masters" and communicate with them. This is also a telepathy phenomenon.

What we need to understand is that telepathy is not a supernatural power. The people that telepathists communicate with are not necessarily gods. Maybe they are just ordinary life in other dimensional spaces.

Chapter 20

A Spiritual Journey in the Mundane World:
Human Beings Are to Cultivate Their Souls in this Virtual System.

We discussed two of the three ultimate issues, and now we can explore the last question: "What is the meaning of life?"

What is the meaning of life? Humans now rely entirely on science to understand the world, but science has failed to answer this question. When science says that the world is like clockwork and everything has been determined in advance, all the efforts of people are in vain. Does life still make sense? When science says that the world is a pile of matter in space, human beings are material machines, and the spirit is the auxiliary function of the brain, even if the spirit itself is illusory, then is it still meaningful to raise such a spiritual question as what is the meaning of life?

Einstein admitted that there were hundreds of people who wrote to him and asked him to reveal the meaning of life, but he couldn't help and couldn't give them more comfort. Alan Guth once said: "There are no mistakes in asking these questions, but you should not expect a physicist to give a wiser answer."

It is precisely because of this that many people no longer pursue the meaning of life from the spiritual aspect, and instead, they pursue material enjoyment.

Can the pursuit of materials give meaning to our lives? Can it give us long-lasting happiness? No, it can't.   Because the pleasure that materials bring us is diminishing. Like what happens to drug addicts, their senses will become numb when the number of times of drug use is increased. If they want to keep the original stimulation, they must continue to increase the doses until their body can't bear it. So, this kind of satisfaction is not sustainable.

I often hear people say, "I have tasted all the delicious food, tried all the funny things, and picked up different kinds of girls, my life is fulfilled and now I can die without any regret. This shows that in contemporary society, many people have

taken the pursuit of material enjoyment as the meaning of their life.

Does life have no meaning at all? No, this is not true. The reason why Modern science makes no progress in the study of the spirit is that it regards matter as the only reality and wants to reveal the essence of the spirit from the perspective of the matter. Modern people simply regard the world as a material one and want to look for the meaning of life in the material world. This is the reason why they failed.

In other words, we can't find the meaning of life from the materials, and we can only find it from the root of the spirit, the soul. This requires further clarifying the truth of the soul: Where does the soul come from and what is the soul?

Where does our soul come from? To answer this question, we have to start with the notion of *space*.

People will usually say that a zero-dimensional space is a point and it has no direction; a one-dimensional space is a line and it can only have two directions, that is, front and back; a two-dimensional space is a plane, and it can have four directions of front and rear and left and right; a three-dimensional space is a three-dimensional space we are in now, and it can have six directions of front and back, left and right, and up and down.

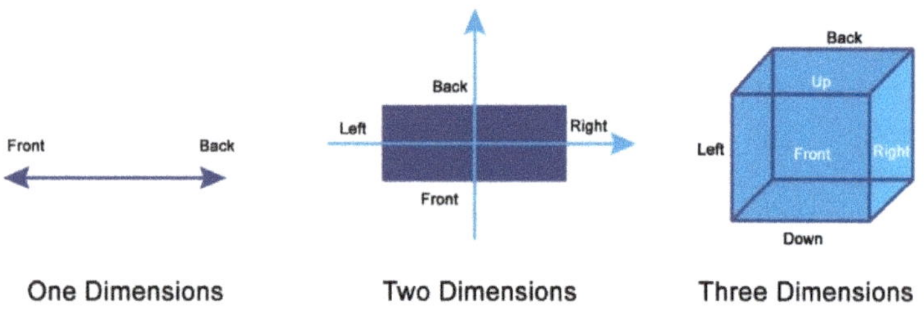

| One Dimensions | Two Dimensions | Three Dimensions |

In theory, space can be completely four-dimensional, five-dimensional, or even multi-dimensional. But in reality, we only know that we are in three-dimensional space. As for whether higher-dimensional space exists, the physics community has not found any evidence to prove it. Even the question of where two-dimensional space and one-dimensional space exist is rarely mentioned.

Speaking of two-dimensional space, there is a question we have to ask: "Where is two-dimensional space?" Can we see the existence of a two-dimensional space in our three-dimensional space? Even the thinnest plane will have a thickness, so it is not strictly two-dimensional. So, where can we find a plane without a thickness?

If you can figure out this, you will understand the true meaning of the relationship between different spaces. The video game world on the computer display is a standard two-dimensional space, which is a plane with only four directions of front, back, left, and right, and with no thickness. What is the relationship between the space in which the video game world is located and the three-dimensional space we are in? It turns out that they are just virtual spaces in our eyes, virtual worlds.

What is the physical meaning of the relationship between a high-dimensional space and a low-dimensional space? The two-dimensional space is a virtual space in the three-dimensional space, and the three-dimensional space we are in is a virtual space in the four-dimensional space, and the four-dimensional space is a virtual space in the five-dimensional space.

Can this growth in several dimensions continue indefinitely? We do not know. Perhaps there is only one real space in the end and there is no dimension attribute in this space. All other spaces are just layers of virtual spaces.

Some science fiction novels have plots of travel from a low-dimensional space to a high-dimensional one, just like the Taoist priest in *Legend* broke through the space boundaries through practice and came to our real world. Is this kind of thing possible?

This issue has to be seen separately. Life is composed of two parts: the body and the soul. They are independent and interdependent. In our opinion, the flesh is a physical thing, and the soul is a virtual thing, which is why we never found the existence of the soul when dissecting the human brain, just like when we opened the computer, we could not find the software in it.

In the past, there was a movie called "The Fair in the Painting," which told the story of a painting hanging in a poor student's home. The fairy in the painting would come out to help him cook and wash clothes and finally became his wife. Can this kind of love exist in reality? Can the characters in the video game world jump out of the screen and live in the real world with us?

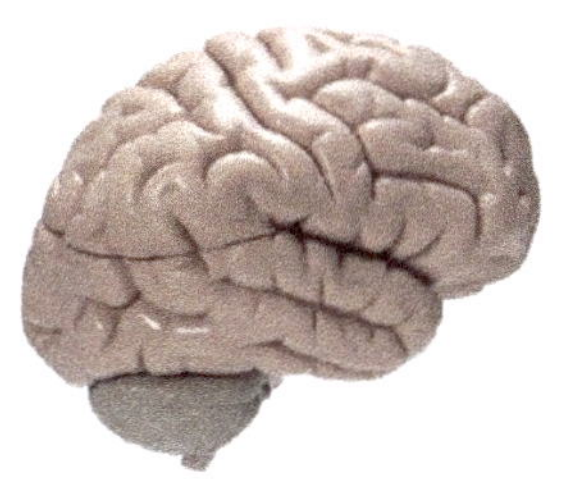

An astronaut did not believe in the existence of God and said, "I have been in outer space, but I have never seen God." A surgeon retorted him: "When I was doing surgery, I often opened the head of the patient, but I never see the mind." A computer engineer can also say: "When I went to repair the computer, I opened the computer, but I never saw the software inside."

Physical matter must exist in time and space, but the virtual thing is different. Its existence is not limited by time and space. Objects in a two-dimensional space are virtual in our view and cannot be brought into the real world, but the software in the two-dimensional space is no different in nature from the software in the three-dimensional space.

From this point of view, our flesh can't break away from time and space, and it can't travel through into high-dimensional space. But the soul is not bound by this. The Swiss psychologist Carl Gustav Jung once said: "I believe that a certain part of the human soul is not subject to the laws of time and space."

Is it possible for the human soul to go to a higher dimensional space? In the movie *The Thirteenth Floor*, Doug's flesh is still left in the real world, but his soul can enter the body of people in the lower dimensional virtual world or reach the higher dimensional space of the future world. In theory, since the soul can ignore the limitations of spatial rules, it can travel between different spaces. It can travel between different spaces and reach higher or lower dimensional spaces.

Relying on virtual reality technology, our consciousness can enter the virtual space and experience what is close to the real experience. The US military uses virtual reality technology to simulate the battlefield environment and conduct individual soldier combat simulation training, which is based on this principle. This fact has inspired me a lot: Is it possible that our soul comes from outside of the universe to be trained in this world?

To increase the sense of the presence of the experience in the virtual reality system, it is necessary to isolate the sensory perception of the experience from the world outside the system. If our soul is to exercise in this world, then its original function must be sealed away and cannot be perceived.

Interestingly, this inference can be confirmed in many ways. Whether in modern psychology, Taoist classics, hypnotism, or Buddhist scriptures, we can all see the same thing: Some parts of the soul are indeed sealed, and our consciousness is not able to detect them.

In 1899, Freud put forward the concept of the *subconscious* in *An Analysis of Dreams*. He believes that the composition of human consciousness is like an iceberg, and only a small part of it is above the water's surface, that is, *consciousness*; most of the other parts are hidden underwater, that is, *the subconscious*. The subconscious mind controls most of the spiritual activities, but our consciousness cannot sense the existence of the subconscious.

He wrote in the book, "The subconscious is the real spiritual reality. But we still do not understand its intrinsic nature, just as we do not understand the real external world."

Taoism believes that there are two kinds of "gods" that govern the actions of people. One is called "the knowing god" and the other is called "the primordial god." The knowing god is the consciousness in the human brain that can control life behavior. It is attached to the "vigor" and controls the conscious world of human beings. The primordial god comes from the Land of Eternity, which is born from the moment when the sperm and the egg are combined. It is attached to the "soul" and controls the unconscious world of people.

According to Taiyi Jinhua Zongzhi, a Taoist classic of internal medicine, "The heavens and the earth regard humans as insects, and the great Tao regard the heavens and the earth as bubbles. Only the true spirit of the primordial god exists eternally." These words say that the primordial god is an eternity beyond the heavens and the earth. "When a mortal reincarnates, the primordial god is in the upper part and the knowing god is in the lower heart." The primordial god and the knowing god are born upon reincarnation.

Knowing God is equivalent to the consciousness that Freud talked about. The primordial god is equivalent to what he called the subconscious. Just as Freud believes that the subconscious mind is the real spiritual reality, Taoism also believes that the primordial god is the "true spirit" that is permanent.

The Taoist viewpoint is so close to modern psychology that in 1927 someone translated *The Taiyi Jinhua Zongzhi* into German, named *The Secret of Golden Flower,* and asked Jung to write a preface to it. Jung immediately compared it with his psychological research and wrote a long review, which caused great repercussions in Western academic circles.

Compared with psychology and Taoism, hypnotism makes a deeper understanding of the soul.

I once watched *The Hypnosis Night*; a variety show hosted by He Jung. The hypnotist from Canada had hypnotized more than a dozen audiences live on the spot. The hypnotized audience felt conscious but lost control of themselves. The hypnotized audience said whatever the hypnotist told them to say and did whatever the hypnotist told them to do; and whatever the hypnotist asked them, they answered honestly. This is easily reminiscent of the "broilers" that have been planted with the Trojan viruses. Although there are no abnormalities on the surface these computers have been remotely controlled via the Internet.

Michael Newton is a certified hypnotherapist with a Ph.D. in psychology in the United States. He received the annual award from the National Association of Hypnotherapists in 1998. In 1968, during the treatment of a patient named Yuna, he accidentally had an encounter with the soul world. He was stunned by the patient's vivid description of this world. Since then, he had devoted himself to researching and designing a working model for exploring the soul world. And based on the research findings he wrote the book *The Journey of the Soul.*

In many years of hypnosis practice, Michael Newton discovered that the human mind is divided into three levels. The outermost layer is *consciousness*; the second layer is *sub-consciousness*; the third layer is the core layer, which can be called *super-consciousness*. Normally our consciousness cannot perceive the existence of the subconscious, but the hypnotist can penetrate deep into the subconscious of the hypnotized person in hypnosis and control their behaviors through their subconscious. At this time, the hypnotized person, like those computers that have been planted with a Trojan virus, still maintains a clear consciousness but does not know that he is already under control.

When compared with Taoism and psychology, Michael Newton further discovered that *the subconscious* or *the primordial god* can be divided into two parts: *the subconscious* and *the super-conscious*. He also found that the memory of this life is recorded at the level of consciousness, which is the source of judgment, analysis, and reasoning in real life. On the subconscious level, all the memories of past and present life are buried, where we can use hypnosis to discover hidden secrets. On the super-conscious level, we cherish our true ontology. It is the total control of the self, and what hides here is the ultimate truth of the soul.

Michael Newton used instruments to measure changes in the brainwaves of hypnotized people. He found that in the awake state, the brain wave is in the ß state; when sleeping, the brain wave is in the state; in the meditation phase of the hypnosis process, the brain wave is in the state; and when hypnotized, the brain wave eventually enters the θ state. In the state of being hypnotized, consciousness is not ignorant, and information can be received and transmitted, and all memory channels are open. These measurements provide a degree of scientific evidence for his findings.

However, shocking the discoveries of psychology, Taoism and hypnotists are, compared with Siddhartha's teachings, they are all worth nothing.

There is a clearer description of the human mind in the Buddhist scriptures. Siddhartha said that people have "eight consciousnesses" in total. The first five consciousnesses are: eye-consciousness, ear consciousness, nose consciousness, tongue consciousness, and body consciousness, the sixth consciousness is mind consciousness, the seventh consciousness is *manas* consciousness, and the eighth consciousness is Alaya consciousness.

It makes sense that Siddhartha further subdivided what people usually think of consciousness into six consciousnesses. The first five consciousnesses depend on the existence of mind consciousness, but there is indeed a difference between them and mind consciousness. For example, ear awareness allows us to hear the ups and downs of the sound, but the meaning contained in the sounds must be distinguished by mind consciousness. Only mind consciousness knows whether it represents popular songs or ethnic music. And when mind consciousness exists, the first five senses may be closed. For example, when I concentrate on writing on the computer, I can't hear the sounds from the computer speakers, and I don't know what song it played afterward. This indicates that my ear senses are temporarily closed.

Based on the idea that "people have eight senses," Siddhartha has painted a strange picture, in which "there are three realms in the human mind and all the laws can be learned through human senses."

In the movie *The Matrix*, when Neo understood the truth, he entered virtual reality again to experience it. He touched the chair with his hand and asked unsurely: "Is it not true?" Morpheus replied: "What is true? If you mean taste, touch, smell, hearing, and vision, they are the electronic signals that the brain receives. What you think of as the real world is a matrix," a virtual world.'

In Siddhartha's view, the entire world system of the Three Realms and Six Paths is all virtual, a huge "matrix." It is said in *The Sutra of Origin*: "The origins of all the laws come from emptiness and are not created by any lord; through peace of heart one can achieve the origins of the heart, and this is called Shramana." This sentence means that the laws of the three realms are all caused by karma, which are all illusions, not true realities, only Alaya consciousness is real; it is the origin of the laws of the three worlds. Only when we understand this point can we attain Shramana.

Alaya consciousness can also be referred to as bodily consciousness, fetal consciousness, seed mind, tathagata, and true being" Siddhartha believes that it is a kind of existence with no beginning and no end. It is said in *The Abhidharma Mahayana*: "There is a world of no beginning, where all laws are followed, and all kinds of interest are born; and only when one reaches Nirvana can he prove such pursuits." This means that Alaya's consciousness has existed since the very beginning, and the manifestation of all laws of the Three Realms is dependent on it; it is precisely because of it that we have all kinds of phenomena in the Three Realms, and it is precisely because of it that we can achieve Nirvana.

In the virtual systems of US military combat training, the soldier's consciousness comes from outside the system, and it enters the virtual system to receive training. Siddhartha believes that Alaya is also from outside the Three Realms, and it also comes to receive exercise. Alaya can hold seeds of cleansing, and practitioners can accumulate the seeds in continuous reincarnation and cleanse the contaminated habits until they become a buddha. It is said in *The Secret Sutra of Mahayana*: "Alaya's consciousness is the seed of cleansing of buddha, and it is contaminated in the mortal life. When a Bodhisattva gets rid of the habits, they become the Buddha"

How does Alaya know how to operate in the Three Realms? Just as the soldier's consciousness enters the virtual system, to be realistic, it is necessary to shield away his original sensory functions. The original function of Alaya is also blocked away after entering the Three Realms when "the eighth consciousness of Alaya" became the seventh consciousness of Manas."

The eighth consciousness appears in the form of the seventh consciousness in the Three Realms. There are six reincarnations in the Three Realms, and the seventh consciousness is constantly reintroduced in the Six Paths. However, in the specific reincarnation of each world, some functions of the seventh consciousness of manas were blocked, and only the memory of this world has become the sixth consciousness "the mind consciousness."

In Buddhism, people with the heaven-eye ability can see that after a good man dies, he will go to the place for a good life, and after a wicked person dies, he will go to the place for a wicked life. If you have fortune-telling ability, you can know your past experiences. Just like a hypnotist can see the pasts and presents of the hypnotized persons in their subconscious.

People in the "maternal body" cannot touch the real world, nor can the first seven consciousnesses touch reality. All its experiences in the Three Realms are simulated. It is said in *Yogācāra-bhūmi-śāstra*: "Or there exists one color, which is resulted from the proper function of the eyes. Or there are two kinds of color, that is, the inner color, and the outer color"; Here "outer color" refers to the information that the eye obtains from the physical world, and "inner color" refers to the image that is simulated in the brain. Everything a soldier sees in a virtual system is an image of the analog signal sent by the system into his mind. The images that the first seven senses can perceive in the three realms are all simulations, which are called "the realm of self-heart" by *the Lankavatara Sutra.*

The purpose of Siddhartha's creation of Buddhism is to guide sentient beings to discover the truth, to change the behavioral orientations of body, mouth, and mind, to eliminate all troubles, and finally to get rid of the constraints of the Three Realms and return to the concrete reality. Just like a soldier entering a virtual system, the purpose is to get his consciousness to be exercised. After reaching the goal, he will exit the virtual system and return to the real world.

But how can we discover the truth? We can't directly observe the Alaya consciousness. Only through its role in the exercise of all laws in the Three Realms can we see the nature behind it and feel its existence. *The Diamond Sutra* says: "All phenomena are illusions. When you see beyond the phenomena, you will see the Tathagata." It means that all phenomena in the Three Realms are illusory. If you can see through these phenomena, you can see the Alaya consciousness hidden underneath.

Regrettably, in reality, the vast majority of people will regard everything in front of them as real, and the five aggregates as their true selves. This is called "seeing by oneself" in Buddhism, which is also called "seeing my body."

When Descartes said, "*I think so I am,*" he regarded the sixth consciousness as the real "I." This view is easy to refute. People are not conscious when they sleep or are in a coma. They don't think, but they are still alive and there, so it is obvious that Descartes is wrong.

There is an unchanging subject in the cycle of life and death, that is, the eighth consciousness, which is called "I" in *the Agama Sutra* and "Alaya Consciousness" and "Tathagata" in the Mahayana Sutra. It is written in *The Diamond Sutra*:

"If you see me with color and beg me with your voice, you are doing evil ways, and you cannot see the Tathagata." Here, "I" and "Tathagata" both refer to Alaya Consciousness, which means if you regard all the sounds and colors in front of you as true, it is impossible to see Alaya.

At the time of reincarnation, Alaya entered the body of a baby, so it was also called "human fetal consciousness." *Dirghagama-sutra: Mahanidana-sūtra* mentioned the "conception consciousness" when it talked about the "consciousness" of the tenfold karma method.

Alaya is the reason why all beings have self-awareness and can realize their existence when they are in the cycle of reincarnation in the Three Realms and Six Paths. Therefore, they are also called the consciousness of "holding the body." However, our consciousness does not know the existence of Alaya's consciousness and doesn't know that it is the reason for our various experiences in the Three Realms. Therefore, It is said in *the Ekottaragama-sutra*: "This consciousness is the most original, which makes people be born, get old, become sick, and die, but don't know the causes of these phenomena of life."

Although the experience of the soldier in the virtual system is false, the impact of these experiences on his consciousness is real. Although the sixth consciousness can have the memory of this world it cannot bring the memory to the next world; however, the behavioral habits of this world have already been recorded in the seventh consciousness and will be brought to the next world. More importantly, these actions will have a real impact on the Alaya consciousness.

If the troubles of this world are not eradicated, they will be brought into the next world, and more sorrows and distress will arise. But if there is a world where one can get rid of all the troubles, the seventh consciousness will be extinguished and no longer enter incarnation in the six paths. This is the "nirvana with nothing left." It is said in *the Lankavatara Sutra*: "Nirvana means the extinction of delusions." This means that the extinction of delusions or the first seven senses is the "nirvana with nothing left.," and the person who achieves this realm is called *Arahant*. This is like the soldier having attained the expected goal of exercising awareness and coming out of the virtual system.

But Alaya's consciousness will not be extinguished. It is said in *The Lankavatara Sutra*: "The extinction of the Alaya consciousness is nothing different from arguments of extraneous reasoning and arbitrary judgments of other schools of thought." If anyone thinks that the Alaya consciousness can be extinguished, that is the concept of extinction advocated by other schools of thought.

Therefore, it is said in *the Mahāyāna śraddhotpada śāstra*: "According to the Tathāgatagarbha, there exist life and death and incarnation of mind. When life without death and life with death are integrated into neither a state of unity nor separate states, there appears the Alaya consciousness. The Alaya consciousness will not be born and destroyed; but the seventh and sixth consciousnesses, which depend on the Alaya consciousness, will be born and destroyed in reincarnation in the Three Realms. The Alaya consciousness that does not die out contains the seventh and sixth consciousnesses that go through the cycles of birth and death. They are not the same thing, but we cannot say that they are different things, because they are closely linked.

Soldiers enter the virtual system to exercise their awareness and improve their ability to adapt to the battlefield environment. What are we going to exercise in the Three Realms? We go to the Three Realms to exercise Alaya, or to exercise our hearts and mind.

Many practitioners have a deep understanding of this. The German meditation master Ayya Kema said in *The Sequence of Meditation*: "Through Zen, we have experienced a high level of state of mind, showing that we are only in this world, but do not belong to this world. We know that although we have this body and mind, we can still surpass it."

Our behavior in worldly life is meaningful; it is related to the promotion of Alaya. There is a complete evaluation mechanism behind the six paths, which many Indian religions call *karma*. Every good and bad thing we do will become our "industry" for evaluation. This kind of evaluation determines whether we will be in the place where the good dwell or the place where the evils dwell in the afterlife, or whether we will go to heaven to be heavenly people or we will be condemned to hell to suffer, or whether we will continue to fall in the six paths of reincarnation or to leave the Three Realms after Nirvana to attain the ultimate freedom.

The material temptations and sensory stimulations in our worldly life are a test for us. It is not worth pursuing. It is not the meaning of our life. The meaning of life is the improvement of the mind and soul. The true practice is to pursue peace of mind and heart in the sensual world. As Zen Buddhism believes, it is the training of your heart and temperament in the routines of daily life such as fetching water, cutting firewood, wearing clothes, and taking regimens.

A life experience is a journey of spiritual practice. Spiritual practice is everywhere. To live a good life is to practice, to solve the current problems is to practice, to improve yourself through study is to practice, and to temper yourself through setbacks is also to practice. No matter what you are doing, as long as you concentrate on it, it can help to improve your heart and mind until you are fulfilled.

Michael Newton recorded a large number of conversations with the hypnotized people in *The Journey of the Soul*. These conversations show that after death, the soul will leave the body of flesh and embark on the path to the soul world. Newton vividly describes the soul world and the experience of the soul, which tells us that the fundamental purpose of the existence of life is to practice and through practice, the perfect soul will gain eternal peace. Therefore, on the cover of his book, he wrote these words: "The evolution of life in the world is truly the practice of the soul."

Multiple Personality Disorder

Multiple personality disorder is a mental illness. The official name is "dissociative identity disorder." It is manifested as a person with more than two personalities, just like several souls living in one body.

Each personality of person with multiple personalities is independent. When one personality appears, other personalities will automatically exit. At any time, only one personality is in control, and there will be no confusion of several personalities competing for control. At a specific time, what personality dominates one's actions? This completely follows the principle of "whatever personality is best suited to the environment and needs at the time, this personality is initiated and emerged." This is a bit like a *chameleon* that adjusts the color of its body to suit the environment.

People with multiple personalities will use a confident personality to cope with a competitive environment, and a weak personality to win sympathy. There used to be such a case. In addition to the normal personality, a certain person had three different personalities in his body: a refined and rational one, a gentle and passionate one, and a cruel and cold one. The first personality often appeared when he was working hard; the second personality appeared because his mother liked to dress him up as a girl when he was a child, though he longed to be a man; the third personality would appear when he was beaten.

Multiple personalities are terrible in reality. There are several famous movies with this theme, such as *Shutter Island*, *Psycho,* and *Identity*; almost all of them are horror movies. After the personality transformation, people with multiple personalities are like persons who have changed completely. The personality has changed, the memory has changed; some have become left-handed; some originally had squint eyes, and now they become normal!

This question was difficult to explain at first, but after reading the teachings of Siddhartha, it should be easy to understand. Under normal circumstances, people have only the sixth consciousness in the world, but there may be exceptions. Since the seventh consciousness can give you different consciousness in each round of reincarnation, it is entirely possible to give you several different consciousnesses in the same world. Of course, this confusion is not the normal behavior of the system. This malfunction will occur only after the system has been strongly stimulated when confusion appears.

Chapter 21

Who Is the Creator?
Who Built the Huge Virtual System
of *Three Realms and Six Paths*?

Who is the creator? This question is more difficult to answer than all the previous ones. If there is a creator, it is clear that it can't be in this universe. Where can we go to find its clues? Many ethnic groups have myths of creation. In ancient China, there was the story of "Pangu creating the heaven and earth," Legend has it that in the beginning, the world is chaos like a big egg, and only Pangu is sleeping inside. One day he woke up. When he looked around, he found it was very dark. He was very uncomfortable. He lifted a giant axe and cut it apart. The big egg was divided into two halves. The clean gases rose to make up the sky; the turbidity sank to become the ground. His body became the sun, the moon, the stars, the mountains, and the rivers...

But, if we follow up on this story, some questions are not answered here. Where did the original world like the big egg of chaos come from? Where did Pangu come from?

This myth says that everything in the world evolved from Pangu's body. This represents a view of the world: God is the world, and God is nature. Many philosophers have said so. Thales, an ancient Greek philosopher in the 6th century BC, who was known as the first philosopher in the West, declared that "there are Gods in all things." Plotinus, an ancient Roman philosopher in the 3rd century AD, even believed that everything in the world is integral and God is in everything. Plotinus even said that he once had the experience that his soul was united with God as one. People often call this experience a "mystical experience."

But the more common belief is that the creator is personified into God, an omnipotent God of creation.

According to the Genesis of the Old Testament, the world was created by Lord Jehovah. However, if we continue to ask questions, there will also be a problem: If the world is created by God, then where does God come from?

The answer given by Christianity is that God exists without a beginning and an end, so there is no need to ask where it comes from. Logically speaking, this can only be answered in this way; otherwise, the questions will be endless.

This kind of answer is not a Christian patent, and Taoism also said this when explaining the origin of the Tao. Lao Tze himself did not answer the question of where the *Tao* came from. He honestly admitted that "I don't know whose son it is", saying that he did not know where it came from. However, Zhuang Tze answered the question about the origin of "*the Tao*": The heaven and earth were born of themselves, and they came into being since the primeval times; Gods and spirits gave birth to heaven and earth. There cannot be any height higher than that before the Taiji; there can't be any depth deeper than under the six poles; there cannot be any longevity longer than the heaven and earth, and there cannot be any time older than the oldest time." As "it came into form since ancient times," it is the existence of no beginning and no end; since "it was born of itself", it can create itself by itself and on its own. You don't need to answer the question of where it came from.

From the perspective of modern people, the previous statements of the creation myth are not true, for the description of the creation of the creator is far different from what we have learned from modern science.

Some people have long made guesses about the way that the creator created the world. Pythagoras, a philosopher of ancient Greece in the 6th century BC, said that God uses numbers to create everything in the universe, so everything is a number. He believes that through the study of the logarithm, we can understand the mysteries of the universe, sublimate our souls, and unify them with God because God rules the universe through numbers.

This statement used to look ridiculous, but now we can feel its unique charm. Anyone who has studied computer programming knows that the programming language is ultimately a bunch of binary codes consisting of 0 and 1. Since the creator makes the world like designing computer games, then everything in the world is a bunch of programming codes. So, everything Pythagoras said may be true.

Even though scientists have discovered that the creation process described in the creation myth is wrong, can we deny the existence of the creator? We can't. We have not found the answer to this question until now.

Many philosophers believe that there is indeed a personified God. Aristotle believed that all activities on Earth are affected by the operations of planets, and these planets must be manipulated by certain forces to set them to work. He calls this power "the prime mover" or "God." Newton was influenced by his idea and firmly believed that "the prime mover" did exist.

Pythagoras believes that everything is a number. Before the invention of the computer, the average person regarded it as a joke; but now people have gradually realized its deep meaning of it.

Now we can fully explain the problem of the prime mover with the setting up of the "creation program," But Aristotle's logic still holds. Everything has its first cause. We can't avoid this question in the end: Where did the creator come from?

Of course, some people are trying to find other explanations. They believe that the creator is not a personified God but something else.

Some people think that the creator is just a kind of reason or some kind of supreme wisdom. The ancient Greek philosopher Heraclitus discovered that there is a *universal reason* in the world that guides everything that happens in nature. He believes that this is the source of all things, and he called it "God" or "logos," The Stoic school in Athens around 300 BCE also believed that there is some axiom in the world, which can be called the "law of God", and that it is built on the long-standing rationality of ancient times and will not change at any time. All natural phenomena follow this unchanging rule.

But what they have found is not the creator, but the natural law of our world. Because the laws of nature also govern the world, just as the creator governs the world, they mistake the laws of nature for the creator.

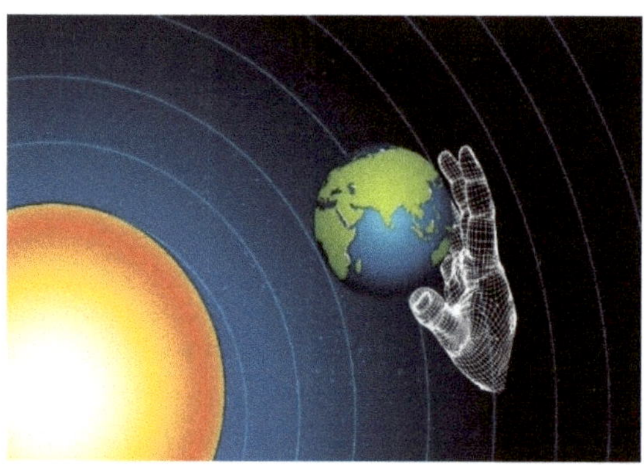

The moon rotates around the earth, the earth rotates around the sun, the sun rotates around the center of the galaxy, and everything in the universe is spinning. How did they initially begin to spin? Who set this process to work? This is the "prime mover" problem that has intrigued countless people since the primeval times.

Siddhartha did not believe that there was a personalized creator but thought that Alaya is born of the three realms and six roads. According to the *mahā-vaipulya-buddhavata* sutra, "the heart is like a painter, it can draw the entire world, the five embodiments are all born of it, so are all the laws." This means that Alaya is like a painter, and it can draw all the life in the three realms and six roads; the five embodiments are all caused by it and all the laws of the three realms are created by it.

The Avatamsaka Sutra also said: "The heart is the main focus of the three realms, and those who can see the heart will be free, and those who can't see it will be sinking. The hearts of all beings are like the great earth, where the five fruits and five crops are born. Such ways of heart practice give birth to the creation and annihilation of the world, the good and evil, and the five interests, ignorance or wisdom, the attainment of Bodhisattva and Tathagata. Because of karma, the three realms are dictated by the heart, which is called the land of all things." This sentence means that the five fruits are all grown from the ground, and the mind of the sentient beings or the Alaya consciousness is like the earth and can produce the "the laws of the world" and "the laws out of the world", including the sentient beings of the five interests, sound hearing, predestined consciousness, Bodhisattva, and Buddha. As the Alaya consciousness can give birth to all the phenomena in the three realms, so "everything is created by the heart" and the "heart" is the land that can generate the three realms.

The *Mahāyāna śraddhotpada śāstra* also said: "This insight has two meanings; that is, it can govern all the laws and it can produce all the laws." This means that the Alaya consciousness has two meanings: one is that it governs all laws, and the other is that it generates everything. Siddhartha's view is similar to that of Heraclitus except that it considers something non-personified to be the creator. But we can't avoid this question either: where does it come from, be it the logos that Heraclitus talked about or the Alaya that Siddhartha suggested?

The answer to the question given by Christianity is that "God exists with no beginning and no end." Buddhism is no exception. It is said in the *Abhidharma Mahayana*: "There is no beginning to the world on which all laws are dependent." This means that Alaya has existed since the very beginning and there is no need to consider the question of where it came from.

Are these statements correct? Who is the creator? What is his form? Is there a personalized God, or is it just a mysterious source?

When I first realized that the creator had made our world in the same way as designing computer games, I suspected that the creator was a programmer dwelling in a high-dimensional space. But in reality, the computer game in the real world is the result of a team of programmers working together instead of the result of development by one person. So, I think the creator may not be just one, but a group, or a team. Among them are project managers, system analysts, job designers, needs descriptors, software architects, specific programmers, and test engineers...

But after I had learned about Siddhartha's teachings about Alaya through reading *Introduction to Empirical Buddhism* by Lu Zhenguan, I found that the situation was not that simple. If the three realms and six paths are all a huge virtual system, then the creator may not be in the high-dimensional space, but outside the three realms and six paths, for the high-dimensional space is also a virtual world.

If that is the case, the sentient beings in the high-dimensional space, like us, are all in the three worlds and six paths and are all in reincarnation. Compared with us, their life forms may be more advanced than ours. But this is nothing remarkable, just as a person with a visual acuity of 1.5 can see farther and clearer than one with a visual acuity of 0.5, but there is no qualitative difference between them.

It is not surprising that some people may have the ability to engage in telepathy with life in other dimensional spaces. But it is completely wrong for them to think that they are talking to Gods and that they have got the *Revelation*.

I am very doubtful of the statement that Siddhartha believes that Alaya has created the three realms. Because all the experiences of American soldiers in the virtual system are generated when the soldiers' consciousness enters the system, it cannot be said that the soldiers' consciousness has created this virtual system. This system was built by the US military, not by the soldiers. By the same token, the three realms and all the laws are manifested by the existence of Alaya, but it cannot be said that Alaya has created the virtual system of the three realms and six paths.

I suspect that this is what Siddhartha meant. And later generations misunderstood his teachings. But who is the creator? Who built the huge "mother body" of the three realms and six paths? Siddhartha did not explain further. He usually considered such philosophical problems as "nonsense," Even if someone asked him, he would not answer.

According to the *Arrow Sutra*, a young Buddhist disciple named "the bearded child" came to visit Siddhartha. He consulted the master on 14 questions, including "Does the world ever exist?" "Does the world have a boundary?", and "Will Buddha exist after he dies?" Siddhartha said, "I will not answer such questions as they are not beneficial to practice." He gave an example to illustrate his point. Just like someone was shot by a poisoned arrow. As the members of his family quickly sought medical treatment for him, the wounded man thought that there was no need to rush to take the arrow out and treat the poisoned wound. Instead, he wanted to know what the name of the doctor is, what he looks like, what his identity is, who shot him with the arrow, what kind of wood the arrow handle is made of...

This fool insisted on figuring out all the problems before pulling the arrow out for treatment. But he did not know that he would have already been poisoned and died before he waited to figure out all these questions.

Siddhartha said that seeking liberation is the problem we need to solve. Just like for those who have been shot by poisoned arrows, the top priority is to hurry to find a doctor to take out the arrow and treat him. Therefore, he never explored the mysterious problems that have nothing to do with practice.

Coincidentally, many wise men in the world have the same attitude as Siddhartha did. Zhuang Tze said: "My life has a boundary, whereas knowledge is boundless, so to pursue a boundless thing with a limited life will exhaust my limited life." People's lives are limited, and knowledge is infinite. Exploring infinite knowledge with a limited life will only lead to one's exhaustion. Life is limited, time is precious. One should do something meaningful in his life, rather than always asking those silly questions that are meaningless.

Confucius also holds such an attitude. *The Analects of Confucius* writes: "The child does not speak strange things and chaotic ghosts," Just as Siddhartha does not explore issues unrelated to practice, Confucius does not like to talk about ghosts and Gods. His disciples found that they had never heard their Master talking about the mysterious problems. Zigong said with emotion: "The articles of the Master can be obtained and heard, but the essence of the words of the Master and the laws of heavens can't be learned."

When someone asked such questions, Siddhartha always refused to reply. The same is true of Confucius. *The Analects of Confucius* records: "Ji Lu came to ask about the ghosts and Gods. The Master said: "How could you ask about the matters of ghosts before you know about the matters of man?" Ji Lu further asked: 'I dare to ask about death. The Master answered: 'How could you know about death before you know about life?" In other words, Zi Lu couldn't figure out many things and asked the teacher how to get along with the ghosts and Gods. Confucius said, "Why do you want to know how to get along with the ghosts when you don't even figure out how to get along with others?" Zi Lu did not give up and asked what will happen after people die. Confucius said: "Why do you care about what will happen after death when you don't know even how to live well,"

I don't know whether these wise men really don't understand or just don't want to say it. Logically speaking, we may never know the ultimate truth of the world. I don't know what the world is like in the three realms. I don't know who made the three realms and reincarnations in the six paths, just like the consciousness of the American soldier in the virtual world can't know who made this virtual world. It is only when his consciousness exits the virtual system and returns to the real world could it is possible for him to understand this information.

One day, when you are in nirvana and become a Buddha, your Alaya consciousness will return to the original world outside the three realms, and then you may understand everything.

The attitude of the wise men on this matter is undoubtedly correct. The American soldiers come to the virtual system not to find out who made the system but to exercise their consciousness and return to the real world after reaching their goals. We should also do this. We don't have to be obsessed with such questions as who the creator is and who made the world. Instead, we should care more about how to cultivate ourselves and improve our hearts and minds.

It is precisely because the ultimate goal of the practice of all beings is to cultivate their hearts and minds and enhance their consciousness of Alaya that Buddhism does not encourage the cultivation of magical powers, even if some supernatural powers look very powerful.

Based on Siddhartha's eight insights of man, I believe that the magical power is a normal function of Alaya, which has been sealed off after one enters the three realms. Some people have magical powers because the seals are partially opened. So, the magical powers of those people are often seen after being struck by lightning or being rescued from near death.

The most important task of the soldier in the simulation system is to exercise his consciousness, instead of trying to remove the sensory function that is shielded to increase the sense of reality, which has no practical significance. The same is true of the sentient beings of the three realms. Instead of being obsessed with supernatural powers and working hard to lift the seal of Alaya to restore its function, they should focus on training their hearts.

In the past few years, I have met many people with supernatural powers. But to be honest, quite a few of them are not well-cultivated. The magical powers they possess have not improved their hearts and minds, nor have not brought any benefits to their lives; instead, some of them even have brought a lot of confusion and disturbances.

Perhaps because of this, Buddhism does not encourage the cultivation of supernatural powers. There are two ways to practice Buddhism. The first is "meditation." Starting with meditation, it is possible to obtain supernatural powers; but according to Buddhism, there is no benefit in doing so, for even if you have attained meditation, you will still be unable to escape from the shackles of the three realms if you don't hear the correct Dharma and be born through Jhana after death. Having magical powers may even affect your practice, just as a soldier restores the sensory functions that were blocked off in the virtual system, but this will affect his training performance, and the effect of training of consciousness will be greatly reduced.

Another way of practice in Buddhism is "contemplation," If you start with contemplation, once you break the three binding knots, achieve the first result, and improve your character, your insight will never be lost. Even if you no longer practice in this life, you can escape from the sea of suffering at most seven times, far better than those who have achieved success in meditation. So now many Buddhist monks only cultivate the mind but not concentration. Although they don't have the magical powers we imagine, they have a great capacity for the cultivation of hearts and minds.

Plotinus and the Mystical Experience

"Mystical experience" refers to a mysterious experience in which the soul and the supreme spirit merge into one. Most people who have had this experience are mystics with a strange knowledge of the world. These people believe that we cannot obtain truth and wisdom from the real world through our senses. To achieve this goal, we must close the eyes of the flesh, open the eyes of the soul, detach ourselves from foreign objects, and return to ourselves. Only in this way can we achieve deep feelings and insights into the contemplation of the mind.

Religions generally emphasize that God is superior to the world it creates, but the mystics don't think so. They think we can be one with God. Many of them have had this experience. In a special state of mind, when self-consciousness disappears, they can feel the existence of a greater ego. They think that this greater ego is God, or "the heart of heaven and earth," According to them, God exists in all things. So, when you eliminate your self-awareness and merge into the world of all things, it feels like a drop of water flowing into the ocean or a wandering traveler returning to the embrace of his mother.

An Indian mystic described his experience this way: "In the past, when my self-consciousness existed, I could not feel God; now I feel the existence of God, and I disappeared." Valencia, a Christian mystic in the 17th century, said: "When every drop of water flows into the ocean, it becomes an ocean; in the same way, when the soul finally rises, it becomes God."

For most people, loss of self-awareness is a terrible experience, so people are afraid of death. But mystics believe that it is not terrible to lose yourself. At this time, you will find yourself becoming larger and greater. The self in front of me will pass away one day, but the bigger ego is like a mysterious flame that will burn for eternity.

Mystic experience is not something that can be obtained casually. It needs to be realized through practice. The general way is to live a simple life and practice meditation so that one day you can communicate with God.

Mysticism is not limited to a certain religion. This phenomenon can be seen in all major religions in the world. What's strange is that the mysterious experiences depicted by people of different cultures and beliefs are often very similar. Even many people without religious beliefs have had mysterious experiences. They would suddenly feel the existence of some kind of "consciousness of universe ", and their consciousness would be merged with it, and they seemed suddenly transcend time and space and feel the world with an unprecedented vision.

Plotinus is the most famous philosopher of Neo-Platonism. He is a mystic. It is said that he had had many mysterious experiences. He once joined the Roman legion on an expedition and went to India to study Eastern philosophy. His doctrine combines the ideas of Pythagoras and Plato, as well as Eastern mysticism. He believes that the highest spirit, "the Supreme One", is the source of all things, and the goal of life is to return to the "the Supreme One" and become united with it.

Chapter 22

The World as the Place of Practice: Achieve Harmony Between Man and Nature, Between People, and Between Man and Oneself, so as to Shift Mankind to a Higher Level.

When the American soldier was initially trained in the virtual system for individual combat capabilities, he was a lone fighter with no comrades. Is the same true for all beings in the three realms and six paths? Is it true that this could be done by improving just one individual's heart and mind? If this is the case, then practice is just a matter of an individual himself and has nothing to do with others. Many chicken soup stories are persuading us: "There is no one outside you except yourself."

Primitive Buddhism, Theravada Buddhism, and the present Southern Buddhism all peach this. With self-improvement and relief as the mission, they advocate the practices of discipline, meditation, and wisdom, and believe that wisdom can be gained by observing discipline and practicing meditation. They believe in the practice of the "eight correct ways" of thinking and acting. Among them, the *sravakayana* starts with the pursuit of the "four truths," and the highest level that one can attain is Arhat, which will rid people of troubles of the three realms, and transcend them beyond the reincarnations of six paths; *pratyekabuddhayana* starts with the twelve causes and the highest level to attain is the *pratyekabuddha*.

This Buddhist sect emphasizes the practice of the individual on his own. By taking the elimination of life and death as the original intention, the rise out of greed as the foundation, and the transcendence of body and mind as the mission, its followers hope to eliminate all troubles through practice and achieve personal relief and deliverance in the end. The followers are all practitioners who have abandoned the materialistic life in the world, and they focus on their relief instead of the relief and deliverance of all other creatures. Therefore, the followers of this sect of Buddhism are considered to be *self-attainers*. Hence, this Buddhist sect is called *Theravada Buddhism*.

But, it is very unlikely that you fight alone on the battlefield. Teamwork is far more important than individual combat, so later the virtual system is used more to train the team fight. The same is true of the sentient beings in the three realms. Practice is not just a matter of one person in which only self-improvement is pursued. Instead, the collective practice focusing on overall cooperation is required to attain consummation.

Around the first century CE, a new sect was born of Indian Buddhism. The followers of this sect believe that the Buddhist teachings they believed in are like a large boat, by which the sentient beings will be delivered from the world of reincarnations of life and death to the world of Nirvana. The purpose of their practice is to deliver all sentient beings to become Buddhas. This Buddhist sect is known as

Mahayana Buddhism.

In Mahayana Buddhism, practice is not just a person's self attainment; but more importantly, it is to benefit all beings. To become a Buddha, all sentient beings must first practice becoming Bodhisattva. They make big determinations that they will save all sentient beings from the sea of suffering. The most important is "the Four Vows": "the vow to deliver all sentient beings without a boundary, the vow to rid of all the troubles that are endless, the vows to learn the laws that are infinite, the vow to attain the way of Buddha that is the supreme."

The purpose of Mahayana Buddhism can be summed up as "to seek the Buddhist truth to relieve from the reincarnation of life and death, and to deliver all sentient beings from the sea of sufferings." Therefore, in addition to the requirements of study and practice of the three studies and the eight correct ways for self-improvement, it is more important to practice the six ways and the four takings required of becoming a Bodhisattva. The six ways refer to giving, precepting, forbearing, advancing, meditation, and wisdom. These six ways are the methods to get out of the sea of life and death, the path to Nirvana. The four takings refer to the principles that need to be observed when dealing with others, namely, giving to others, loving words, beneficial deeds, and cooperation with others. These are the principles and methods that a Bodhisattva should follow when saving sentient beings.

If the world is generated by the creator in the same way as the programmer develops a computer game, then the three realms and six paths become a huge playground where the Bodhisattva is to improve his wisdom through practice and lead the people to play the game well together. When the game is won, the purpose of the sentient beings to exercise in the three realms is fulfilled, so they will not be condemned to the reincarnations of the six paths. Instead, they will be able to leave the game to attain Nirvana and eventually become a Buddha, returning to where we are from.

This easily reminds me of what Confucius once said. When Zigong asked him what makes a gentleman. Confucius gave his answer to this question on three levels: self-cultivation to pay respect to oneself, self-cultivation to cultivate others, and self-cultivation to save all people. Self-cultivation to pay respect to oneself means self-improvement and cultivation, and self-cultivation to cultivate others and self-cultivation to save all people all mean that based on self-improvement one should strive to help deliver all the sentient beings.

Because of this, Mahayana Buddhism advocates the practice of entering the world, i.e., practicing in the sensual world and practicing at home, unlike Hinayana Buddhism, which asks the practitioner to leave his home to be a monk.

The earth is just a small copy of the big game of the three realms and six paths. What is being played here is not a single-player game, but a multiple-player group game. The human world is a huge dojo, a place of practice. The best practice for mankind is to find and practice the ways to turn it into a beautiful and loving paradise. And those who can make the great determination to lead all beings to achieve this goal together will become bodhisattvas.

But what should we do specifically? Apart from some principles and methods, there is no specific implementation plan in the Buddhist scriptures. You can't do things just by a wish. Or you may do bad things with a kind heart. Just like some people who release animals for life nowadays, they put foreign species in the local natural environment. Because there are no natural enemies in the environment, these species will reproduce wildly, thus posing a huge threat to the local species and messing up the local ecosystem. Is this a release to life or a killing of life?

How can we build the earth, the common home of mankind, into a paradise for man? We can draw from the wisdom of the great sages of history. The wise men of the "Axis Age" have already answered, but they only talked about one aspect. We need to combine their thoughts and form a complete system to guide us to win through the game.

The first problem to be solved is the harmony between man and nature. The earth is the common home of human beings, animals, plants, microbes, and other creatures, not just belonging to humans. However, the development of human civilization has caused tremendous damage to the earth's ecology and is triggering the sixth wave of mass extinction of species. Countless creatures that had lived on the earth for a long time before the birth of human beings are disappearing. This is bad karma caused by mankind. If we do not correct our behaviors in time, mankind will suffer from its reckless actions. When the Earth's ecosystem collapses, mankind itself will become extinct.

This issue has attracted the attention of intellectuals for a long time. Thoreau, the 19th-century American thinker and author of the world literary masterpiece *Walden Lake*, had already seen the problems that would arise as early as in the age when industrial civilization had just expanded globally. Thoreau pointed out, that while industrialization in the form of mass employment of machines can bring a prosperous material life, intoxication with material enjoyment will make people lose the sense of the true meaning of life, and that the supremacy of materialism triggered by this will lead to spiritual poverty and emptiness. Therefore, he advocated and practiced the lifestyle of "returning to and integrating into nature" throughout his life, standing for a simple life in nature.

Thoreau anticipated the serious consequences of logging, destroying virgin forests, polluting rivers, and hunting animals. He said: "It is an outdated and wrong idea that man would conquer nature. The harmony between man and nature is key to the survival of human beings on this planet.

But Thoreau was not the first to realize this problem. As early as more than 2500 years ago, the Taoists represented by Lao Tze in China had already understood the law that "what is strong is bound to become old and be on the decline," and put forward the concepts of "Tao follows nature" and "harmony between man and nature," advocating a simple and natural lifestyle. There is a complete theory in *Tao Te Ching* that guides human beings on how to live in harmony with nature, which can be considered a *successful strategy* for playing the game copy of the earth.

Regrettably, although Lao Tze pointed out the problem a long time ago and also gave a solution, his suggestions have not been implemented yet. Now that environmental pollution, climate change, resource depletion, and species extinction have become harsh realities, more and more people are aware of the need to protect the environment. There abound environmental protection public service advertisements on TV, and environmental issues are discussed everywhere in the media,   all the textbooks teach children to take good care of the environment, and the World Conference on Climate has been held many times. However, more people are shouting out lofty slogans than taking concrete actions. People talk what they talk and do what they do. While worrying about the consequences, they continue to destroy.

Environmental protection has become the consensus of almost everyone. Everyone knows that this problem has been exacerbated to the extent that the survival of the entire human race on the earth is in danger. But, for such a problem that endangers the fundamental interests of all mankind, why is there no real action? why cannot we see any hope of a solution?

The place where I was born and the place where I first started working are both in mountainous areas, but the scenes of the two places are completely different. In one place, the mountains are lush, full of uncut virgin forests, and the ecology is very well preserved; in another place, the mountains are bare, and it is rare to see a few big trees, for all of them have been cut down by the villagers.

After comparison, I found that the reason is quite simple. The folk customs of the two places are different. In the latter place, the folk customs are not very good. The relationship between people is not harmonious, and they don't care much about each other, and they often scramble for land and other things. The trees on the mountain suffer because the villagers are rushing to cut the trees first, for fear of being taken advantage of by others. In the former place, the folk customs are very good. The relationship between people is harmonious, and they don't make a fuss with each other, and no one wants to take advantage of others and cut off and took back the trees on the mountain for his use.

This incident made me understand a truth: to achieve the goal of harmony between man and nature, we must first achieve harmony between people.

Do the countries of the world act in the same way as the villagers of the good village did when they are wrangling with each other on the issue of environmental protection and climate change? They always care about whether they will suffer, and they are always worried about whether the resources will be seized by others. They wish to turn the world's natural resources into money and put it into their wallets. They have never wondered how other sentient beings can survive when natural resources, which are the basis for the survival of human beings and other creatures on the earth, have been taken into their own pockets. How can you survive without the survival of others? Think about the rich landlord holding a big bag of gold in a great flood. Doesn't he understand that he would starve to death without any bread and that his hoard of gold cannot be eaten as food?

Confucius's *Analects* and Plato's *Republic* both discuss how to achieve harmony among people. Unfortunately, though everyone wants to live in a world of harmony and no fighting, an ideal country of fairness, justice, and order, they are constantly subjected to bloody conflicts, discrimination, bullying, and a sheer financial divide between the rich and the poor in the real world.

Society is made up of individuals. If everyone wants to have a world of great harmony and is willing to strive for it, how can our wishes not be realized? Why is it so difficult to achieve harmony between people in reality?

Later, I figured out the reason for this problem. The disaccord between people is rooted in the disharmony in everyone's heart. People's hearts are full of contradictions and conflicts. Although reason tells us that a world of harmony and no disputes is an ideal country, our emotions and desires often drive us to satisfy our desires and to take actions that are against public interests or even may harm others.

From this perspective, if you want to achieve harmony between people, you must first achieve harmony between the soul and the flesh in each person. This brings us back to the origin of the problem: the effect of joint practice will ultimately depend on everyone's practice. Therefore, a Bodhisattva should not only focus on his practice; instead, he must deliver all living beings and lead everyone to practice together to attain the perfect state of consummation.

How to achieve harmony in one's heart? It is through faith. Generally speaking, people with faith can easily achieve richness, peace, and harmony in their hearts. They will not worry about unsatisfied desires. What can help us most in this regard is the teachings of Siddhartha. Its core content is to teach us how to subdue the evils of our hearts.

The biggest problem in our society now is the lack of faith. With the rise of science, the major religions of the world have suffered greatly. Today's world is already dominated by science, and faith has been marginalized to the corners of society. When a person lacks faith, he will naturally think: "I only need to be responsible for myself, and I must never treat myself wrongly. As for ethics and social responsibilities, let them go aside. I don't care whether the world will be destroyed by a big flood or any other catastrophe."

For this reason, a Buddhist said: "If people believe that there will be an afterlife after this life, their entire life will be completely changed, and their responsibilities and morals will be clear. If people don't believe in an afterlife after this life, they will inevitably create a society with seeking short-term interests as the goal, and they will not think about the consequences of their actions. At present we have created a cruel world, a world with little real compassion, isn't it? Isn't the above mentality the main cause?"

It is precise because many people have lost their faith and awe that human beings gradually become self-centered and demand relentlessly from nature, causing devastating damage to the ecological environment. In social life, people are slowly embarking on a path of only caring for themselves at the expense of others, only pursuing material enjoyment instead of spiritual satisfaction. Social morality is gradually deteriorating.

The role of faith in enriching one's spiritual world cannot be replaced by other things. Faith is not only a personal pursuit but also the foundation of the entire social moral system. The lack of faith will cause serious social problems.

In today's world where science has enjoyed great development and dominated our way of thinking,   how can we rebuild our faith worldwide, so that it can serve as a spiritual beacon of light to guide us out of the quagmire of materials?

The first thing to do is to change the concept of "emphasis on materials over spirit". If people do not change their ideas on this if they still believe that the world is nothing more than a simple pile of materials and refuse to recognize the existence of the soul, then what is the point of talking about spiritual pursuit? Since only material is real, why not put the pursuit of materials first?

Once materialism prevails, chasing after money becomes people's top priority, and many people will do whatever it takes to make money. Among people who are frantic about money, the decline of social morality will become an inevitable trend.

A materialistic civilization will inevitably be unscrupulously greedy, relentlessly exploiting nature and being unable to curb the urge to expand abroad, which will harm not only the entire world but also itself. A materialistic world is bound to become hell on earth.

The Austrian philosopher Steigmüller said in his book *The Mainstream of Contemporary Philosophy* that it may be one of the biggest mistakes in the 20th century to place materialism in a dominant position in the world and regard materials as the only real reality.

The choice of what kind of faith to build is also a big issue. Historically, different religions formed in different regions of the world due to geographical isolation and lack of exchange of information. These religions may have conflicting doctrines, which are difficult to harmonize. And many contents of these religions even have been refuted by science. No matter what religion we choose to believe in, it will inevitably cause dissatisfaction from the followers of other religions and disdain from people who believe in science. The result is only to make the conflicts even more intense.

How to solve this problem? I think that whether it is philosophy, science, or any kind of religion, they all reflect the same world. Each angle can be different, but there can only be one truth, so they have a basis for unity.

Today, as the Internet has unprecedentedly narrowed down the distances between people, physical distance is no longer an obstacle to information exchange. As information is more and more interconnected, we can fully achieve the interconnection of knowledge and bring together human wisdom from different historical periods, thus breaking through the barriers between philosophy, religion, and science, and establishing an inclusive theoretical system that truly reflects the truth of the world.

This theoretical system should be an open rather than a closed one. It should allow questions and not be unquestionable. It should be capable of modification rather than be unchangeable. This system should not only reflect the wisdom of the past generations but also leave room for contributions and modifications by future generations. It can not only cover all the existing discoveries but also guide the direction of human progress.

For this reason, I am willing to start by presenting a theoretical framework. In this book, we have discussed the three issues of where the universe comes from, where humanity comes from, and what is the meaning of life. These matters will reveal the nature of the world and the meaning of life. This is just the beginning. We will have to further discuss how to achieve harmony between man and nature, harmony between men, and the harmony of soul and flesh.

How can human beings live in harmony with nature so that the entire population can thrive on the earth for an immeasurable long time without falling into the danger of extinction? All will be discussed in future books.

The Axis Age

The Cambrian life explosion is an unsolvable mystery in biology. Species appeared in an explosive concentration in a short period, which is incredible. But what is even more incredible is that in the history of human thought, there is the same phenomenon as the Cambrian life explosion. In a short period, the greatest thinkers in human history appeared in a concentrated manner, like the shining stars in the dark sky. Their light illuminated the entire sky of that era. This is the "Axis Age". The concept of the axis age was put forward by the German philosopher Jaspers in The Origin and Goal of History published in 1949. He found that between 800 BC and 200 BC, especially around 500 BC, there was an axis era in human civilization. The area where this phenomenon occurs is probably between 25 degrees and 35 degrees north latitude. Human civilizations in different regions made breakthroughs almost simultaneously during this period.

In the Axis Age, great spiritual teachers appeared in various civilizations. There were Socrates, Plato, and Aristotle in ancient Greece, the Judaic prophets in Israel, Siddhartha in ancient India, and Lao Tze and Confucius in China. Their ideas have shaped different cultural traditions and continue to have great influences on people's lives. And more importantly, although China, India, the Middle East, and Greece are separated by mountains and rivers, their cultures in the Axis Age have many similarities.

In that era, the cultures of ancient Greece, Israel, China, and India all had the awakening of ultimate concern. People began to face the world rationally and morally. At the same time, religions emerged. The Israelis created Judaism, which later gave birth to Christianity and Islam; Lao Tze created Taoist ideas, which later gave birth to Taoism in China; Siddhartha founded Buddhism. These religions have had an indelible impact on mankind and have affected the entire process of human civilization.

The lights of their wisdom have been shining so brightly that it can even be said that human thinking has not surpassed that of the Axial Age.

Such breakthroughs made their cultures transcend the primitive stage. The types and frameworks of these cultures were shaped at that time, which determined the different cultural forms of the West, India, China, and Islam today, just like the biological genera were formed during the Cambrian explosion of life and have not undergone any fundamental changes so far. Those cultures that made breakthroughs in the Axis Age have continued to this day, while other ancient civilizations that have not achieved transcendence, such as the Babylonian culture and the Egyptian culture, although large in scale, are difficult to escape the fate of extinction, and eventually become cultural fossils.

I have a feeling that the emergence of the Axis Age is no accident like the Cambrian explosion of life. The thoughts of Lao Tze and Siddhartha completely surpassed the normal level of human wisdom in that era and contained a certain apocalyptic element. Just as the Cambrian explosion of life was the system's concentrated delivery of species, maybe the phenomenon of concentrated emergence of the great thinkers in the Axis Age is a reminder of the system for the game.

But now we can hardly count on the apocalypse anymore. The new axis age can only rely on human wisdom. If we want to clear the hurdles and win the game, I am afraid we can't count on the savior. The only thing we can only rely on is our practice.

Siddhartha said, "Everyone has a Buddha in his heart, and everyone can become a Buddha". Every one of us can be a savior so long as we embark on a journey of practice.